I0816422

ANYTHING GOES?

Berlin Architecture in the 1980s

Edited by Thomas Köhler and Ursula Müller

With texts by Esra Akcan, Andreas Butter, Wolfgang Kil, Kathrin Meissner, Marco De Michelis, Anna-Maria Nitschke, Verena Pfeiffer-Kloss, Emily Pugh, Philine Schneider (Guerilla Architects), Florian Urban, Georg Vrachliotis, Julia Wigger, Antonia Wolff, Gerd Zimmermann

KERBER

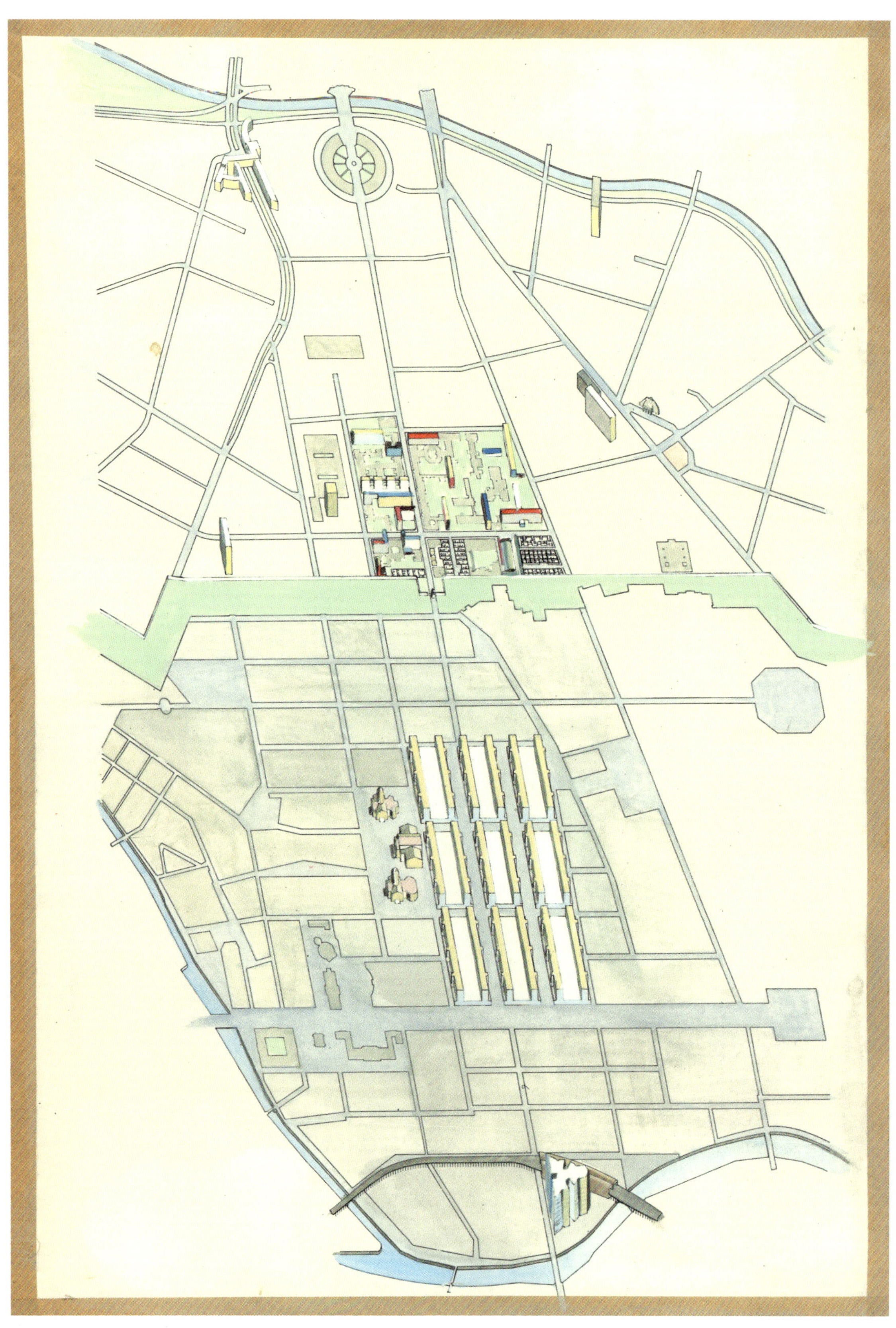

Office for Metropolitan Architecture (OMA), Elia Zenghelis, Matthias Sauerbruch, residential building at Checkpoint Charlie, site plan, 1980

WELCOMING REMARKS FROM THE GERMAN FEDERAL CULTURAL FOUNDATION

In Herrmann Zschoche's feature film *Insel der Schwäne* (Island of Swans)—which forms part of this exhibition's accompanying program—the young protagonist Stefan is in danger of falling into the elevator shaft of an unfinished building. The scene takes place in a development of new buildings in the Marzahn district of Berlin. In the film, all turns out well in the end. But the possibility that a large socialist housing development under construction can pose a deadly threat to young people resulted in harsh criticism from the state in 1983 and led the newspaper *Neues Deutschland* to judge it a "distorted view of our reality."

But what did it look like, the undistorted reality of the divided Berlin of the 1980s? Neither the eastern nor the western part of the city possessed the certainties that had marked the architecture of the postwar period: that the old was ugly and had to be removed with the pomp and ornament of a bourgeois architecture; and, since the 1970s, the promise of architecture had also become shaky. The stony desolation and cubic monotony of large housing developments offered sufficient reference points on both sides of the Berlin Wall for critical assessments in film, painting, and literature.

The urban planning polarities of tradition and modernity, of socialist and Western aesthetics, which were already laid out in 2015 by the exhibition *Radically Modern,* are echoed in this most recent project of the Berlinische Galerie. The museum once again sets out to write the history of the city. Its title—*Anything Goes?*—not only stands for the postmodern turning point in the history of architecture. It can also be justly applied to the historical breadth of this exhibition—without the question mark, in the latter case, thanks to a provident collection policy. For the first time, the history and significance of building activity in Berlin before the fall of Communism can be viewed from both eastern and western perspectives. In the process, it becomes clear that as the competition between political systems continued, even in the areas of architecture and urban planning, both parts of the city pursued, each in its own way, the same "postmodern" goal: harmonizing the principles of the modern city with local cultures, traditions, and human needs. Both parts of Berlin were, moreover, shaky economically and were searching for guidelines for a contemporaneous urbanity with international appeal.

In both places, it was the historical impetus connected with the 750th anniversary of the city that started the motor of building activity. And, once again, in competition: with the IBA on the western side and the *Bauausstellung der DDR* on the eastern side of the Berlin Wall—that supersign in the politics of architecture that would finally fall with the peaceful revolution of the late 1980s, at the end of this significant decade. Thirty years later, other signs of this period are beginning to disappear: the residential complex on Lützowplatz in West Berlin by Oswald Mathias Ungers, built in the context of the IBA, for example, has since been demolished. For that reason, it would appear to be high time to get to know this architectural epoch of divided postmodernism, and at the same time to discover the mark it left behind on the art of its time.

The German Federal Cultural Foundation thanks the Berlinische Galerie, its director, Dr. Thomas Köhler, and his team, as well as the head of its architectural collection, the curator Ursula Müller, and her entire staff for undertaking an exhibition project on the 1980s that opens a new chapter in the history of the city and architecture of Berlin. It impressively reveals how an era's urban planning, architecture, design, painting, photography, and, last but not least, film can interact.

Hortensia Völckers
Executive Board /
Artistic Director

Kirsten Hass
Executive Board /
Administrative Director

Fig. 1 View from the south of the historical area of Luisenstadt, ca. 1965, photo: Otto Borutta
In the foreground, the Deutsches Patentamt (German Patent Office) on Gitschiner Strasse. To the left of center, the low-rise of the newly constructed glass warehouse can be seen, still surrounded by large vacant lots. Since 2004, this has been the site of the Berlinische Galerie.

ARCHITECTURE EXHIBITIONS AT THE BERLINISCHE GALERIE

> Beyond that, it would also have offered an opportunity to speak about all sorts of bureaucratic stupidity and even maliciousness, and it would certainly also be time to reveal the fact that many of the "participants" are, on the one hand, opportunistic owing to party politics and, on the other hand, incompetent on the subject matter, which has repeatedly led to dubious decisions or pointed them in the wrong direction.[1]

This criticism could scarcely have been expressed in a more prominent place: in his foreword to the publication for the Internationale Bauausstellung 1984/87 (International Building Exhibition), its director, the architect Josef Paul Kleihues, offered a thorough accounting. Reading it, one immediately understands the effort that must have been required to turn this ambitious and visionary project into reality. Endless planning phases and processes had worn down the people involved. It is therefore that much more of a pleasure that it was possible to realize large parts of this project on urban space, which was based historically on Interbau 1957, even if substantial changes were required in some cases.

In contrast to archives, collections, and museums that concentrate exclusively on architecture and its history, the Berlinische Galerie always views its engagement with architecture and urban planning in a dialogue with its collection of modern and contemporary art. We managed to achieve this compellingly in 2015 in the exhibition *Radically Modern: Urban Planning and Architecture in 1960s Berlin,* and that led to a desire to approach the architecture of the 1980s in a similar way. The goal was to focus not only on the question of how the ideas of urban repair and future housing were conceived and realized in (East and West) Berlin, but also on how we can understand today the living spaces that resulted.

Answers to that are provided not only by a selection of original documents from the period, but also by current installations and groups of works by the Berlin artist Isa Melsheimer, whose work scrutinizes selected "postmodern" buildings in the city and opens up for viewers new perspectives on an architectural trend that remains controversial.

The Berlinische Galerie is located in an area that had been selected as one of the centers of the IBA. The immediate vicinity has buildings by Hans Kollhoff and Arthur A. Ovaska, Arata Isozaki and Frowein & Spangenberg. The warehouse for glass that was converted into our museum had been built in 1964 and thus is one of the few new buildings from the postwar era in the area. Until the 1980s, the neighborhood was still marked by vacant lots and a few residential buildings (fig. 1). There were a few historical buildings as well, such as the Kollegienhaus (Supreme Court Building), the former headquarters of Victoria-Versicherung (Victoria Insurance), and residential buildings from the Gründerzeit (late nineteenth century). It is part of the southern Friedrichstadt, which was essentially based on plans by Friedrich Wilhelm I and his architect Philipp Gerlach, construction on which began in 1732. The Friedrichstadt was destroyed almost entirely in World War II and only a small part of it has been rebuilt.

This monumental insurance building represents an important element of urban planning. It was built from 1893 to 1913 by the construction engineer Karl Bernhard based on plans by the architect Wilhelm Walther in the neo-Baroque style. The continuous expansions ultimately led to this complex extending from Lindenstrasse to Alte Jakobstrasse, thus taking up an entire block. All that survived the massive wartime

1 Josef Paul Kleihues, "Vorwort: Fünf Jahre sind vergangen," in *Internationale Bauausstellung Berlin 1984: Die Neubaugebiete; Dokumente, Projekte,* vol. 1: *Modelle für eine Stadt,* ed. Vittorio Magnago Lampugnani (Berlin, 1984), p. 7.

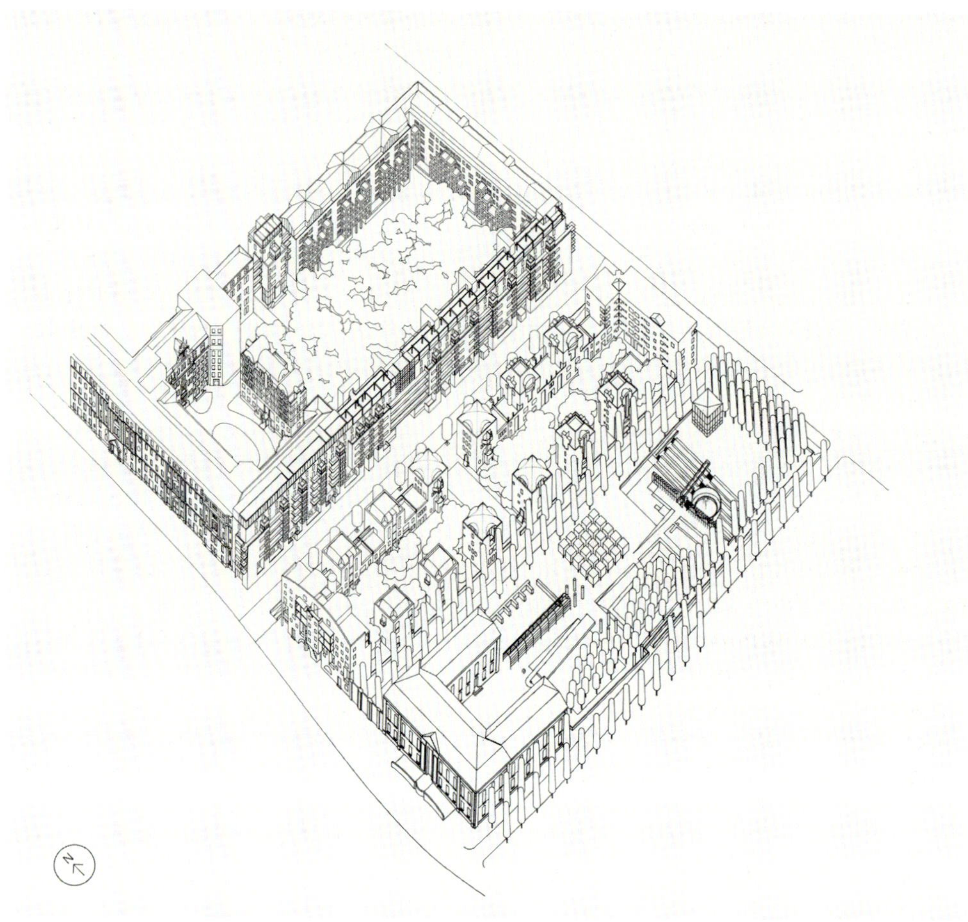

Fig. 2 Hans Kollhoff, Arthur A. Ovaska, Wohnpark am Berlin Museum (Residential Park at the Berlin Museum), construction, 1984–86, axonometric drawing, 1986

Fig. 3 Dieter Frowein, Gerhard Spangenberg, residential complex on Alte Jakobstrasse 129–133, Wohnpark am Berlin Museum, view from the northeast, 1986, photo: Siegfried Büker

destruction was a building volume of three wings on Lindenstrasse. The insurance company left the building at the end of World War II, moving its headquarters to Düsseldorf. In the years that followed, the building was used by a variety of institutions. Numerous decorative elements from the historical building can still be found as used spolia for IBA buildings.

The Berlinische Galerie is located immediately adjacent to the so-called Wohnpark am Berlin Museum (Residential Park at the Berlin Museum). The latter, in turn, originated as an important part of the southern Friedrichstadt demonstration area; and, after winning an ideas competition, the Hans Kollhoff and Arthur A. Ovaska planning collective was commissioned in 1980 to continue the urban development of the area. As so often, the original concept for the architecture was realized only partially. The block between the street Am Berlin Museum and the Berlinische Galerie consists of four different, decidedly diverse components (fig. 2): a slab apartment building facing the street, designed by Kollhoff and Ovaska themselves, who were also responsible for the residential tower facing the Berlinische Galerie; a residential building by Arata Isozaki & Associates; and an apartment building by Frowein & Spangenberg, which was also commissioned to design the grounds.

The last-named building closed off the L-shaped block-perimeter structure on its northern and eastern sides (fig. 3). The northern crossbar, which borders on the grounds of the Berlinische Galerie, forms the interface between housing and culture—originally between housing and commerce, since the glass warehouse was operating until 1998. The façade facing the museum is decorated with glazed white square titles and diagonal stripes of red tiles. Its architecture was thus clearly referring to the design of historical commercial complexes in Berlin, many of which can be found in our Kreuzberg neighborhood. After a building by Oswald Mathias Ungers on Lützowplatz, built for the IBA in 1987, had been demolished, only to be replaced by a mediocre new building—and against the backdrop that the cultural heritage of architecture from the GDR of that same period was treated none too gently—it seemed appropriate to us to emphasize this difficult-to-categorize era in the history of architecture as well.

For the past three years, the curator Ursula Müller has been preparing the exhibition and tracking down clues, especially where the projects in the eastern part of the city are concerned.

The success of her efforts is especially evident from the thirty-nine original models, elegantly executed on a scale of 1:200, that document the plans to develop Friedrichstrasse north of the Checkpoint Charlie border crossing. Only partially completed before the fall of the Berlin Wall in 1989, existing but still unfinished buildings were demolished as part of redesigning Berlin to be the German capital again. With the generous support of the DKLB-Stiftung and funding from the German Federal Cultural Foundation, it was possible to buy these models back from a private collection and restore them to a state in which they could be presented in order to preserve an overall impression of the ideas that were planned at the time and to show them to the public. We hope that this exhibition will contribute to a conscientious approach to buildings from this period, which is not yet far behind us.

Anything Goes? is based on the considerable original holdings in the museum's collection and was supplemented by numerous loans. I am sincerely grateful to our lenders for their trust in us. Despite considerable restrictions on the use of archives, despite reduced lending and diverse guidelines and rules connected with the pandemic regulations, it was possible for us to complete the research necessary for the exhibition and to satisfy all of our relevant wishes.

I would like to take this opportunity to emphasize our colleagues at the Leibniz-Institut für Raumbezogene Sozialforschung in Erkner (IRS), namely, its director, Oliver Ibert, as well as Andreas Butter, Kai Drewes, and Anja Pienkny. Having previously worked with this institute on the *Radically Modern* exhibition, we were able to continue our dialogue on the occasion of *Anything Goes?*.

Our colleagues at the Landesarchiv Berlin continued to be constructive supporters of our activity despite difficult circumstances.

I thank most warmly Ursula Müller, the busy head of our architecture collection, for her research achievement and her élan in reappraising this era in architecture. She was able to present a scholarly work in this catalogue that has the makings of a standard work on the subject. She was energetically supported in her work by the research interns Nuno de Brito Rocha, Anna Nitschke, and Antonia Wolff, who made an essential contribution to the success of the exhibition and of the catalogue. They received committed assistance from Verena Pfeiffer-Kloss, who was also responsible, along with Linus Lütcke, for developing the web app, and from Frank Schütz, who knows the holdings of our collection like few others and helped to organize the loans.

I would like to thank the designer of the catalogue, Lars Egert, for his clear and cogent graphic concepts. It was a great pleasure to communicate with him, even over a great distance.

The architect David Saik found a compelling form for the diverse exhibition material, for which we are very grateful to this long-standing partner of ours.

The head of administration, Birgitta Müller-Brandeck, and the head of finance and controlling, Susanne Teuber, supervised the budget of the project and ensured that the subsidies entrusted to us were used properly.

Ulrike Andres, as head of our Communication and Education Department, was responsible for the corresponding public perception of this exhibition project. I am very grateful for her professionalism and contributions to the related subject matter.

Guerilla Architects—namely, Nike Kraft, Shahrzad Rahmani, and Philine Schneider—worked with the photographer Phil Dera and our curator of outreach, Christine van Haaren, to implement an education project based on dialogue with residents of buildings from the 1980s. I wish to thank them sincerely for their great commitment to actively encouraging enthusiasm for the subject of architecture—not just in the stratum of the population with little contact to museums—and also for expanding an archive that is accessible in proximity to the exhibition by adding to it materials from regular workshops with visitors. I very much hope that many similar projects will follow.

This exhibition was possible only thanks to a substantial grant from the German Federal Cultural Foundation. I therefore thank its directors, Hortensia Völckers and Alexander Farenholtz, as well as the latter's successor, Kirsten Hass, and its board. Without the foundation's support, we would not have been able to present the exhibition in this form.

Now that the Berlinische Galerie has dealt with the decade in the history of architecture that preceded the fall of the Berlin Wall and German reunification, which was such an epochal event for the city, we must gain perspective on the period that followed. How Berlin tried to reinvent itself above all in the 1990s must be studied in a future research project.

Thomas Köhler
Director

	Kriterien zur Gegenüberstellung der Prinzipien	MODERNE	POSTMODERNISMUS
Arch. u. Gesellschaft	Verhältnis zur Gesellschaftsstruktur	Architektur als gesellschaftsverändernde Strategie	Soziale Passivität
	Verhältnis zum Privateigentum	Privateigentum als Hindernis einer rationellen Projektpolitik	Konformismus zum Privateigentum
	Problem des Nutzers	Professioneller Architekturzentrismus	Hinwendung zum Nutzer
	Soziale Ausrichtung	Architektur für die gesamte Gesellschaft	Sozialer Konformismus
	Verhältnis zum technischen Fortschritt	Industrielle Technologie als Basis	Deklarierter Antitechnizismus
Stadt	Städtische Funktionen	Monofunktionale Zonierung	Mischgebiete
	Entwicklung des städtischen Skeletts	Verkehrsfunktion bestimmend	Benutzung historischer Planungsstrukturen
	Strukturierung der städtischen Bebauung	Unstetigkeit der städtischen Räume	Historische Kontinuität der städtischen Bebauung
	Begriff von der städtischen Ordnung	Architektur als rationelle Ordnung	„Chaos" als höhere Stufe der Organisation der Umwelt
	Verhältnis zur bestehenden Umwelt	Radikale Umgestaltung	Anpassung an die bestehende Umwelt
Formgestaltung	System der Formensprache	Morphologischer Monismus	Morphologischer Pluralismus
	Verhältnis zur Funktion	Funktionalität als Grundlage der schöpferischen Strategie	Indifferenz zur Funktion, ihre Unterordnung
	Verhältnis zur Konstruktion	Form konstruktiv determiniert	Unterwerfung der Konstruktion unter die Form · Trennung
	Verhältnis zur Dekoration	Ablehnung des Dekorativismus „wahre Erscheinung"	Dekorativität als schöpferisches Prinzip
	Architektonisches Erbe	Absage an historische Prototypen der Form	Allusionismus und die direkte Reproduktion des Erbes
	Träger der architektonischen Form	Ästhetische Anpassung der industriellen Technologie	Historisch-kultureller Symbolismus

Modernism and postmodernism compared, excerpts from Peter Anatolyevich Ratschkow's dissertation, "On Theoretical Concepts of Postmodernism," ca. 1982, translated by Christian Schädlich

ANYTHING GOES?
Ursula Müller

Berlin's architecture of the 1980s is evidence of an important but also controversial phenomenon in recent architectural history that is usually classified under the heading "postmodernism." A multilayered architectural idiom continuing the tradition calls into question previous ideas of a modern lifeworld. Without using what has been passed down as a direct model, it creates a broad spectrum of fictive images of the city and its buildings, streets, squares, and parts that simulate a history.[1]

Imaginative façade motifs, contrasting materials and colors, intertwined, highly structured, or clear formulations of space, and architecture with unusual manifestations that are based on new design concepts now stand directly side by side. This rich variety of design is supplemented by a different way of dealing with the existing building fabric: rather than defining urban renewal as demolition, now reuse, alteration, and expansion with the participation of the residents become the goals of planning.

These complex, multiple new approaches in urban development, architecture, and landscape planning resulted from responses to urgent sociopolitical and spatial problems. The existing models available to address the housing shortage since World War II were neither affordable any longer, nor could they provide the necessary accommodations in sufficient numbers and with a consistently acceptable design. Moreover, there were still rundown vacant lots in central urban areas: the southern Friedrichstadt and the Spreebogen (Bend in the Spree River) in West Berlin; and the northern Friedrichstadt and the Gendarmenmarkt in East Berlin. The result was growing discontent in the population with, for example, the plans for extensive demolition of old buildings as part of blanket urban renewal (in West Berlin) or the rational austerity of modern postwar architecture.

In order to improve the respective image of each part of the city, for both domestic and international politics, the two governments undertook far-reaching measures to remedy this deplorable state of affairs. With the Internationale Bauausstellung (International Building Exhibition, IBA) of 1984 in West Berlin, which was initiated in 1978, and the preparations for the architecture exhibition in East Berlin, the capital of the German Democratic Republic (GDR), the city was transformed into a kind of architectural laboratory, with results intended in each case to demonstrate the superiority of its respective side.

When these two architecture exhibitions opened in 1987, on the occasion of Berlin's 750th anniversary, the innovation and diversity of the methods, styles, and functions of the architecture they presented would shape international discourse for more than a decade. Whereas the approaches adopted in the capital of the GDR and IBA-Altbau (Old Buildings)[2] received most of the attention,[3] the solutions of IBA-Neubau (New Buildings) met with a contradictory response from the media.

Whereas *Time* magazine in New York praised this part of the exhibition as the "most ambitious showcase of world architecture in this generation,"[4] journalists from the West German press accused those responsible of being out of touch with reality[5] and of "stultifying the awareness of architecture,"[6] asserting that the projects narrated "not history but little stories."[7] Leading architectural theorists of the GDR, such as Bernd Grönwald and Christian Schädlich, also recognized in "postmodernism" a fundamental lack of socially relevant context that was said to be irreconcilable with socialist ideas.[8]

In the 1990s, after the fall of the Berlin Wall, the phenomenon of postmodern architecture was initially

1 The question of how to define postmodernism in architecture and the specific forms it took in Berlin is addressed by Gerd Zimmermann in his essay in the chapter "Urban Diversity."

2 Following the urban development of the neighborhoods of new and old buildings, the IBA was divided into the sections IBA-Alt and IBA-Neu.

3 The ambitious plans in East Berlin to develop part of Friedrichstrasse into an "attractive socialist cosmopolitan boulevard" looked better when compared to the West Berlin "challenge to untidy Kurfürstendamm." And even the Nikolaiviertel, which was resurrected in the historical center of the city, triggered more enthusiasm than criticism, despite its wild mix of historical imprecision, eclecticism, and prefabricated production. See Florian Urban, *Berlin/DDR neo-historisch: Geschichte aus Fertigteilen* (Berlin, 2007), pp.126–27; Karl Heinz Krüger, "Strasse des Luxus und der Moden," *Der Spiegel*, April 20, 1987, www.spiegel.de/spiegel/print/d-13523050.html (accessed August 24, 2020); Falk Jaeger, "Schaufenster der Weltarchitektur," *Der Tagesspiegel*, August 16, 1987.

4 Kurt Andersen, "Design: Rebuilding Berlin—Yet Again," *Time*, June 15, 1987, pp.48–50, esp. p.48.

5 Jaeger, "Schaufenster der Weltarchitektur" (see note 3).

6 Rolf Lautenschläger, "Verzierte Geschichte: Dokumentation zum 'Prager Platz'," *taz*, August 11, 1989, https://taz.de/VERZIERTE-GESCHICHTE/!1802425/ (accessed August 24, 2020).

7 Wolfgang Pehnt on Rob Krier's reconstruction of the Feilner residence, quoted in Dieter Bartetzko, "Stadtmontage: Das Berlin der Internationalen Bauausstellung," *Deutsche Volkszeitung / Die Tat*, August 7, 1987.

8 Bernd Grönwald, "Architekturprogrammatik für die 80er Jahre," *Architektur der DDR* 31, no. 6 (1982), pp.335–39, esp. p.336.

banished from the public sphere. Today, the most recent concepts of it in exhibitions, events publications, and artworks confirm a reawakening of interest.[9] In the foreground of this debate is the question of the topical relevance of this architectural movement and whether it should be regarded as a closed chapter in history.[10]

Our exhibition *Anything Goes?* takes up these inspirations and explores for the first time the architectural events of the 1980s using the example of Berlin the divided city on the front of the Cold War (fig. 1). In six thematic chapters, it examines the reasons behind the content and aesthetics of the architecture built and traces the field of tensions between global and local requirements within which both architects and decision makers operated.

The exhibition addresses the events liberated by this rethinking and the occasionally pioneering strategies, experiments, and positions that had already formed in the context of a European debate over the design of the city in its first chapter, "Impulses and Confirmation." The photographs, posters, and drawings in the exhibition not only document exemplarily the aforementioned critique by citizens of the ahistorical construction activity of recent decades; they also refer to the first realized architectural experiments, which created identity by engaging with the past and were intended to signal political concessions. The spectrum, discussed here, of new international architectural trends pertaining to a direction to take in the future is illustrated by example of a previously unknown graphic series by Christian Schädlich. For research and teaching in the GDR, he copied architecture from Western countries being reviewed at the time in journals and other publications—meticulously recording the source in each case—and recommended, rather than adopting this new trend, continuing to follow the "historically important concept of the modern movement of the 1920s, which has great potential for evolution."[11] This was in keeping with efforts in the GDR from the mid-1970s onward to put high modernism in the service of state policy, which went hand in hand with the claim that this architectural movement enjoyed historical interpretive authority (→ pp. 12, 29).

The chapter "Beautiful Old City" is dedicated to the complex relationships between urban planning and architectural design influenced by the Cold War and the necessity of citizen participation. It is a motley mix of materials that reveal different types of historical accounts—on the one hand, through images of the preserved tradition of the city and its renovated and redesigned architecture and, on the other hand, through documents of historicizing new buildings that engage creatively with the local structures, forms, and motifs. Both exemplify a new design for historicity that characterizes Berlin's urban development today.

Until now, little has been known about the opposition to architectural developments in East Berlin in the 1980s. An exciting account of the protests by residents and the early days of the self-organization of tenants in Prenzlauer Berg is concerned with the question of whether the GDR addressed the housing stock, and thus encountered critique from its citizens, for economic reasons alone, or whether it indeed represented a conscious appreciation of existing old buildings.[12]

Under the chapter title "The City as a Whole," the capriccio of the modern and the historical is developed further using examples of urban-planning activity in the capital of the GDR. The goal of creating unmistakable places motivated planners to use the most modern technologies to rebuild badly damaged public squares in the center of the city, such as Gendarmenmarkt, with the Schauspielhaus (Theater), the Deutscher Dom and Französischer

9 On this, see *Times Are Hard, but Postmodern,* a series of photographs with works by the artist Isa Melsheimer, in the epilogue to the present volume.

10 Postmodernism has been discussed again recently in the following exhibitions and publications: *Postmodernism: Style and Subversion, 1970–1990* (published in 2011), Victoria and Albert Museum, London, September 24, 2011 to January 15, 2012; *Mission: Postmodern; Heinrich Klotz und die Wunderkammer DAM,* Deutsches Architekturmuseum, Frankfurt am Main, May 10 to October 19, 2014; Martino Stierli and Mechtild Widrich, *Postmoderne: Zur Genealogie und globalen Aktualität eines umstrittenen Konzepts,* lecture series, Universität Zürich, February 26 to May 28, 2015; Claudia Kromrei, with photographs by Thomas Bomm and Manfred Hamm, *Postmodern Berlin: Wohnbauten der 80er Jahre* (Salenstein, 2018); "Charles Jencks: Über die Aktualität der Postmoderne," interview by Stephan Becker and Friederike Mayer, *Baunetzwoche* 509, March 29, 2018; Isa Melsheimer, *Der unerfreuliche Zustand der Textur,* KINDL – Zentrum für zeitgenössische Kunst, Berlin, March 22 to July 5, 2020.

11 Christian Schädlich, "Der Postmodernismus—eine alternative Architektur?," *Architektur der DDR* 31, no. 6 (1982), pp. 340–46, esp. p. 346.

12 On this, see the essay by Andreas Butter, Julia Wigger, and Kathrin Meissner in this volume.

13 On this, see the essay by Wolfgang Kil in this volume.

14 Margrit Kennedy, ed., *Öko-Stadt,* vol. 1: *Prinzipien einer Stadtökologie,* and vol. 31: *Materialien zur Internationalen Bauausstellung (IBA)* (Berlin, 1986), p. 76.

Fig. 1 Tseng Kwong Chi, Keith Haring mural at the Berlin Wall, 1986

Fig. 2 Raimund Abraham with Heike Buttner, Claus Neumann, residential and commercial building at Friedrichstrasse 32–33, 1985–87

Dom (German Church and French Church), and the monument to Friedrich Schiller, in a hybrid of original, copy, and re-creation and also motivated them to fill in—in a transformed way—the gaps in the surrounding block-perimeter structures. There were also impressive attempts to use prefabricated concrete-slab construction to approximate the small-scale quality of neighborhoods of prewar buildings in, for example, Marzahn.[13]

This section of the exhibition transitions into images of varied built and also unbuilt projects, their often contradictory, sometimes elusive formulations leading to this decade in architecture being accused of advocating that "anything goes." The chapter "Urban Diversity" raises for discussion once again projects realized in West Berlin, among other places, by especially theory-oriented architects such as Raimund Abraham (fig. 2), John Hejduk, and Hans Hollein (→ pp. 117 and 122). Highly regarded internationally, they belonged to the faculties of leading academies and universities, and the IBA gave them the rare opportunity to turn their ideas into reality. In addition, we remember not only newly introduced design elements and urban housing types, such as the frequent decorative motif of columns and the still-popular "multifamily villa," but also the emergent style of deconstructivism in the designs of, for example, Zaha Hadid and Daniel Libeskind in West Berlin (→ pp. 126–127, 140, 188–189).

The chapter "Beautiful Old City" already suggests that the ambitious goal of creating individual and yet inexpensive housing in the center of the city can be achieved step by step not only through new construction but also and above all by renovating older buildings, improving social and functional structures, and taking into account ecological perspectives. The chapter "Architecture for the People" studies this more closely using the example of the IBA. One essential foundation of success in this area was the participatory strategy of Hardt-Waltherr Hämer's "Behutsame Stadterneuerung" (Cautious Urban Renewal), which even today is resulting in valid changes to the standards for urban renewal and the social protection of the character of neighborhoods. There was also the innovative "Ökologie and Energie" (Ecology and Energy) research department under the direction of Margrit Kennedy. In addition to the use of environmentally friendly materials, it addressed above all how to improve microclimates by planting greenery in courtyards and on roofs and façades, trash recycling, alternative concepts for water use, and energy savings.[14]

The final chapter, "A Future from the Past," is dedicated to the question of how both parts of the city grappled with their past and specifically with the architectural problems inherited from the "Third Reich" and the architectural results of their sometimes heated debates over the culture of memory, influenced by ongoing competition between ideological systems. A comparison of the separate celebrations in East and West Berlin of the city's 750th anniversary shows that antithetical objectives for it even further codified the existing independence of the two sectors and provided no hint that the Berlin Wall would fall two years later.

The six chapters are followed by references to a film program that accompanies the exhibition, presenting cityscapes of Berlin in the 1980s through inspiring new reflections. In addition, recent groups of works and installations by the Berlin artist Isa Melsheimer open up additional perspectives.

Finally, the text by the collective Guerilla Architects, which is accompanied by photographs by Phil Dera, tell of the origins of a process-based, open-ended educational experiment for the exhibition. Commissioned by the Berlinische Galerie, this project attempts to enter into a dialogue with our neighbors concerning the subject matter of the exhibition.

Anything Goes? is supported by an advisory committee of scholars that includes Andreas Butter, Marco De Michelis, Stanislaus von Moos, Kerstin Wittmann-Englert, and Gerd Zimmermann. I wish to thank them very sincerely for the critical support and enthusiasm they have brought to this project from the outset.

This exhibition was made possible by the great dedication of private and public lenders in Germany and abroad. Above all others, they deserve my profound thanks. In order to impart architectural principles and concepts visually, while also making them accessible to people with impaired vision, tactile models were developed in collaboration with the Modell+Design department of the Technische Universität Berlin and members of the Allgemeiner Blinden- und Sehbehindertenverein Berlin e.V. (ABSV). I am sincerely thankful to all involved for their work in creating these exhibition stations.

My gratitude also goes out to the authors, whose professional and very inspiring contributions have ensured the success of this book.

I am especially grateful to the German Federal Cultural Foundation for supporting this project.

IMPULSES AND CONFIRMATION

Brandenburg Gate with Berlin Wall, postcard, 1960s
Children playing by the Berlin Wall in West Berlin, picture postcard, ca. 1970

Jürgen Holtfreter, poster for the exhibition *Diagnose: Zum Bauen in West-Berlin* (Diagnosis: On Building in West Berlin), 1968

Gerd Wessel, *damit man es nicht so sieht* (so that it's not so visible), ca. 1985

Hasso von Werder, Uwe Pompinon, Klaus Beyersdorff, townhouse at Herderstrasse 16, 1970–72,
photo: Siegfried Büker, ca. 1972

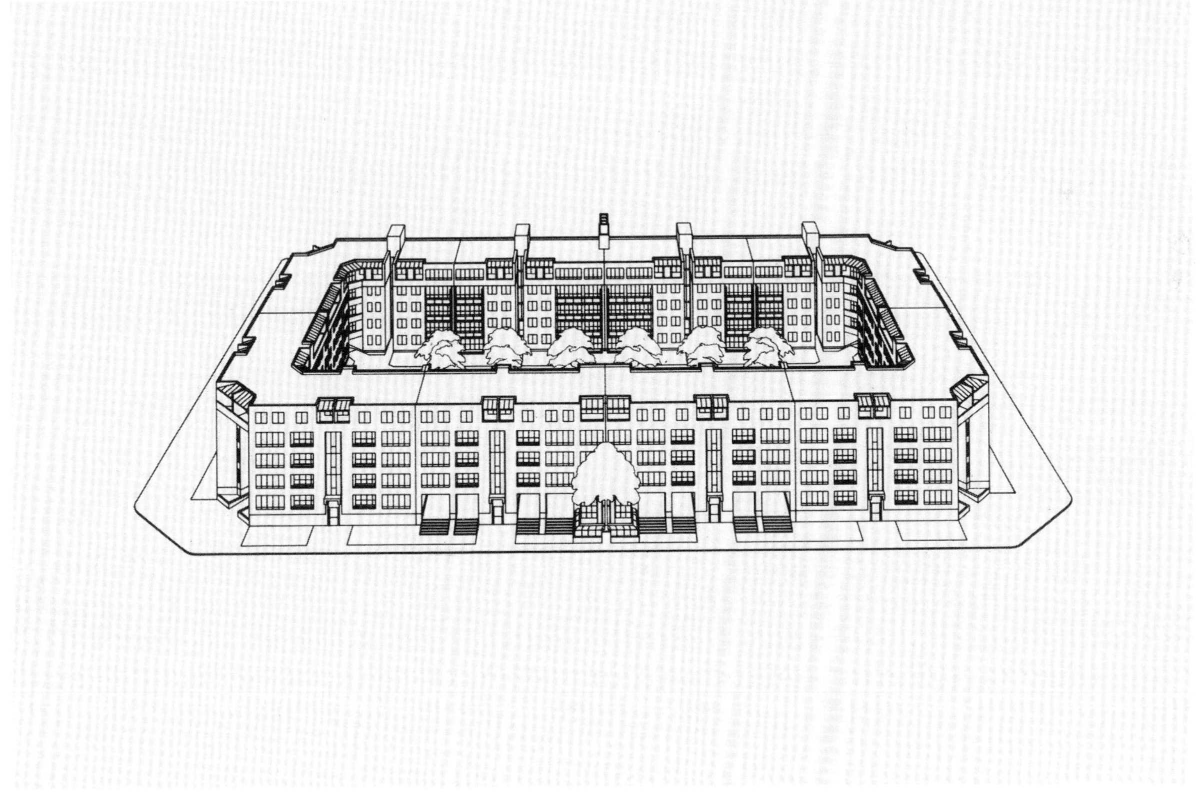

Josef Paul Kleihues, Manfred Schonlau, residential block of new buildings on Vinetaplatz, 1971–77, photo: Hélène Binet, ca. 1986, isometric drawing, ca. 1971

Dorothea Krause, Ernst Kristen, Karl-Heinz Megow, Manfred Zache, Hans-Jürgen Mücke, Jürgen Schulz
Revitalization of Arnimplatz, 1972–84, photo: Siegfried Nitsch, 1974

Residential and commercial building at Nehringstrasse 30, before and after renovation, 1975 and 2020
This prewar building in Charlottenburg is part of Block 118, which was revitalized as part of the European Architectural Heritage Year. Photos: Mieterinitiative (tenant initiative) Sanierungsgebiet Klausenerplatz (top), Gottfried Schenk (bottom)

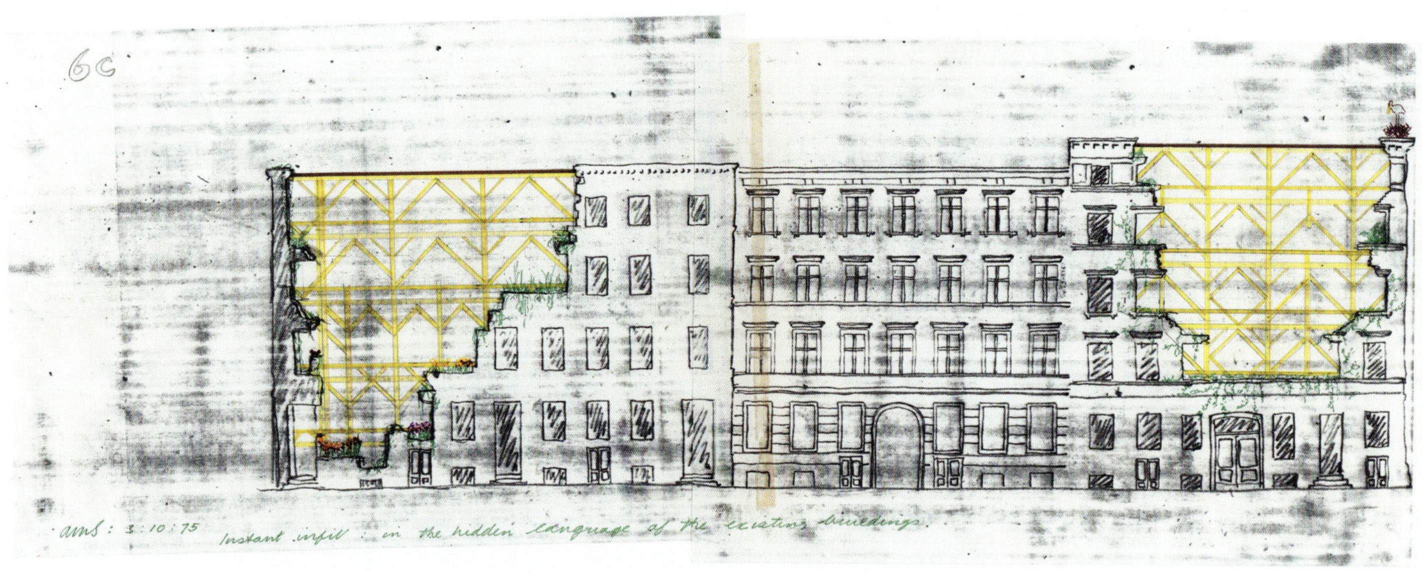

Alison Smithson, revitalization of residential buildings on Adalbertstrasse, study as part of the “Entwerfen in der historischen Strasse” (Designing on the Historical Street) week of events by the the Internationales Design Zentrum Berlin (IDZ), 1975

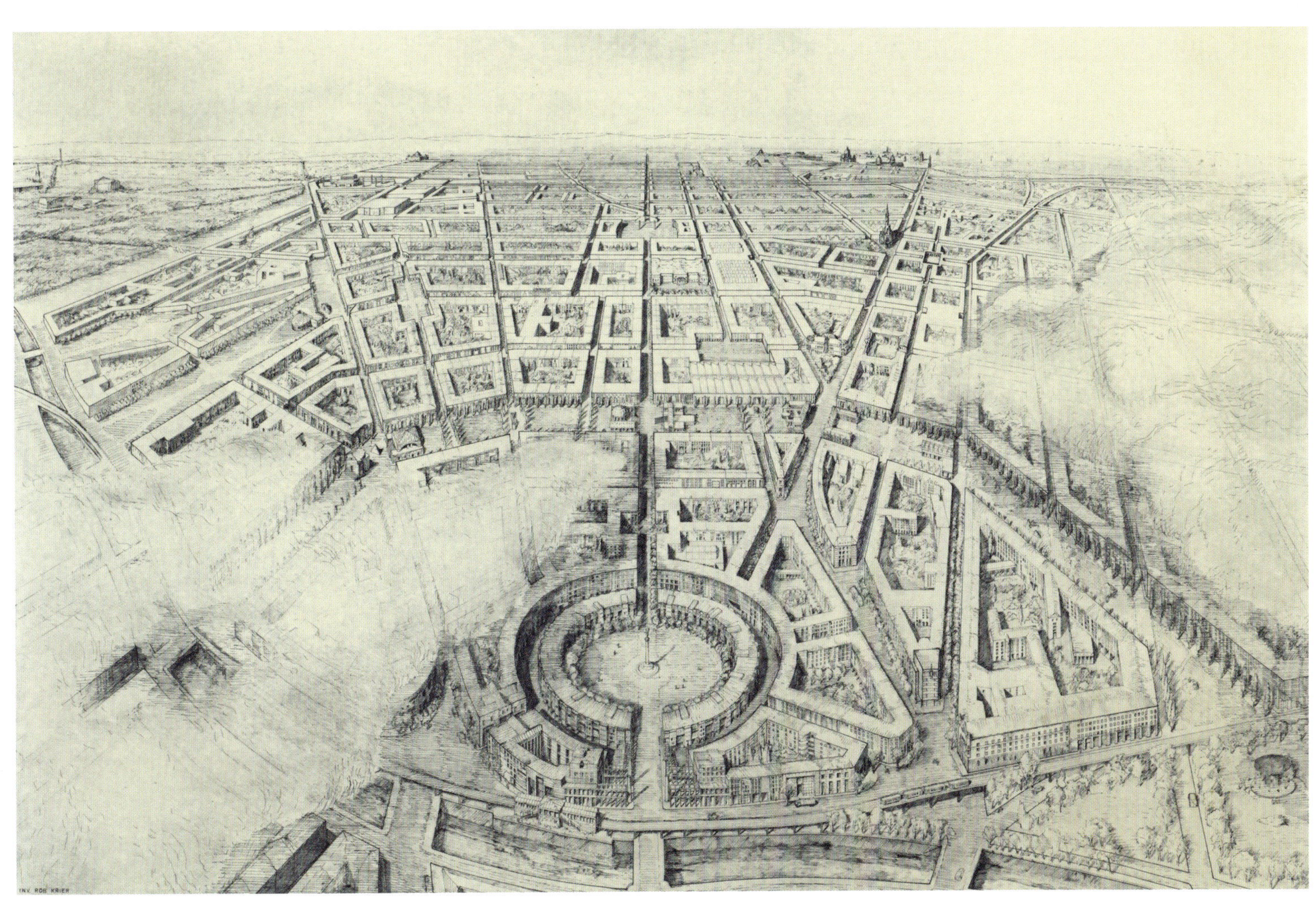

Rob Krier, idealized plan for the southern Friedrichstadt, 1977

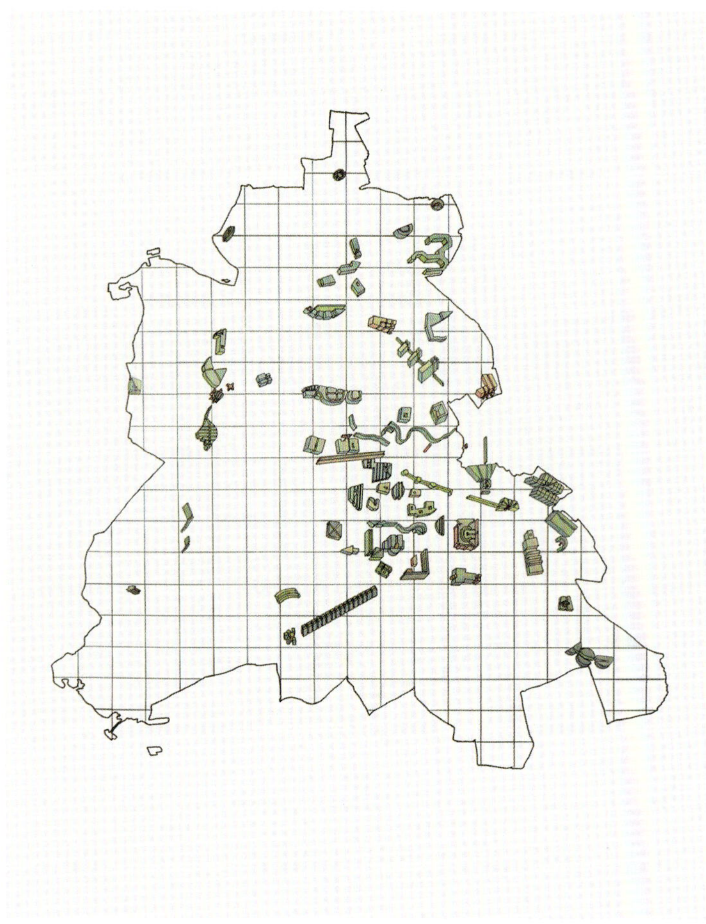

Oswald Mathias Ungers, Peter Riemann, Die Stadt in der Stadt: Ein grünes Archipel (The City in the City: A Green Archipelago), Cornell Summer Academy in Berlin, 1977

Peter Riemann, urban islands, Cornell Summer Academy in Berlin, 1977

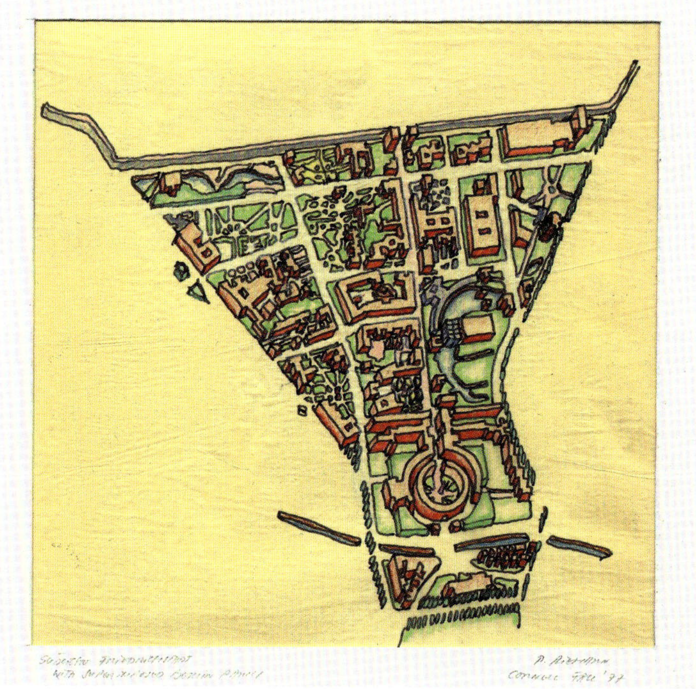

Peter Riemann, concept for the southern Friedrichstadt, Cornell Summer Academy in Berlin, 1977

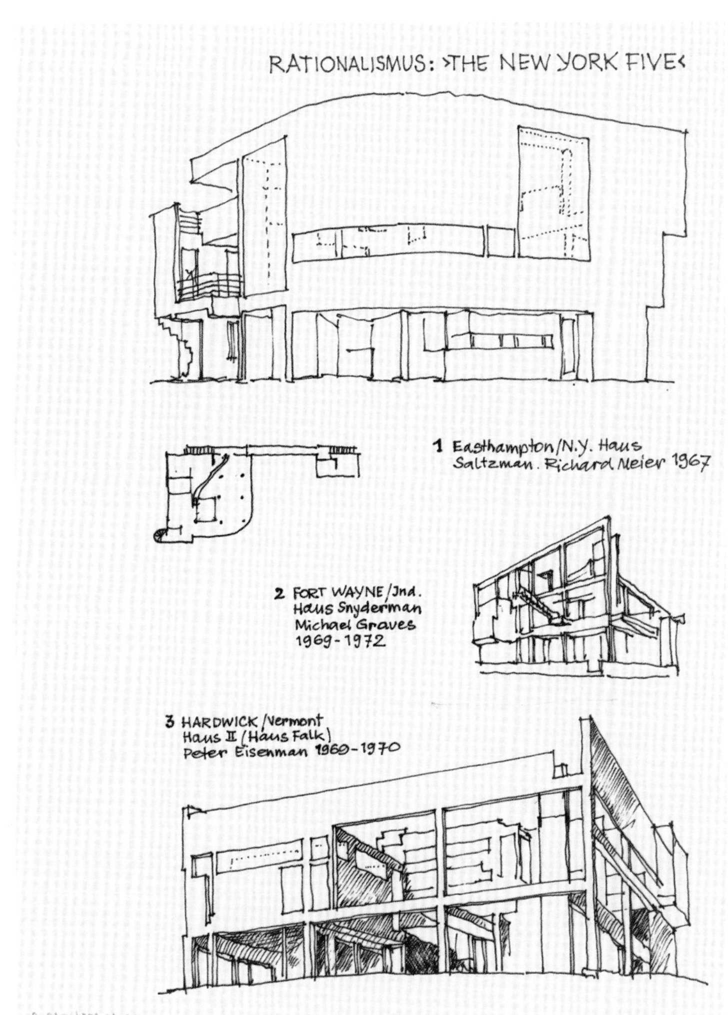

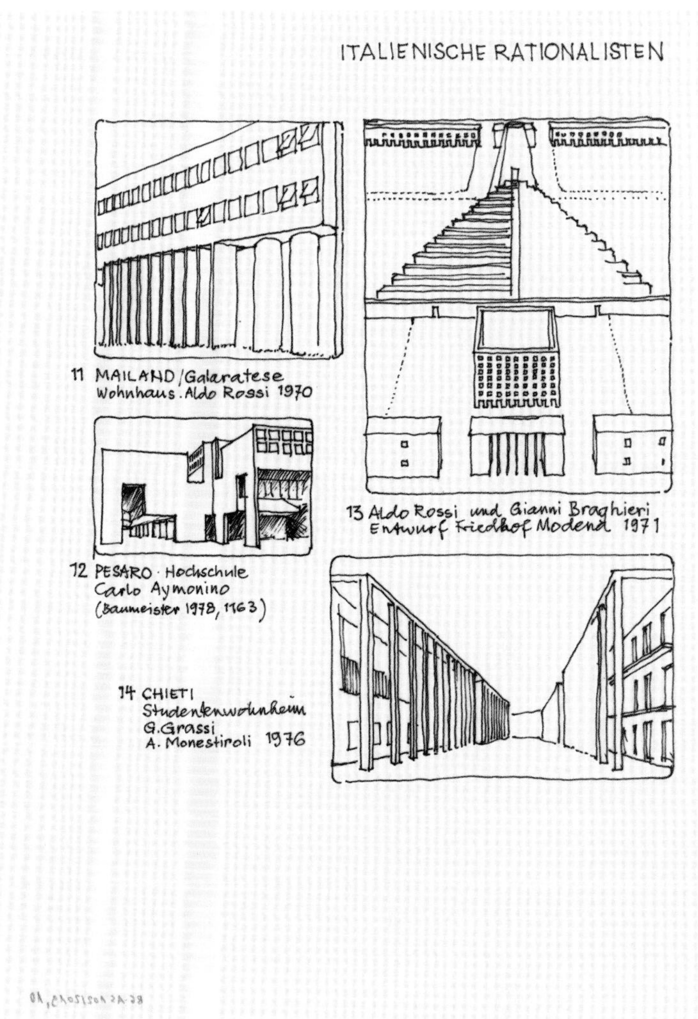

Christian Schädlich, “Italienische Rationalisten” (Italian Rationalists) and “Rationalismus: The New York Five” (Rationalism: The New York Five), two sheets from a series of drawings on postmodernism, ca. 1982

“BETWEEN SOCIAL ISSUES AND ARTISTIC RESPONSIBILITY”

Architecture in West Berlin until the IBA

Marco De Michelis

THE DIVIDED CITY

Historically, Berlin has been characterized by a complex and often incoherent structure since its earliest days, when there were two twin cities, Berlin and Cölln. The expansions in the following centuries were no more than additions to the initial system, especially the baroque Friedrichstadt, still recognizable in today's city maps due to its triangular geometric outline. Berlin's polycentric character became even more distinct in 1910, with the Greater Berlin Competition. Its aim was to give a unitary, metropolitan shape to an existing system of cities and suburbs, which each had their own specific settlement patterns. The "Berlin of stone" still coexisted with the "green Berlin" of villa districts in the western suburbs of the city. However, Berlin's destiny cannot be considered separately from the disastrous historical events of the twentieth century: the horrifying destruction from the last months of the war; a hasty reconstruction, incapable of dealing with the city's history; the unprecedented tragedy of the city's division into the different occupation zones by the victors of World War II until 1961, when the construction of the Berlin Wall inaugurated a completely new situation within history. A large city was suddenly forced to split in two and to become two cities, with settlement morphologies, representative functions, centers, and peripheries that were completely impermeable.

From 1961 on, two parallel and completely separated histories began. In the East, Berlin was to take on forms and functions of the capital of a German state as part of a "socialist" political and economic system, oriented toward the East of Europe and of the world. East Berlin comprised a significant part of the old city, which, however, was characterized, until the 1980s, by traces of the war, in the form of wastelands, ruins, and vacant lots. Brisk construction activity redensified the city's periphery in order to accommodate the large numbers of inhabitants to be expected in a capital. East Berlin therefore had a traditional morphological system: a center and an urban area developing around it, with almost endless potential to grow. The enclosed West Berlin, on the other hand, had to comprise its different characters within the large, but still limited perimeter of its political boundaries: the green Berlin; the large, just recently completed residential areas such as Märkisches Viertel and Gropiusstadt; the nineteenth-century fragments along the eastern city border. Within this context, any possibility of organic growth was excluded, and a policy of uninterrupted financial support was necessary in order to prevent relentless economic and cultural asphyxia.

The architectural scenery reflected this condition. In the early postwar years, and again at the beginning of the 1960s, Hans Scharoun had been the advocate of the heroic season of modernism: his "Kollektivplan" (Collective Plan), developed in 1946, had to some degree anticipated the total dissolution of the city's historical structure and envisioned in its place a linear settlement, stretched along the Spree's course, where alternating production and residential zones were separated by green areas. Here and there, isolated fragments of historical Berlin remained visible, such as Unter den Linden, Charlottenburg Palace, and the Museum Island. Scharoun would remain true to this idea of *Stadtlandschaft* (city landscape) until 1958, when he participated in the urban planning competition Hauptstadt Berlin. Likewise, Scharoun's project for the Kulturforum in the Potsdamer Platz area, with the Philharmonie and the posthumously erected buildings Staatsbibliothek, Musikinstrumenten-Museum, and the small Philharmonie, defined an urban scenery in which the buildings were freely distributed along the new course of the Potsdamer Strasse,[1] which now made it impossible to reconstruct the original settlement structure.

1 To this day, the prolongation of Potsdamer Strasse to the north, as implemented in the late 1960s, constitutes a physical barrier between the Staatsbibliothek and the cultural institutions around the Matthäikirche, thus reinforcing the insular character of the Kulturforum. See: https://harald.bodenschatz.berlin/texte/deutschland/berlin/berlin-auf-der-suche-nach-dem-verlorenen-zentrum/5-versuch-um-versuch-zentrumserweiterung-west (accessed June 23, 2020).

TOWARD A NEW ARCHITECTURE

It is no coincidence, then, that with Scharoun's death Berlin architecture (and, more generally, German architecture) started playing a marginalized role within the architectural debate. In the 1960s and 1970s, the focus was, for example, on Aldo Rossi's ideas. He understood the city as an architectural artifact, regulated by rules of morphology, typology, and, soon, from a postmodern perspective, also by broad themes such as the relationship between architecture and history.

In 1960, Oswald Mathias Ungers, whose work a young Aldo Rossi was interpreting in terms of the polarity between "illuminismo e misticismo" (enlightenment and mysticism), as well as between traditionalism and modernism,[2] wrote a manifesto "for a new architecture"[3] together with Reinhard Gieselmann. The authors polemicized with the functionalism dominant at the time and suggested a notion of architecture as a primarily artistic and spiritual practice instead. Three years later, Ungers published *Die Stadt als Kunstwerk* (The City as a Work of Art),[4] where he argued that the city is essentially an architectural phenomenon mediating between tradition and society. He thereby proved the affinity already suggested by Aldo Rossi: just three years later, Rossi's *Architettura della città* (The Architecture of the City) was centered on the identity of city and architecture, and consequently also on the notion that the past subsists in the present.[5]

In December 1967, during an international congress on architectural theory at the Technische Universität Berlin (TU Berlin), Ungers tried to situate the question of what architecture is within reflection on its theoretical foundations. The aim was thus to provide groundwork for the practice of designing that was aware of the demands of architectural form, and to redefine the relationships tying a building and its typology to the city's settlement structure.[6]

However, the turbulent atmosphere that led—also in Germany—to the events of 1968 set other priorities: Ungers left his position at the TU Berlin to move to the United States, where he became head of the architecture department at Cornell University. Until 1978, when he ultimately returned to Germany, he did not design one single building. He never stopped reflecting on architecture and on urbanism, especially that of Berlin, but did so only in the form of several competition entries, projects, and theoretical writings.[7]

THE MURDERED CITY

In the early 1970s, Berlin's architecture developed in terms of several isolated episodes, architectural thoughts, and projects—fragments rather than complex strategies that slowly started to shape a new city project.

Ten years after the construction of the Berlin Wall, the situation of the enclave West Berlin appeared more and more problematic. The war's damage seemed finally removed, even though countless scars were still dramatically visible; on the other hand, the city risked suffocating within the unnatural and impenetrable bounds of the Wall. West Berlin seemed condemned to the destiny of a "shrinking city": its population kept decreasing, and with it, inevitably, its productivity. The debate on the city seemed to have lost all vitality. Hans Kollhoff noted some years ago:

> In the field of urban planning and also that of architecture, the 1970s had reached the lowest intellectual level imaginable. It was the end of functionalist ideas, and the land use plans were nothing more than futile attempts to slow down urban decay. The most beautiful buildings in Berlin were destroyed and gigantic satellite cities built in their place.[8]

2 Aldo Rossi, "Un giovane architetto tedesco: Oswald Mathias Ungers," *Casabella Continuità* 244 (October 1960), pp. 22–35.

3 Oswald Mathias Ungers and Reinhardt Gieselmann, "Zu einer neuen Architektur," *Der Monat* 15, no. 174 (1963), p. 96. The manifesto is dated 1960, but it was published in 1963.

4 Oswald Mathias Ungers, "Die Stadt als Kunstwerk," *Werk* 50, no. 7 (1963), pp. 281–83.

5 Aldo Rossi, *L'architettura della città* (Padova, 1966). English translation: Aldo Rossi, *The Architecture of the City*, trans. Diane Ghirardo and Joan Ockman (Cambridge, MA, 1982).

6 Cf. Jörg Pampe, ed., *Architekturtheorie: Internationaler Kongress in der TU Berlin* (Berlin, 1968).

7 Marco De Michelis, "Architectura artificialis," in *O.M. Ungers: 1991–1998* (Milan, 1998), pp. 9–18. Unfortunately, the article was not translated in the German and English versions of the volume.

8 Hans Kollhoff, "Eine aufregende Übung: Hans Kollhoff im Gespräch mit Florian Hertweck und Sébastien Marot, Mai 2009," in *Die Stadt in der Stadt: Berlin; Ein grünes Archipel*, ed. Florian Hertweck and Sébastien Marot (Zurich, 2013), pp. 153–61.

Wolf Jobst Siedler and Elisabeth Niggemeyer had already focused on this issue in their book *Die gemordete Stadt* (The Murdered City):[9] they denounced, more than the useless destruction of documents of Berlin architecture, "the extinguishment of the truly urban." A few years later, in September 1968, students at the TU Berlin organized an exhibition entitled *Diagnose zum Bauen in West-Berlin* (Diagnosis of Building in West Berlin), which took place in the shell of the faculty building begun by Scharoun. They openly criticized a policy based on "their declared goal of letting the city degenerate into a huge property offering a return on investment."[10] This was also the essence of a manifesto published on this occasion and signed by seventy architects, including many of the future protagonists of 1980s architecture in Berlin.[11]

In 1975, it was the turn of the Internationales Design Zentrum Berlin to organize, at the initiative of Heinrich Klotz and François Burkhardt, a debate on "Entwerfen in der historischen Strasse" (designing in the historical street) (→ p. 26). From this year onward, thoughts began to emerge—more or less in the open—on whether it was convenient to organize a new Internationale Bauausstellung (International Building Exhibition) in Berlin. The strategy was no longer to stage an exhibition in the form of a model quarter, as had been the case at Interbau 1957 and as the case would have been for the Landwehr Canal in the Tiergarten according to the plans for a—soon forgotten—"Interbau 1981." Instead, the slogan was now "Stadtreparatur" (Urban Repair): the plan was to intervene on the existing city, analogously to the new conservation strategies applied to old Italian city centers at the time (especially Bologna)[12] and to the studies and theories discussing the European city in those years.

On behalf of the Senate, Josef Paul Kleihues had elaborated a *Berlin-Atlas* of Charlottenburg and Kreuzberg, which constituted the cognitive foundation for a future restoration program.[13] Between 1971 and 1977 he also experimented with the theme of housing blocks, with his project for the Vinetaplatz in Berlin (→ p. 23). Its success contributed, on the one hand, to reintroducing housing solutions from the time between the nineteenth and twentieth centuries; on the other hand, it demonstrated that a morphological approach to urban architecture was feasible when critically aware of the preexisting settlements and of the visible traces of the city's history.

The complex renovation of Block 118 by Hardt-Waltherr Hämer between 1974 and 1980 dealt with similar problems, although with very different means of expression (→ p. 25). This project had successfully recovered a fragment of the nineteenth-century city, while considering both the needs of the residents and the settlement's original architectural character: by eliminating superfluous additions, transforming the inner courtyards into semipublic green areas, modernizing the housing facilities, and safeguarding the rights of the tenants.

MODELS FOR A CITY

All of these topics converged in a series of articles by the title "Modelle für eine Stadt" (Models for a City) published by Kleihues and Siedler in the newspaper *Berliner Morgenpost*. The clear objective was to support an exhibition model that was not limited to an isolated construction project, but instead engaged with the complexity of an existing urban fabric, and required an integrated series of restoring, repairing, and completing activities.[14]
The same architects who were involved in other initiatives of those years—Carlo Aymonino, Heinrich Klotz, Aldo Rossi, Peter and Alison Smithson, James Stirling, Rob Krier, Wolfgang Pehnt—contributed to abandoning the original theme "Wohnen in der Innenstadt" (living in the city center), focused on a single central area, in favor of a deeply comprehensive intervention. It was

9 Wolf Jobst Siedler and Elisabeth Niggemeyer, *Die gemordete Stadt* (Berlin, 1964).

10 "Diagnosen zur Architektur," *Arch+* 1, no. 3 (1968), pp. 63–68; *Diagnose zum Bauen in West-Berlin, Ausstellung der Aktion 507, 1968: Zusammenfassender Rückblick von Hinrich Baller*, June 2017 (unpublished typescript); Andreas Schätzke, "Ein Anliegen der Polis: Stadt, Architektur und Öffentlichkeit in der Bundesrepublik Deutschland," in *Josef Paul Kleihues: Stadt Bau Kunst*, ed. Paul Kahlfeldt, Andres Lepik, and Andreas Schätzke, exh. cat. Hamburger Bahnhof – Museum für Gegenwart, Berlin (Berlin, 2003), p. 57.

11 Next to Josef Paul Kleihues, Oswald Mathias Ungers, and Ludwig Leo were Hinrich Baller, Jonas Geist, Goerd Peschken, and Jan Rave. They were all among the twenty-seven people portrayed in the August 1968 issue of the *Deutsche Bauzeitung*: "Junge Berliner Architekten," *Deutsche Bauzeitung* 102, no. 8 (August 1968).

12 Pier Luigi Cervellati, Roberto Scannavini, and Carlo de Angelis, *La nuova cultura delle città* (Milan, 1977).

13 Josef Paul Kleihues, *Berlin-Atlas zu Stadtbild und Stadtraum* (Berlin, 1973).

14 Vittorio Magnago Lampugnani, "Von den Grosssiedlungen in der Peripherie zur Rekonstruktion der Innenstadt: Urbanistiche Debatten in Deutschland 1960–1980," in Kahlfeldt et al., *Josef Paul Kleihues: Stadt Bau Kunst* (see note 10), pp. 67–88.

Fig. 1 Aldo Rossi, Fabio Reinhart, Bruno Reichlin, Eraldo Consolascio, “La Città analoga” (The Analogue City), 1976
In this contribution to the Venice Biennale, Rossi summarized visually his theory of the urban.

15 Abgeordnetenhaus von Berlin, June 30, 1978, printed matter.

16 Magnago Lampugnani, "Urbanistische Debatten" (see note 14).

17 Rossi, *The Architecture of the City* (see note 5).

18 Ezio Bonfanti, Aldo Rossi et al., eds., *Architettura razionale* (Milan, 1973).

19 On IBA-Alt versus IBA-Neu, see also the article by Gerd Zimmermann in this volume.

20 Philipp Meuser, "1977. Rob Krier: Idealplan der südlichen Friedrichstadt," in *Das ungebaute Berlin: Stadtkonzepte im 20. Jahrhundert*, ed. Carsten Krohn (Berlin, 2010), pp. 209–11.

described in a policy document on "planning and realizing an international building exhibition in Berlin in 1984," approved by the Senate of West Berlin in the summer of 1978.[15]

The initiative's new title was "Die Innenstadt als Wohnort" (The City Center as Domicile) and was supposed to affect an area of around 250 hectares. Its aim was to build about 9,000 housing units, based on nine theses that were formulated, inter alia, as follows: "Berlin is many cities—a city within the city"; "The basic historical structure of the city must become a foundation for urban development"; "The city as constant, the building as variable"; "The city as domicile"; "New tension between social issues and artistic responsibility."[16]

The influence of Aldo Rossi's ideas on this new strategy was evident (fig. 1): his *L'architettura della città* was published in Italy in 1966 and translated into German in 1973 and into English in 1982,[17] precisely as the debate on urban architecture reached its peak. In 1973, the Milan Triennale inaugurated the section on international architecture of its fifteenth edition, where Aldo Rossi introduced—under the umbrella of "Tendenza"—the group of architects that was shaping the next IBA. Among them were Oswald Mathias Ungers, Josef Paul Kleihues, Rob and Léon Krier, as well as the New York Five.[18]

The IBA was divided between the topics of "cautious urban renewal," focused on the problematic Kreuzberg district, which was forced by the Berlin Wall into a position of extreme marginality, and that of "critical reconstruction,"[19] used by Kleihues as a basis to define the reconstruction especially in the Tiergarten and in the Südliche Friedrichstadt. However, despite the continuous polemics accentuating these differences, from today's perspective the IBA seems in fact characterized by a consistent morphological approach. Its aim was to reclaim the entirety—meaning both the settlement structure and the architectural elements—of those central areas in Berlin where the scars of war and reconstruction were the most visible.

In 1977, before Kleihues was named director of the upcoming building exhibition together with Hämer, Rob Krier had elaborated an ideal project for southern Friedrichstadt on behalf of the building commissioner Hans Christian Müller (→ p. 27). There, Krier adopted the morphological approach that would later be at the center of the IBA, and he even suggested the same project strategy that he was applying to the residential complex on Ritterstrasse for the whole Baroque city (also beyond the border of the Wall, a boundary the IBA would never cross) (figs. 2–3). In his ideal project, Krier outlined a path based on the reconstruction of the historical roadway and on the regular succession of city blocks, distributed uniformly onto a rectangular pattern. He also envisioned a broad boulevard exactly where the originally planned route of the motorway in the 1960s would have definitely destroyed the urban unity of the Baroque city, as well as the reconstruction of some architectural "emergencies" such the Böhmische Kirche or the Jerusalemer Kirche, which had been destroyed after the war. The large, unfulfilled monument designed in 1797 by Friedrich Gilly in honor of Frederick II was also to be seen in the background of the bird's-eye view of his project, at the center of the octagon of Leipziger Platz.[20]

DELIRIOUS BERLIN

In 1972, *Casabella* launched a competition for new urban visions. Among the participants was a young Dutch architecture student named Rem Koolhaas, who had just transferred from the AA School in London to Cornell University.

The project, conceived with Elia Zenghelis, Madelon Vriesendorp, and Zoe Zenghelis, was entitled *Exodus, or the Voluntary Prisoners of Architecture*.

Fig. 2 Rob Krier, Ritterstrasse residential complex, building types, 1977

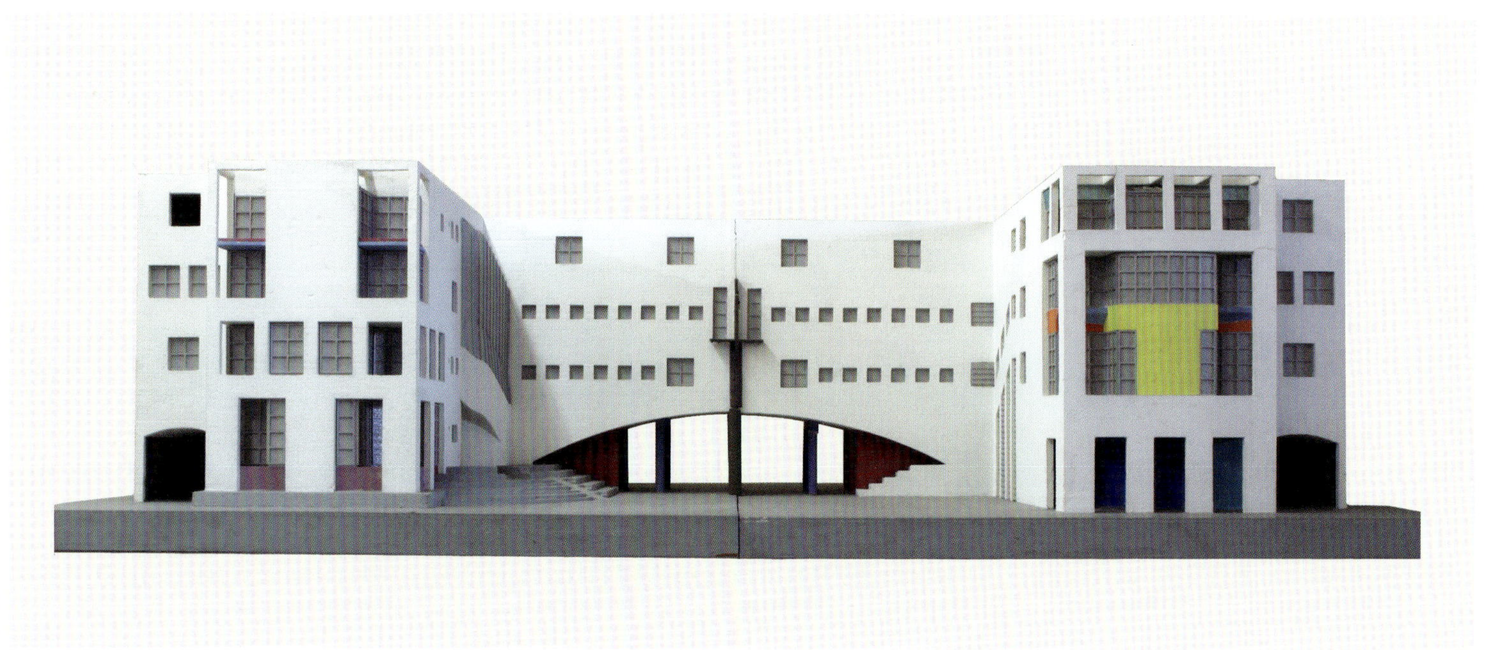

Fig. 3 Rob Krier, Ritterstrasse residential complex, gate building, model, 1977

It focused on the Berlin Wall and offered a new interpretation of it: as an intermediate architectural space inhabited by voluntary prisoners, who are enthusiastic about the freedom given by their architectural boundaries. The Wall's no man's land was transformed into a strip of "intense metropolitan desirability, … like a runway, a landing strip for the new architecture of collective monuments."[21] Koolhaas and Zenghelis thus anticipated their 1980 project for Friedrichstrasse/Kochstrasse within the context of IBA, where the two architects seemed to foresee the fall of the Wall, by designing a linear park along the course that at the time still defined the impassable frontier between East and West Berlin (→ p. 4).

It comes as no surprise that Koolhaas and Ungers crossed paths, attracted as Koolhaas was, in the early 1970s, by the simple repertoire that Ungers sought to develop, and the relationship between history and modernity with which he was playing.[22] Until around the end of the 1970s, their two careers developed in parallel.

From his "exile" at Cornell, Ungers observed Berlin and the discussions shaping the upcoming building exhibition closely. In 1977 and 1978, he organized two summer academies together with Rem Koolhaas, Hans Kollhoff, Peter Riemann, and Arthur Ovaska, all students or collaborators at Cornell University at the time. The topics of the academies were the "Urban Villa" and the "Green Archipelago": a city "which is neither conserved nor reinvented, but which is created from the extant through the paradox of a selective tabula rasa, a collection of existing urban morphologies created by selection and elimination, together forming a new order."[23]

The proposal was therefore neither to ignore nor to conserve the historical city. The conceptual plan was radically different from the "morphological" approach of urban renewal and from the implied possibility of integrally restoring a homogeneous cityscape. According to Ungers, the city had to be interpreted as a system of inconsistent places—of urban islands (→ p. 28)—chosen for their specific qualities and compared to various preexisting models that originated from completely different historical or geographical contexts. The ideal plan of Karlsruhe thus was compared to the rotunda of Mehringplatz at the southern end of Friedrichstadt; Central Park in New York with the abandoned area of Görlitzer Bahnhof; Ivan Leonidov's project for a linear city in the Soviet city Magnitogorsk with the straight route of Unter den Eichen, and his unbuilt Palace of Culture designed in the early 1930s for Moscow was taken into consideration for Berlin.[24]

The city would become an open system of urban islands, interspersed in an open city landscape, where the islands themselves were characterized by a typological inconsistency, based on the hybridization of open (peripheral development) and closed architectural structures (urban villas).

It was an endeavor aimed at thinning the urban space and dissolving the city's original structure into what Ungers called an "urban garden" with floating enclaves, each having a specific typological, political, and sociological character. The main reason for this approach was evidently the economic and demographic crisis of West Berlin, which had lost more than 200,000 inhabitants in the 1970s, equal to a tenth of its population. As the first version of the *Berlin Manifest*, written by Rem Koolhaas at the beginning of the seminar, stated: "Any future planning for Berlin must plan for a shrinking city."[25]

Ungers himself justified his renewed interest in the typology of the urban villa with an alarmed statement:

> The city is now competing, particularly as far as the environmental qualities are concerned, with the life in the country. The future of the city therefore depends entirely on the solution of the dichotomy

21 Rem Koolhaas and Elia Zenghelis with Madelon Vriesendorp and Zoe Zenghelis, "Exodus, or the Voluntary Prisoners of Architecture, 1972", in *Perfect Acts of Architecture*, ed. Jeffrey Kipnis, exh. cat. The Museum of Modern Art, New York, and Wexner Center for the Arts, Columbus (New York, 2001), pp. 14–33.

22 "Ghostwriting: Rem Koolhaas im Gespräch mit Florian Hertweck und Sébastien Marot, April 2010," in Hertweck and Marot, *Die Stadt in der Stadt* (see note 8), pp. 131–43.

23 Wilfried Kühn, "Oswald Mathias Ungers, Grünes Stadtarchipel," in *Das ungebaute Berlin: Stadtkonzepte im 20. Jahrhundert*, ed. Carsten Krohn (Berlin, 2010), pp. 206–8.

24 In Rem Koolhaas's typescript "Berlin: A Green Archipelago," p. 5, he mentions the "insertion of Leonidov's Palace of Culture into the Kreuzberg area," later corrected by hand into "Ernst-Reuter-Platz." The text was published in Hertweck and Marot, *Die Stadt in der Stadt* (see note 8), pp. 12–13.

25 Hertweck and Marot, *Die Stadt in der Stadt* (see note 8), p. 12.

> between city and country. If the city is going to survive as a social, political, economic, and not the least, as a cultural entity, the survival is only possible if living and environmental conditions can be provided in the city similar to those of a more natural environment.[26]

The per se contradictory concept of the urban villa had the role of implementing a necessary compromise between city and countryside that Ungers saw realized in the romantic landscape in Glienicke, inhabited by Schinkel's architectures and Lenné's gardens.

It should be noted that such topics were neither isolated nor marginal. On the contrary, they were a part of Berlin's history, starting from a polycentric layout in which *Zwischengebiete* or intermediate zones are crucial for defining the plurality of characters present in the city. Many earlier projects can be interpreted in this regard: the most significant entries to the competition of 1910, such as the one by Hermann Jansen with his *Grünflächenprojekt* (Green Spaces Project); Bruno Taut's and Martin Wagner's projects for large housing developments in the 1920s; the "green city" in which nature and urban phenomena merged, as described in Leberecht Migge's *Das grüne Manifest* (The Green Manifesto);[27] and the most important input by Scharoun, Jørn Utzon, and the Smithsons for the 1958 competition Hauptstadt Berlin.

In his project for the residential complex at Lützow Platz in 1979—an unfortunate project, just recently demolished—Ungers had tried to realize a city within a city. This individual "island" combined a solid front facing the city and an open structure of urban villas blending with nature at the back (figs. 4–5).

The twenty-four sessions in Ungers's summer academy show how much he was counting on this occasion to elaborate a valid alternative to Kleihues's proposal for the next building exhibition, as it would have led inevitably to a concealment of the city's problems: the last thing a "postindustrial" city in the middle of a demographic crisis needed was more housing areas!

The whole "neorationalist" movement that Aldo Rossi had tried to form in his exhibition at the Milan Triennale was now gathering around the topic of the urban villa.[28] Among them was, of course, Rem Koolhaas, who was just putting the theme of "city within the city" into practice in New York, with an archipelago of islands coinciding with single city blocks, divided not by straits, but by impetuous traffic streams running along the regular street net.[29]

CRITICAL RECONSTRUCTION OF THE CITY

It has been recently observed that the complete history of Berlin can be summarized around two opposing tendencies:

> The first boiled down to centralization, densification, and homogenization: examples of this are the Baroque Berlin, the Hobrecht Plan, Wilhelm's Berlin, the IBA, and most especially the critical reconstruction of reunification. The other approach tried to decentralize and loosen up the city: Schinkel's Berlin project, Taut's dissolution of cities, Scharoun's collective plan, and also the manifesto of the "city within the city."[30]

Between critical reconstruction and the green archipelago, the former would prevail, and Kleihues was appointed as director of the IBA-Neubaugebiete (new building areas). He managed to involve the same group of international architects that had participated in Ungers's summer academy, thanks to the more empirical, maybe less "radical" nature of his proposal, which proved

26 Oswald Mathias Ungers, "'The Urban Villa': A Prototype for Inner City Residences," in *The Urban Villa*, ed. Oswald Mathias Ungers, Hans Kollhoff, and Arthur Ovaska (Ithaca and Cologne, 1977), p.1.

27 Leberecht Migge, *Der soziale Garten: Das grüne Manifest* (Berlin-Friedenau, 1926).

28 Along with the Germans Josef Paul Kleihues, Jürgen Sawade, and Stefan Wewerka, the following individuals were also involved. Kenneth Frampton, Robert Stern, Charles Moore, Peter Eisenman, Philip Johnson, Aldo Rossi, Vittorio Gregotti, Alison and Peter Smithson, Hans Hollein, Rob Krier, Carlo Aymonino, Massimo Scolari, and James Stirling.

29 Sébastien Marot, "Genese eines Hopeful Monster," in Hertweck and Marot, *Die Stadt in der Stadt* (see note 8), pp. 25–43.

30 Hans Kollhoff, "Eine aufregende Übung" (see note 8), pp. 158–59.

In the courtyard of the building at Fehrbelliner Strasse 6, 1980s, photo: Robert Conrad
The blind portal on the rear façade of the former Pfefferberg brewery combines ancient associations with very Berlin ones.

Gasometers, 1984, photo: Gerd Danigel
Numerous photographs and drawings of the three gasometers were taken in 1984 shortly before they were demolished, and they demonstrate the visual significance of the buildings.

Gaudystrasse, 1987, photo: Robert Conrad
The street façades reflected, especially with their traces of wear, the eventful lives of their occupants.

Klaus Pöschk, Helmut Müller, Wigbert Treuter, daycare center on Arnimplatz, 1983
Redesigned open space on the block between Swinemünder Strasse and Zionskirchstrasse. This daycare center was designed as a project for reuse. The mural *Himmelsschaukel* (Sky Swing) is by Jürgen Beidokat.

Werkfabrik (Work Factory), renovation and conversion of a disused steam-powered sawmill for the Regenbogenfabrik (Rainbow Factory) alternative project, Lausitzer Strasse 22, 1983–87

Álvaro Siza Vieira with Peter Brinkert, apartment building on Schlesisches Tor, Kreuzberg, 1983–85
The words “Bonjour Tristesse” were added to the building anonymously in 1984.

VEB Bau- und Montagekombinat Ingenieurhochbau Berlin and HAN Bau, residential and commercial building on
 Leipziger Strasse (at Mauerstrasse), ca. 1987, unbuilt

VEB Bau- und Montagekombinat Ingenieurhochbau Berlin and HAN Bau, reconstruction of the complex of arcades between Friedrichstrasse and Charlottenstrasse, view from Mohrenstrasse, ca. 1987, unbuilt

VEB Bau- und Montagekombinat Ingenieurhochbau Berlin and HAN Bau, reconstruction of the complex of arcades at Friedrichstrasse, view of historicizing façade design of the industrial residential building between present-day Jägerstrasse and Taubenstrasse, ca. 1987, unbuilt

Eisenman Robertson Architects with Thomas Leeser, residential/office building at Checkpoint Charlie, 1985–86, photo: Günter Schneider, ca. 1986

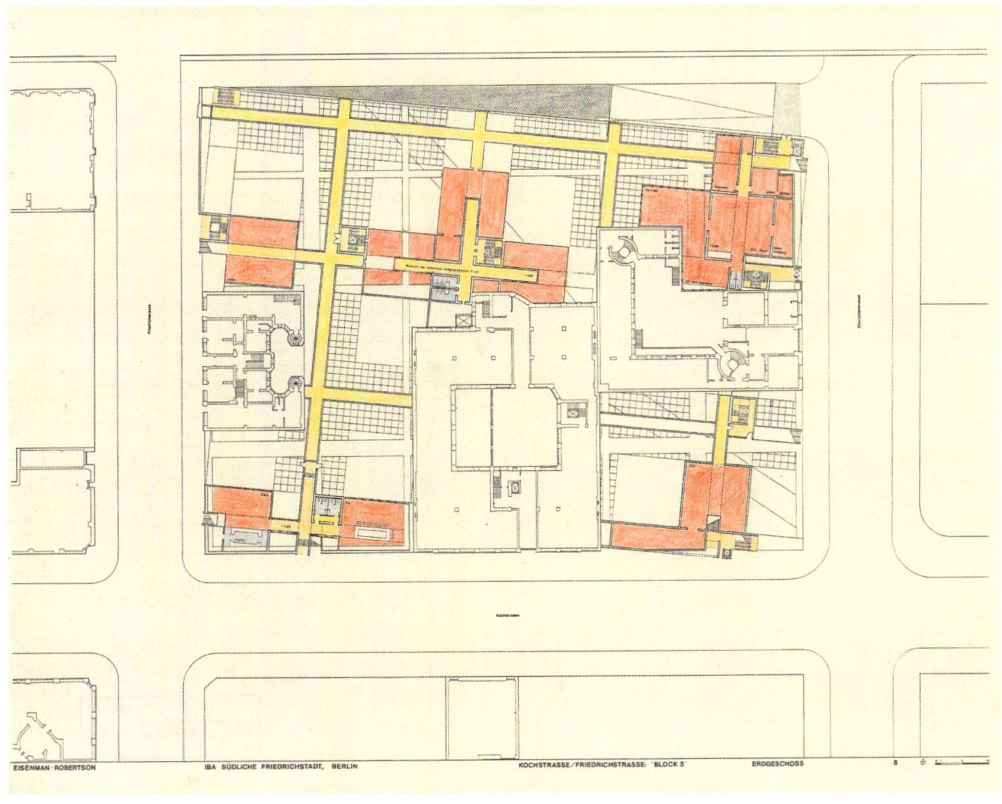

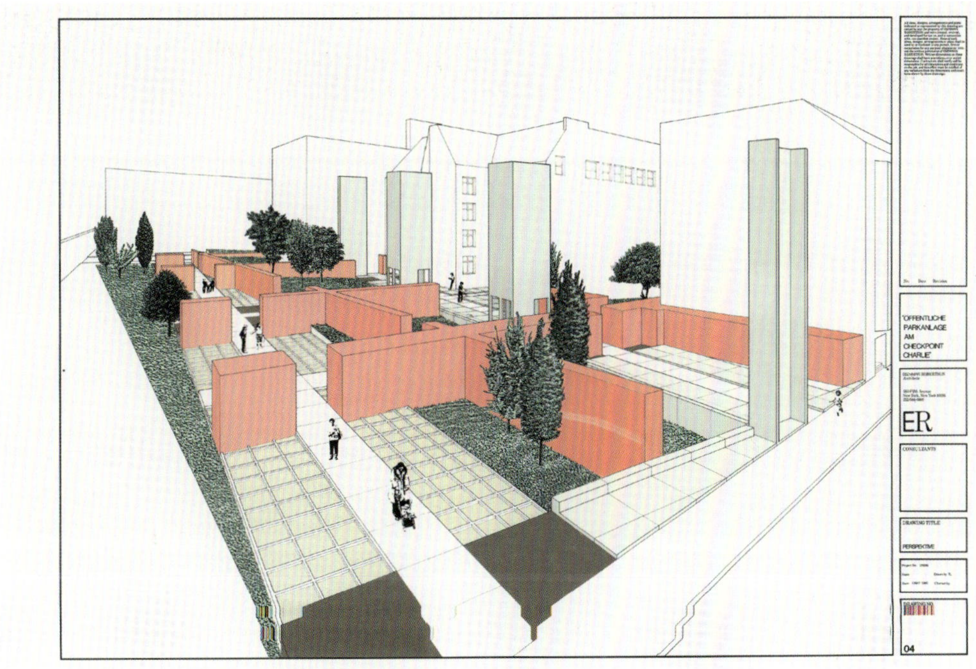

Eisenman Robertson Architects with Thomas Leeser, referential system of two superimposed grids for the new complex at Checkpoint Charlie with the Museum der künstlich ausgegrabenen Stadt (Museum of the Artificially Excavated City), 1985, unbuilt

Eisenman Robertson Architects with Thomas Leeser, public parks at Checkpoint Charlie, May 1, 1985, unbuilt

Kjell Nylund, Peter Stürzebecher, Christof Puttfarken, Wohnregal (Residential Shelving), Admiralstrasse 16, built, 1985–87

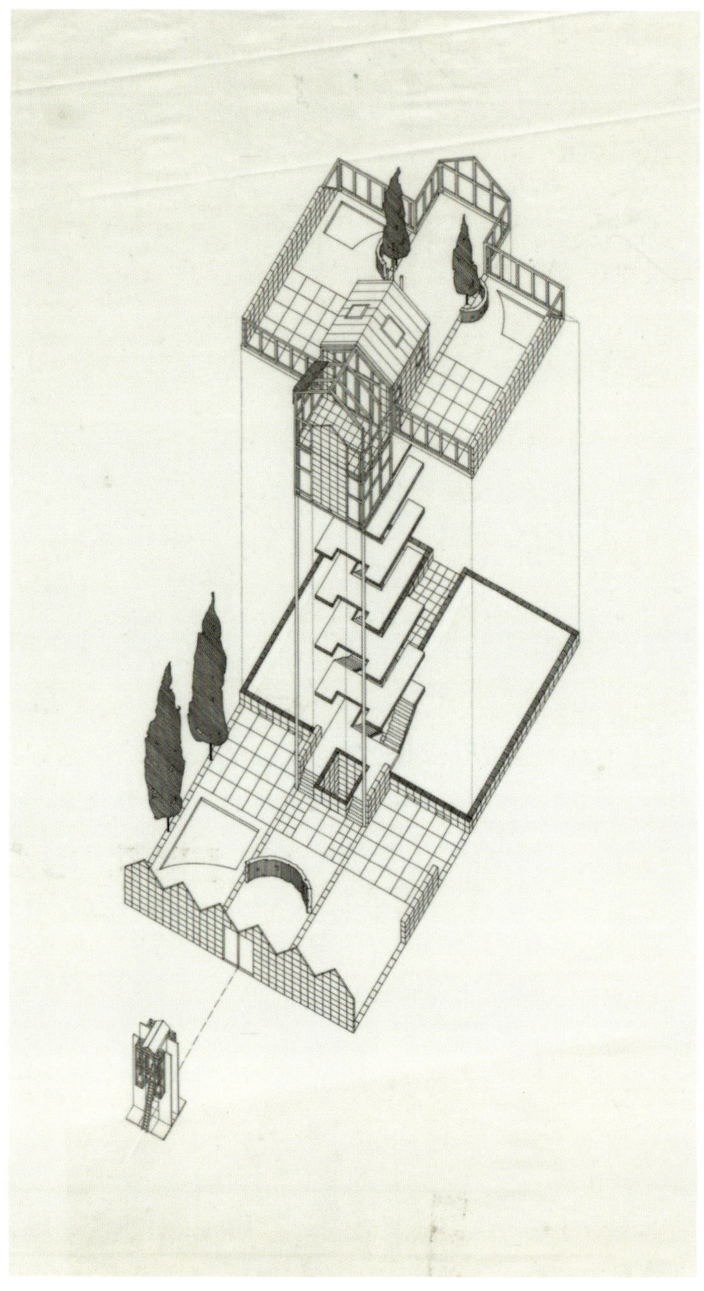

Kjell Nylund, Peter Stürzebecher, Christof Puttfarken, Wohnregal (Residential Shelving), Admiralstrasse 16, built, 1985–87
This drawing shows the building's construction, which resembles a bookshelf with adjustable shelves.

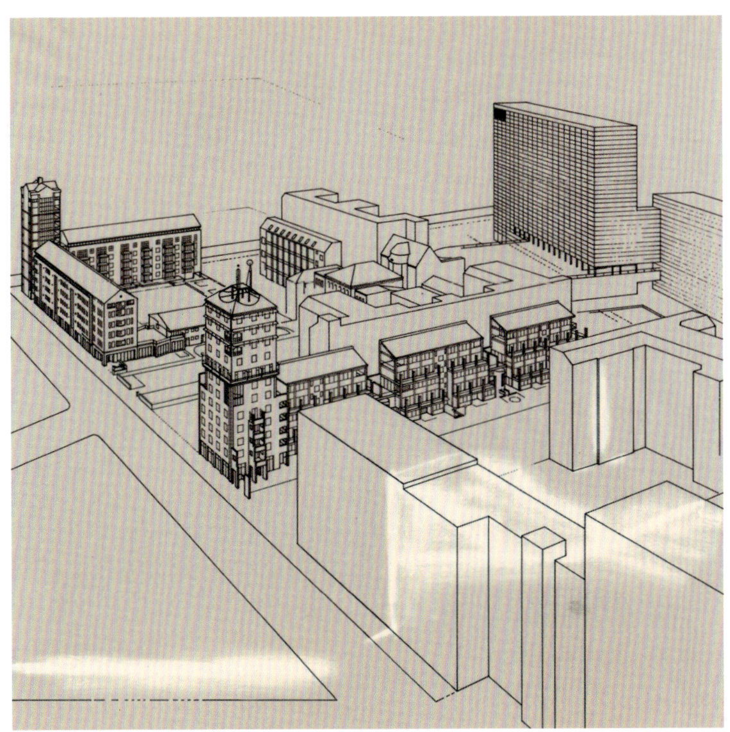

Dietrich von Beulwitz, self built terraces, Wilhelmstrasse 120–121, perspective of the surroundings and model, 1981–87

This apartment building was one of the experimental buildings for the IBA 87. The future residents could lower their rent by doing work themselves.

BEYOND THE BERLIN MYTH

The Local, the Global, and IBA 87

Emily Pugh

In a 1994 article entitled "Berlin: Once and Future Capital," the urban sociologist Hartmut Häussermann and the political scientist Elizabeth Strom discuss the importance of a country's capital city, calling it the place where "national identity in its most tangible form is rooted." They note, however, that if the capital is a "symbolic space, it is also an ordinary town in which rubbish must be collected."[1] What Häussermann and Strom are alluding to are two interrelated aspects of any city, but particularly a capital city: its image, both figurative and literal, in the public imagination, as well as the more mundane side of the city that is often left out of nationalist and/or heroic visions of it, such as the workaday tasks that are a necessary part of urban living.

Perhaps nowhere have these two facets of a city stood in such sharp relief as in West Berlin during the Cold War, where the effort to construct the city in international terms as the "capital of the free world" was complicated by the city's own social and economic problems, many of which were ironically endemic to its unique position at the center of a global conflict. Accounts of architecture and urban planning in West Berlin have, understandably, tended to emphasize the city's symbolic significance over its local urban politics; yet, a complete account of the former is ultimately not possible without a consideration of the latter.[2] With this essay, I will explore what might be characterized as the push-pull relationship between the global and local demands placed on West Berlin, particularly in the 1970s and 1980s, through an investigation of the squatter movement and the 1987 International Building Exhibition (IBA). In particular, I will examine the IBA as a response to the squatter movement and, in doing so, consider the ways that West Berlin's local politics often conflicted with the more lofty goals related to the construction of its global image. Understanding how these two aspects of West Berlin coexisted, often in tension, will help in creating a more nuanced account of the context in which urban planning and architectural policies were created and enacted in the city through these decades.[3]

FROM COLD WAR CAPITAL TO COUNTERCULTURE CAPITAL

Since the end of World War II, governments in the West had gone to great lengths to define West Berlin in international terms, to cast it as a bastion of freedom, democracy, and capitalism: the so-called shop window of the West. However, while there was truth to this image, it was also somewhat exaggerated. For example, although West Berliners certainly enjoyed civil liberties that those in East Germany did not, to speak of freedom in a city that was cut off from the West and, after 1961, barricaded by the Berlin Wall was somewhat ironic. Moreover, the economy of this shop window of the West was from the start heavily subsidized by the West German government, and as a result West Berlin never had an independent economy.[4] Although defined as a symbol of the West as a whole, West Berlin was in many ways a special case, subject to a set of political, economic, and social circumstances that were specific to it.

As an attempt to reconcile the local and global demands placed on West Berlin, the IBA in 1987 was caught between them. Staged as part of the larger celebration of the city's 750th anniversary, the event featured built architectural projects along with an exhibition program, including displays of drawings, designs, and models as well as historic surveys, all of which were intended to encourage discussion about city planning and housing policy on a global scale. However, the IBA was also an attempt to address West Berlin's housing shortage and, in so doing, to respond to the critiques of the city's squatters, who in the 1970s had joined together as part of a broad-based social protest movement.

1 Hartmut Häussermann and Elizabeth Strom, "Berlin: The Once and Future Capital," *International Journal of Urban and Regional Research* 18, no. 2 (1994), pp. 335–45, esp. p. 334.

2 See Kathleen James-Chakraborty, *Modernism as Memory: Building Identity in the Federal Republic of Germany* (Minneapolis, 2018); Stephanie Warnke, *Stein gegen Stein: Architektur und Medien im geteilten Berlin, 1950–70* (Frankfurt am Main, 2009).

3 The material in this essay is covered also in Chapter 6. See Emily Pugh, "Back to Center: Restoring West Berlin's Image and Identity," in *Architecture, Politics, and Identity in Divided Berlin* (Pittsburgh, 2014).

4 Wolfgang Ribbe, *Berlin 1945–2000: Grundzüge der Stadtgeschichte* (Berlin, 2002), p. 132.

5 The most infamous of these construction scandals was the so-called "Garski affair" of 1980–81. See Benedict Ugarte Chacón, "Auf Sand gebaut," in *Untersuchungsausschüsse: Das schärfste Holzschwert des Parlamentarismus? Ausgesuchte Berliner Polit-Skandale*, ed. Benedict Ugarte Chacón, Michael Förster, and Thorsten Grünberg (Berlin, 2019), pp. 93–118.

6 Manfred Görtemaker, *Geschichte der Bundesrepublik Deutschland: Von der Gründung bis zur Gegenwart* (Frankfurt am Main, 2004), pp. 644–45; Margit Mayer, "Social Movements in European Cities: Transitions from the 1970s to the 1990s," in *Cities in Contemporary Europe*, ed. Arnaldo Bagnasco and Patrick Le Galès (Cambridge, 2000), pp. 131–52, esp. p. 132.

7 The image of "stony" Berlin was established by Werner Hegemann's book *Das steinerne Berlin: History of the World's Largest Rental Barracks* (Berlin, 1930).

Fig. 1 Celebration of the third anniversary of the Regenbogenfabrik (Rainbow Factory), March 24, 1984

While other West German cities were also experiencing housing crises, the situation was more dire in West Berlin, partly because of the city's limited amount of space, and it was more visible, given the city's symbolic role. The squatter movement was spurred by a severe shortage of particularly lower-income housing, but also by widely publicized corruption in West Berlin's city government and building industry.[5] The squatters movement in West Germany was in fact one of a number of sociopolitical activist movements developing out of the student protests that took place in the 1960s. Groups of activists espousing a variety of related concerns, from nuclear arms proliferation to women's rights, were linked by communal and/or cooperative "projects" such as bookstores, cafés, and organic food markets. West Berlin's was the largest of these alternative communities, and by 1981 a large network of around 1,500 cooperative projects had been established, collectively known as the alternative scene (*Alternative Szene*) (fig. 1).[6]

The alternative scene generally, and the squatters movement specifically, were centered in the neighborhood of Kreuzberg where, starting in the 1960s, university students and foreign laborers from countries like Turkey and Yugoslavia had moved in search of increasingly scarce affordable housing. The short supply of low-income housing was a result of the building policies that had guided redevelopment in West Berlin following World War II. These policies were designed to correct what were seen as the mistakes of prewar urban development in Berlin that had produced the widely reviled building type known as the *Mietskaserne* (rental barrack). Built in multistory blocks and centered on comparatively small, linked courtyards, *Mietskasernen* had created in Berlin the densely built, "stony" urban landscape for which the city became notorious.[7] In the postwar period, reconstruction generally focused not on renovating such buildings, but on replacing them with large, high-rise housing developments. These developments, one example of which is Gropiusstadt in Neukölln (18,000 units, begun 1962), were for the most part built in the outermost districts of West Berlin, leaving inner-city districts like Kreuzberg comparatively untouched either by urban redevelopment or renovation.

As a result of such policies, there was a decrease in the overall number of new housing units constructed in West Berlin in the 1960s and 1970s, at the same time that government subsidies and other economic incentives indirectly encouraged landlords to leave existing buildings unoccupied and/or un-renovated. By 1982, at the height of West Berlin's housing crisis, almost 10,000 housing units were in empty or partially empty buildings, despite the fact that 70,000 applications for housing were languishing in the offices of the city's housing authority (Landesamt für Wohnungswesen).[8] This shortage of particularly lower-income housing disproportionately affected the city's foreign worker and student populations. In response, activists began illegally squatting in the unoccupied buildings as well as organizing protests against the city's housing construction and urban development policies.

As the movement grew, images of West Berlin's squatters and members of other activist groups began increasingly to replace the images of prosperity and rebirth that had predominated the city's public image in the 1950s and 1960s. In place of photos of the pristine, newly rebuilt Hansa district or of the sleek, modernist Europa-Center rising behind the reconstructed ruins of the Kaiser Wilhelm Memorial Church (fig. 2), the images of the city that filled the West German and international press in the 1970s and 1980s often featured West Berlin's immigrant population, long-haired squatters protesting in the streets, or crumbling tenements festooned with graffiti and antigovernment slogans (fig. 3). In contrast to the earlier photos, these images of the 1970s and 1980s were informed by the local political conflicts that seemed to have overwhelmed the city's grander, globally oriented pretensions. Indeed, press photos of protesters and immigrant residents encouraged the perception that West Berlin was populated with outsiders, a center not of mainstream, Western values, but of aberration, difference, and the critique of such values. As the filmmaker Rosa von Praunheim told the news magazine *Der Spiegel* in 1983, West Berlin had become the "Mecca for all that is extreme and flipped-out."[9]

West Berlin's unrenovated inner-city districts, above all Kreuzberg, featured prominently in such reports and as a result were viewed as the source of the city's problems by many in the press and in the West Berlin and West German governments. For example, because of the high number of immigrant residents in such neighborhoods, journalists worried that the city was no longer truly German, but was becoming what one called a "Turkish city."[10] Protest groups in West Berlin were, according to a 1981 article in *Newsweek*, clearly concerned with "self, not society," happy to spend their days out of work and on the dole.[11] As a result of such "problems," West Berlin was said to be suffering from what was called an "identity crisis," having lost its function and relevance vis-à-vis West Germany and indeed the entire Western world. Moreover the city, argued many, was diseased and dying, kept alive only by the constant transfusion of West German funds.[12] In his 1983 article in the news magazine *Der Spiegel*, journalist Karl-Heinz Krüger did not mince words: "the city is—sad but true—kaput."[13]

Those who regretted West Berlin's "lost identity" saw it as a grave problem primarily in relation to the city's Cold War importance (fig. 4). The fact that the most notorious venue of squatters' and other groups' critique of Western values was the "shop window of the West" was for many difficult to countenance. Indeed, although the media's dire pronouncements regarding West Berlin were no doubt overblown, the negative press was clearly viewed as a liability, in particular by the city's government. The approach of Berlin's 750th anniversary in 1987 was therefore greeted as an opportunity to restore West Berlin's "lost identity," to resuscitate the postwar image of West Berlin as a glamorous European metropolis of international importance, and, in doing

8 Harald Bodenschatz, Volker Heise, and Jochen Korfmacher, *Schluss mit Zerstörung?: Stadterneuerung und städtische Opposition in West-Berlin, Amsterdam und London* (Giessen, 1983), p. 47; Renate Mulhak, "Der Instandbesetzungskonflikt in Berlin," in *Grossstadt und neue soziale Bewegungen*, ed. Peter Grottian and Wilfried Nelles (Basel, 1983), pp. 205–52, esp. p. 205.

9 Karl-Heinz Krüger, "'Ich lerne langsam, dich zu hassen': Über den Niedergang von West-Berlin," *Der Spiegel* 33 (1983), pp. 36–53, esp. p. 40.

10 Joachim Nawrocki, "Wird West-Berlin zum Hinterhof der Nation?: Psychogramm einer siechenden Stadt," *Die Zeit* 34 (July 23, 1976), p. 3. See also Jürgen Engert, "Ist Berlin noch eine deutsche Stadt? Jeder achte Berliner ist ein Ausländer," *Rheinischer Merkur*, December 4, 1981, p. 3.

11 Fred Bruning, "Europe's Dead-End Kids," *Newsweek*, April 27, 1981, pp. 52–57, esp. p. 52.

12 In addition to Nawrocki's and Krüger's, a host of other newspaper articles throughout the period predicted a dire future, not to mention present, for West Berlin, for example "Hauptstadt der Fixer," *Der Spiegel*, January 2, 1978, pp. 51–52; Otto Jörg Weis, "Wohin man schaut: Nichts geht mehr," *Frankfurter Rundschau*, September 3, 1981, p. 3; and "West Berlin: Story of a City in Decline," *US News & World Report*, December 4, 1967, pp. 81–82. Similarly, a number of articles diagnosed West Berlin as suffering from an identity crisis. See, for example, Andreas Cleis, "Westberlin auf der Suche nach neuer Identität," *Neue Zürcher Zeitung*, October 6, 1981, p. 5; Hans-Jürgen Krupp, "Berlin: Eine Stadt auf der Suche nach ihrer wirtschaftlichen Identität," *Aussenpolitik* 37 (1986), pp. 327–41; Otto Jörg Weis, "Identitätskrise einer Stadt," *Stuttgarter Zeitung*, November 10, 1976, p. 1.

13 Krüger, "Über den Niedergang von West-Berlin" (see note 9), p. 40.

Fig. 2 Hardenbergstrasse (Charlottenburg), 1965, photo: Hans Seiler
In the 1950s and 1960s, the image of the partially ruined Kaiser-Wilhelm-Gedächtnis-Kirche (Kaiser Wilhelm Memorial Church)—surrounded by the shops and busy streets along the Kurfürstendamm—came to visually symbolize West Berlin and in particular its resurgence in the postwar period.

Fig. 3 The façade of a squat in Kreuzberg in 1980, photo: Jochen Moll

both, to reassert the city's association with mainstream political and economic values. The IBA 87 was a major part of this effort, designed not only to provide much-needed lower-income housing, but also, according to the Senate of West Berlin, to "work against the widely criticized, inhospitable modern city" and to reestablish "Berlin's preeminence as a cultural metropolis [*Kulturmetropole*]" on a global scale.[14]

THE IBA: PROPAGANDA VERSUS PUBLIC POLICY

The IBA was originally planned for 1984, but debates about the feasibility and expense of the exhibition delayed plans until 1987, at which time the IBA was integrated into the larger, government-organized celebration of Berlin's 750th jubilee. Formally opened in May 1987, the architectural exhibition was divided into two sections: IBA-Neubau or new construction, which focused on buildings constructed as infill at various points throughout the city, and IBA-Altbau or old construction, which entailed the refurbishment of existing buildings. This two-pronged approach, along with the exhibition's themes, "Rettung der kaputten Stadt" (Saving the Ruined City) and "Die Innenstadt als Wohnort" (The Inner-City as a Place to Live), reflected the planners' goals of revitalizing the supposedly "dead" city with new construction but also by paying attention to previously neglected areas. At the same time, drawings and sketches for planned projects were aimed at sparking a global debate about contemporary planning and architecture, and built projects were to make West Berlin a "model city," serving as an urban development blueprint for other cities to follow.[15]

14 "Mitteilung Nr 105: Programm der 750-Jahr-Feier, Internationale Bauausstellung," pp. 10, 11, B Rep 150/416, Landesarchiv Berlin.

15 See, for example, the series of articles in the *Berliner Morgenpost* in which Wolf Jobst Siedler, Josef Paul Kleihues, and others laid out their ideas for the IBA. Wolf Jobst Siedler et al., "Berlin: Modelle für eine Stadt," *Berliner Morgenpost*, January 18, 1977, pp. I–IV. Articles on this subject appeared in the newspaper throughout the year.

In terms of approach, the IBA represented a snapshot of theoretical as well as stylistic trends of the late 1970s and 1980s, especially postmodernism and the style that would later be called "deconstructivism."[16] The IBA projects communicated an overall rejection of modernism, an approach that had of course influenced the design of developments like Gropiusstadt; the postmodern buildings and planning approaches of the IBA were therefore presented as a repudiation of West Berlin's municipal housing policies of the 1950s and 1960s. Rather than zoning areas of the city according to their use, for example, IBA projects often repurposed spaces and/or united residential with commercial and institutional facilities. The architect Abel Volkmann, for example, created designs for a kindergarten and residential building that was to be installed in a former factory (Naunynstrasse 69, 1985), while Gino Valle designed a building intended to house both an elementary school and a wholesale flower market (Block 606, Bessel Park, 1983).[17]

Other projects adhered to the postmodern approach by incorporating historical decorative motifs or referencing past uses of a particular site through layout or design. The plan for Peter Eisenman's apartment and office building, built near Checkpoint Charlie, was an elaborate reference to the city's grid system (1985–88) (→ pp. 52–53).[18] Indeed, the grid, a major leitmotif of postmodern architecture, appears and reappears throughout IBA designs, in Eisenman's building but also in Stanley Tigerman's design for Tegel Docks housing (1985), in O. M. Ungers's design for an apartment complex on Lützowplatz (1979–81, demolished 2008–09 (→ p. 39), and in the IBA-Altbau scheme for "Residential Shelving," built in Kreuzberg (Wohnregal, Kjell Nylund, Christof Puttfarken, and Peter Stürzebecher, 1986) (fig. 5).

In addition to built projects like these, the IBA included conferences, a major historical exhibition entitled *750 Years of Architecture and Urban Planning in Berlin,* and the publication of numerous books, essays, and other literature both in and outside of West Berlin and West Germany. Moreover, the IBA's planners wanted the exhibition itself to embody architecture and urban planning discourse and thus used different styles and approaches to stage a kind of physical "debate" and to encourage discussion around the various proposed urban visions. To help achieve this goal, 20 percent of the exhibition budget was given to bringing the IBA's various urban planning and design ideas to an "intensive confrontation with the public" in the form of exhibition catalogues, pamphlets, maps, printed guides, and walking tours, and architecture and urban planning conferences.[19]

As a result of such initiatives, the IBA was highly visible on an international scale, although its reception, both in the popular and professional press, was—and is—decidedly mixed. Both politicians and the public balked at the exhibition's price tag, and architecture critics charged that its mix of different styles and approaches had turned West Berlin into a postmodern "Disneyland."[20] However, despite such negative assessments, most architecture critics agreed that the IBA marked an important moment for West Berlin in terms of its role as a center of culture. In a more recent assessment of the exhibition, for example, published in *Metropolis* magazine, critic Max Page argues that the IBA "produced no great works of architecture," but that it was nonetheless significant in that it sparked important debates about design and planning and because it gave architects like Peter Eisenman, Zaha Hadid, and John Hejduk their first major commissions.[21]

Indeed, whether one considers the IBA 87 a success or failure depends largely on what one considers its central goal: Was it an attempt to create long-term, practical solutions to housing in West Berlin and throughout the Western world? Or was it primarily an attempt to restore some of the cultural cachet that West Berlin was perceived to have lost in the 1970s and early

16 The term "deconstructivism" would not be coined until 1988, when an exhibition of the same name, which included IBA architects like Peter Eisenman, Zaha Hadid, and Daniel Libeskind, was held at The Museum of Modern Art in New York. See Philip Johnson, *Deconstructivist Architecture* (New York, 1988).

17 Designs for both Volkmann's and Valle's projects, as well as many of the IBA projects mentioned here, are included in Josef Paul Kleihues and Heinrich Klotz, eds., *International Building Exhibition Berlin 1987: Examples of a New Architecture* (New York, 1986).

18 See Peter Eisenman, "Das Symbol," in *Das Neue Berlin: Konzepte der Internationalen Bauausstellung 1987 für einen Städtebau mit Zukunft* (Berlin, 1987), pp. 86–96.

19 Parliament of West Berlin, Section A.3.5, quoted in Wallis Miller, "IBA's 'Models for a City': Housing and the Image of Cold-War Berlin," *Journal of Architectural Education* 46, no. 4 (1993), pp. 202–16, esp. p. 205.

Fig. 4 By the early 1980s, the image of the Kaiser-Wilhelm-Gedächtnis-Kirche had come to symbolize not West Berlin's emergence from the ruins of the past but what many saw as its current-day ruinous state.

Fig. 5 Kjell Nylund, Christof Puttfarken, Peter Stürzebecher, scheme for the Wohnregal (Residential Shelving), 1986

1980s? If one accepts improving housing and housing policy as the IBA's goal, then the exhibition was undoubtedly a failure. One reason for this was that the IBA and the buildings it produced were a product of West Berlin's heavily subsidized and uniquely structured construction industry. Planned and executed under rarefied circumstances, IBA projects were not ones that could be reproduced either in West Germany or in the West generally on a large scale. In addition, the IBA projects were often granted additional dispensations because of their role in the 750th jubilee; this meant that, because of their scale and expense, they were not even reproducible in West Berlin outside the confines of the exhibition.[22]

In addition, although the effort to incorporate many different voices and perspectives was appealing in theory, it had proved difficult in practice. Specifically, the inclusion of so many different groups in the planning and construction processes, from residents to local administrations to credit institutes to property owners and speculators, resulted in what was characterized as a "small war."[23] Even within the IBA's administration, disagreements between the head of the Neubau and Altbau divisions eventually led to a split between the two, so that in the end they functioned as more or less separate exhibitions.[24] As the architecture critic Colin Rowe famously put it, the goals of the exhibition were simply too ambitious and resulted more in a "hostile examination of details" rather than in real, workable solutions.[25]

However, if one considers the goal of the IBA not in terms of architectural solutions but primarily in terms of raising West Berlin's international profile, then the exhibition was a resounding success. It brought not only a huge amount of positive attention to the city, but also an international roster of top-tier architectural talent. Every major Western architectural publication featured articles on the IBA, and some did so twice, in the early 1980s when the exhibition was scheduled for 1984 and again in 1986–87. By virtue of the IBA, as well as all of the events related to the 750th anniversary, West Berlin was once again at the center of significant architectural debates and once again a center of institutionally recognized, as opposed to underground or protest-based, culture. The IBA helped convey the idea, at least to international audiences, that West Berlin had transcended the mire of its local politics, corruption, and infighting and reemerged in the international spotlight.[26]

At the same time, the IBA helped to restore legitimacy to institutions of political and cultural power and thus to provide a response to the critique of these institutions presented by the members of the alternative scene.[27] Throughout the 1960s and 1970s, West Berlin's well-publicized problems with government corruption and mass protests had left the impression that the Senate of West Berlin was ineffectual, "foundering," and had lost control of the city.[28] However in the wake of the 750th celebration, the Senate had to a certain extent restored the faith of West Berliners, West Germans, and the world in its ability to govern the city successfully and without disenfranchising its citizens. Through the IBA, West Berlin's political and architectural leaders had demonstrated their desire to integrate the squatters' critique in official building policy, while at the same time regaining control of the urban space. Moreover, by acknowledging the squatters in such a grand and public fashion, the IBA had blunted the force of their critiques. For all of these reasons, after the events of 1987 it could once again be argued that West Berlin represented mainstream Western values.

Obviously in terms of its main goal, the IBA was both an attempt to raise the city's profile and a genuine attempt to change housing policy in West Berlin. However, West Berlin's political importance in the context of the Cold War meant that the exhibition's function as an international public relations campaign ultimately overwhelmed local considerations. One telling

20 Dankwart Guratzsch, "Introduction," in *Das Neue Berlin: Für einen Städtebau mit Zukunft*, ed. Dankwart Guratzsch (Berlin, 1987), pp. 7–10, esp. p. 7.

21 Max Page, "Checkpoint Check Up," *Metropolis*, March 2005, pp. 106–9, 133, and 135, esp. pp. 133 and 108. Similarly, a 2011 article on the website Exberliner argued that the IBA 87 had "saved" Berlin. On this, see Dan Borden, "Save Berlin: How IBA 1987 Saved Berlin," EXBERLINER.com, December 2, 2011, https://www.exberliner.com/articles/save-berlin-iba/.

22 Peter Hoffmann, "Report from West Berlin," *Architectural Record* 173 (February 1985), p. 67; Manfred Schonlau, "Die Berliner Wohnungsbauförderung," *Baumeister* 5 (May 1987), pp. 20–23.

23 "Immobilien, Baukuhlen und Attrappen," *zitty* 10 (October 1987), press clipping, B Rep 150/461, Landesarchiv Berlin; Karl-Heinz Krüger, "Das Pathos endet an der Haustür," *Der Spiegel*, June 1, 1987, pp. 198–206, esp. p. 200.

24 Krüger, "Das Pathos endet an der Haustür" (see note 23).

25 Colin Rowe, "IBA: Rowe Reflects," *Architectural Review* 1076 (September 1984), p. 93.

26 The contrast between the local and global reception of the IBA 87 was recognized even at the time, as in Falk Jaeger, "Schaufenster der Weltarchitektur: Die IBA als Botschafter Berlins; Im Inland geschmäht, im Ausland gefeiert," *Tagesspiegel*, August 16, 1987.

27 A more recent account of the squatters movement is Alex Vasudevan, *Metropolitan Preoccupations: The Spatial Politics of Squatting in Berlin* (London, 2016).

28 Nawrocki, "Wird West-Berlin zum Hinterhof der Nation?" (see note 10), p. 3.

Fig. 6 The cover of the alternative press outlet for squatters, *Südost Express* (Southeast Express), declared in September 1982 that the IBA was "much paper about nothing."

detail in this regard is the fact that IBA GmbH, the corporation formed to raise money for and execute the exhibition, was not authorized to make any changes to housing policy by, for example, reforming the process by which the government granted housing subsidies. According to the architectural historian Wallis Miller, the city's housing administration "stood firmly between IBA GmbH and the developers, regulating the flow of concept into reality." "Responsibilities to produce an exhibition," she continues, "were not responsibilities to build subsidized housing."[29]

In part because of this administrative constraint, the IBA ultimately did not respond to many of the underlying issues that had spawned the housing crisis and the squatter movement (fig. 6), and thus many squatters viewed the exhibition as what one protest banner called "deception and capital-driven politics."[30] Indeed, a number of West Berlin squats were throughout 1987 decked with similar anti-IBA banners, and protests of the IBA were held throughout the 1980s, in one instance disrupting a formal ceremony celebrating the exhibition.[31] Not only the IBA, but the entire jubilee celebration was viewed with suspicion and derision by West Berlin's alternative scene, a fact that was clearly evident on June 12, 1987, when 50,000 people filled the streets to protest Ronald Reagan's visit to the city and West Berlin's transformation into the "largest amusement park in the world."[32]

Such protests were, however, ultimately overwhelmed by the international significance of the celebration and of the city itself. For example, although tens of thousands of West Berliners protested his visit, Reagan's speech produced one of the most famous and lasting images of his presidency when, standing in front of the Berlin Wall at the Brandenburg Gate, he exhorted the then-Soviet leader Mikhail Gorbachev to "tear down this wall." This widely publicized image, along with those of newly built and refurbished buildings, provide evidence of the IBA's and the jubilee's efficacy as international PR campaigns. However, to say that these events were primarily PR efforts is not simply to dismiss this as a shallow or unimportant goal. On the contrary, West Berlin's public image was an important part of its survival; fostering the perception that the exclave remained vital and relevant was critical to maintaining the financial support of West Germany as well as the military protection of the former Western allies. Nonetheless, it is also important to acknowledge West Berlin as a place that was not only internationally important, but had its own specific local culture and politics as well, and, in this way, to move beyond the notion of West Berlin as defined only by its symbolic urban image.

CONCLUSION

The IBA 87 was in many ways a microcosm of the city itself: both were supposed to be models or standards on a global scale, but in the end were special and unique, exceptions rather than rules. In fact, crucial to understanding any city is understanding this gap between the material reality of urban space and its ideological construction in the service of national identity or, as in the case of West Berlin, the Cold War. The example of the IBA reveals the tension between the day-to-day reality of life in West Berlin that was a symbolic space and the West Berlin that was an ordinary town, one in which rubbish was collected. Moreover, both are key aspects of understanding West Berlin as it was and, indeed, united Berlin as it is today.

29 Miller, "IBA's 'Models for a City'" (see note 19), p. 207. There remain relatively few histories or assessments of the IBA. One recent exception, however, is this book by the architectural historian Esra Akcan, *Open City: Migration, Citizenship, and the Urban Renewal of Berlin-Kreuzberg by IBA-1984/87* (Basel, 2018).

30 Peter M. Bode, "Kreative Experimente kontra Spekulation," *Abendzeitung* (January 29, 1987), press clipping, B Rep 150/461, Landesarchiv Berlin. For a more detailed account of the IBA-Altbau and the critique of it by members of the squatter movement, see Emily Pugh, "'You Are Now Entering Occupied Berlin': Architects and Rehab-Squatters in West Berlin," *Centropa* 14, no. 2 (May 2015), pp. 189–202.

31 Peter Hoffmann, "Report from West Berlin," *Architectural Record* 173 (February 1985), p. 67; "Immobilien, Baukuhlen und Attrappen," *zitty* 10 (October 1987), press clipping, B Rep 150/461, Landesarchiv Berlin.

32 Joachim Nawrocki, "Gewalt zum Geburtstag," *Die Zeit*, June 19, 1987, p. 5. An account in *The New York Times* puts the estimate of protesters far lower, in the 20,000s. Serge Schmemann, "24,000 Demonstrate in Berlin Against Reagan's Visit Today," *The New York Times*, June 12, 1987.

Originally published as: Emily Pugh, "Beyond the Berlin Myth: The Local, the Global and the IBA 87," in *Berlin Divided City, 1945–1989*, ed. Philip Broadbent and Sabine Hake (New York, 2010), pp. 156–67. Stylistic conventions have been adjusted to conform to the publication at hand.

SAVING PRENZLAUER BERG?

Urban Development and “Self-Will” in the “Special” District of East Berlin

Andreas Butter, Julia Wigger, Kathrin Meissner

The Prenzlauer Berg district—or Prenzelberg for short[1]—of the 1980s will seem strange to non-Berliners and new Berliners: gruff, Romantic about its scene, and half-ironically idealized as a "myth" by those who were there.[2] The atmosphere there was different than in the cleaned-up East Berlin of the official media, and it was rarely put on display. In the *Tourist* architectural guide, published in 1987, only a single example of mass housing from the Gründerzeit era (late-nineteenth-century) was included, a building on Senefelderstrasse. But it can be found, albeit in the less official images of gray cityscapes, whose melancholy cannot have had much appeal to the Berlin mentality.[3]

In this section of the capital, everyday life in the Germany Democratic Republic (GDR)—with standardized social facilities, modestly stocked supermarkets, and privately owned stores along major streets—countered an alternative world. Most of the 25,000 vacant apartments counted in a survey in 1990 were located here,[4] in a neighborhood of largely rundown building fabric, where above all people who had not been allocated anything else would move.[5] Entire buildings were unlawfully occupied; despite the shortages of materials, many a vacant lot was converted into a home by someone who had picked up a trowel. As the Kommunale Wohnungsverwaltung (Communal Housing Association, KWV) increasingly lost control, the odds that residents who paid regularly would be offered a rental contract improved.[6] Students, punks, welfare recipients, and candidates for emigration replaced families, who had moved to newly constructed public housing; of the earlier residents, it was primarily the elderly who remained (→ p. 45). They were also intellectuals who were ahead of the time in their nonconformism. Part-time and full-time artists would discuss, paint, and sell in their pads. The neighborhood was a "Durchgangszimmer" (walk-through room),[7] niche, and "utopia"[8] in one; these milieus then met in the bars.

The diversity was based not least on the architectural structure. Densely packed, but opened up here and there by public squares with greenery, the neighborhoods of the "Mietskasernengürtel" (tenement belt) built in the imperial era expanded northward based on James Hobrecht's land-use plan of 1862. In addition to churches, technical structures such as the elevated track of what is now the U2 subway line, the water tower on Kollwitzplatz, and the gasometer east of Prenzlauer Allee provided accents that reinforced residents' connection to their surroundings. The percentage of buildings that had been destroyed in the war was modest compared to other parts of the city. Nevertheless, even forty years later, toilets were often located outside of the units on the half-landings, roofs leaked, and peeling façades characterized the cityscape. The party and the government, which for decades had been fixated on industrial construction methods and an inflexible image of the socialist way of life, seemed to be merely waiting to make a clean sweep.

This area did, however, provide crucial impetus for central urban renewal[9] and resident participation even prior to 1980. This essay is intended to outline subsequent efforts to preserve and design the existing building fabric—in harmony with politicians or the "self-willed,"[10] and this self-will from below had one openly critical and one subversive facet.

BETWEEN TABULA RASA AND OPEN-AIR MUSEUM

In dealing with the historical city, three approaches interact on the planning level: the economy (housing needs, preservation capacity, etc.), design (aesthetics, value as historical landmark, etc.), and the issue of the nature of the desired social environment. There had already been considerable success

1 It has been claimed that the colloquial term "Prenzlberg" was coined by West Germans moving there in the 1990s as a pet name for their new sociotope, implying an exclusion of the previous residents. See Thomas Dörfler, *Gentrification in Prenzlauer Berg?: Milieuwandel eines Berliner Sozialraums seit 1989* (Berlin, 2010), pp. 125–37. In fact, spelled Prenzelberg, it was an authentic term and was common long before that. For example, in 1980 a reading by Hansotto Löggow (1906–1989) was held under the title "Jeschichten vom Prenzelberg" (Stories from Prenzelberg). See "Geschichten um den Prenzlauer Berg," *Neues Deutschland*, March 25, 1980, p. 8.

2 Wolfgang Kil, "Prenzlauer Berg: Aufstieg und Fall einer Nische," in *Die Stadt als Gabentisch*, ed. Hans G. Helms (Berlin, 1992), pp. 508–20.

3 In photography, above all the work of Jürgen Hohmuth, Robert Conrad, Harald Hauswald, Gerd Danigel, and Harf Zimmermann, and in painting and graphic art that of Konrad Knebel and Manfred Butzmann, have become influential.

4 Ernst Kirsten, "20 Jahre Modernisierung und Rekonstruktion in Berlin Ost," in *Stadterneuerung Berlin: Erfahrungen, Beispiele, Perspektiven*, ed. Senatsverwaltung für Bau- und Wohnungswesen (Berlin, 1990), pp. 73–82, esp. p. 82.

5 The allocation of the limited housing supply was based on employment, marital status, and number of family members. Those with greater professional responsibilities or good contacts received preferential treatment.

6 Dietmar Wolf, "Schwarzwohnen in der DDR: Mit stillen Besetzungen gegen den Wohnungsmangel," *MieterEcho* 12, no. 392 (2017), www.bmgev.de/mieterecho/archiv/2017/me-single/article/schwarzwohnen-in-der-ddr.html (accessed August 8, 2020).

7 Barbara Felsmann and Annett Gröschner, eds., *Durchgangszimmer Prenzlauer Berg: Eine Berliner Künstlersozialgeschichte der 1970er und 1980er Jahre in Selbstauskünften (Berlin, 2012).*

8 As an act of self-empowerment, around 5,000 people celebrated the founding of the "Republik Utopia" on Kollwitzplatz on the night of October 2–3, 1990. See Kil, "Prenzlauer Berg" (see note 2), p. 508.

9 The present text has benefited from preliminary work in the context of two project alliances at the Leibniz-Institut für Raumbezogene Sozialforschung (IRS) in Erkner, Germany: *Mediatisierungsprozesse in der städtebaulichen Planung*

Fig. 1 This Bauakademie planning guideline from 1977 recommended widespread gutting of buildings over the next twelve years (yellow); entire blocks had to disappear, and that was to be continued in the 1990s (buildings shown in outline). Only around Arnimplatz, at the top left, was the high-density courtyard structure to have been preserved over the longer term.

und Veränderungen der öffentlichen Sphäre (MedPlan) / The Mediatisation of Urban Development Planning and Changes to the Public Sphere (MedPlan) and *Stadterneuerung am Wendepunkt—die Bedeutung der Bürgerinitiativen gegen den Altstadtverfall für die Wende in der DDR*.

10 The German term *Eigensinn* (self-will), in the context of sociohistorical research, as an expression of subjects' self-empowerment, should be understood not just vertically in the sense of the exercise of power but also horizontally as an expression of competing interests. See Thomas Lindenberger and Alf Lüdtke, "Eigensinn: Handlungsräume und Herrschaftspraxis; Zur Einleitung," in *Eigen-Sinn: Życie codzienne, podmiotowość i sprawowanie władzy w XX wieku, tłumaczenie*, ed. Thomas Lindenberger and Alf Lüdtke (Poznań, 2018), pp. 1–31, https://eigensinn.hypotheses.org/ (accessed August 8, 2020).

11 Roman Hillmann, "Tradition und Typ: Lückenbauten und Kleinensembles in Berlin-Weissensee, 1955–1960," in *Ostmoderne: Architektur in Berlin, 1945–1965*, ed. Andreas Butter and Ulrich Hartung (Berlin, 2004), pp. 100–113.

12 Ulrich Hartung, "Zu Seiten der Stalinallee: Innerstädtischer Wohnungsbau in Berlin Friedrichshain, 1953–1958," in *Projekt sozialistische Stadt: Beiträge zur Bau- und Planungsgeschichte der DDR; Debatten, Fallbeispiele, Stadtbausteine, Biographien*, ed. Holger Barth (Berlin, 1998), pp. 219–25.

13 On this division into periods, see Simone Hain, "Kritische Rekonstruktion 'Made in GDR,'" in *Archäologie und Aneignung: Ideen, Pläne und Stadtkonfigurationen; Aufsätze zur Berliner Stadtfiguration nach 1945*, vol. 10: *Regio, Beiträge des IRS* (Erkner, 1996), pp. 117–19.

14 A formulation by Hans Gericke, quoted in Yasmin Katzer, "Die Traditionsinsel 'Komplex Alt-Berlin' am Märkischen Ufer: Städtebauliche Denkmalpflege der 1960er-Jahre" (master's thesis, Technische Universität Berlin, 2018), pp. 98 and 121.

15 Klaus Pöschk, "Städtebauliche Umgestaltung und Rekonstruktion des Wohngebietes Arkonaplatz in Berlin," *Deutsche Architektur* 20, no. 10 (1971), pp. 602–9. More detailed information is found in an interview with Klaus Pöschk on April 2, 2020.

16 Jürgen Schechert, Hannelore Vetter, and Helmut Müller, "Vom 'Milljöh' zum Milieu: Modernisierungsgebiet am Arkonaplatz in Berlin," *Architektur der DDR* 33, no. 4 (1984), pp. 196–201.

in the 1950s filling in wartime damage to perimeter blocks. As in Weissensee[11] and Friedrichshain,[12] in Prenzlauer Berg the existing layout of the streets and the eave heights were retained, for example, on Schwedter Strasse and the lower stretch of Schönhauser Allee.

From 1964 onward, there was increasing refurbishment of individual buildings in the area around the Zionskirche. For example, toilets were installed in apartments; the windows facing the courtyard were double-glazed; and (sometimes desolate) stucco was replaced with a scratch coat. It was the era in which a broadly conceived modernism determined central planning. The demolition of the small streets on the Fischerinsel would be compensated for with an "island"—more accurately, "row"—"of tradition"[13] with renovated and staggered reconstructed burgher homes on the Märkisches Ufer. Planning was directed by Klaus Pöschk and was intended to represent an element of equal importance within the "cybernetic system of the city."[14]

This approach of adapting the existing fabric to current needs for its use, while preserving historical architectural details as much as possible, was applied by Pöschk and his colleagues (Siegfried Kress and Günther Kabus were responsible for urban planning) in the early 1970s to the Komplexe Rekonstruktion project around Arkonaplatz.[15] The urban planning expansion necessitated some persuasion effort on the local council for the Mitte district, and in later years the area was incorporated into the planning for Prenzlauer Berg (fig. 1). Preliminary work began already in 1967; between 1970 and 1984, some 3,100 apartments were modernized[16]—in certain cases with new floor plans and wet cells from the Czechoslovak Socialist Republic. Where it still existed, the façade decoration was preserved; otherwise, its characteristics were replicated with paint. Residents were not only provided with temporary housing during construction but also voted on specific measures such as whether to preserve the historical windows.[17] Not least in order to avoid what turned out to be very complicated moves to temporary housing, in the end the restoration of roofs, apartments, and façades was largely simplified and accelerated by employing industrial "product lines."[18]

The Komplexe Rekonstruktion project on Arkonaplatz was not just about apartments: green open spaces, supplemented by two daycare centers inside the gutted square (→ p. 46), offered new public spaces. The loss of the rear houses and the consolidation of lots took into consideration modernist planning paradigms to improve quality of life.[19] Because of the proximity to the border, however, the announced redesign of Swinemünder Strasse into a pedestrian zone with a cultural center on one end was never realized.

The Volks-, Berufs-, Wohnraum- und Gebäudezählung (Census of Population, Work, Housing, and Buildings) in 1971 made it painfully clear that the new construction could not compensate for the loss of housing from demolition.[20] For that reason, in the large renovation project on Arnimplatz to the north, where the buildings were not as old, many fewer courtyards were removed;[21] "nondisturbing commercial enterprises" were also retained.[22] In 1973, renovation work began under the aegis of Manfred Zache and Dorothea Krause. Over the course of ten years, more than 6,500 apartments in this area could be assigned to tenants[23]—a success that inspired the measures of "Behutsame Stadterneuerung" (cautious urban renewal) activities in West Berlin.

Benefiting from the European Architectural Heritage Year in 1975[24] and studies by Silvio Macetti (pseudonym of Noureddin Kianouri), an exiled Iranian architect, moreover, there were suggestions of a cultural transformation: density, continuity, and the appeal of historical façades were increasingly appreciated as "positive structural and design approaches" to the existing fabric.[25] Although the practice of wearing out and quickly replacing the existing

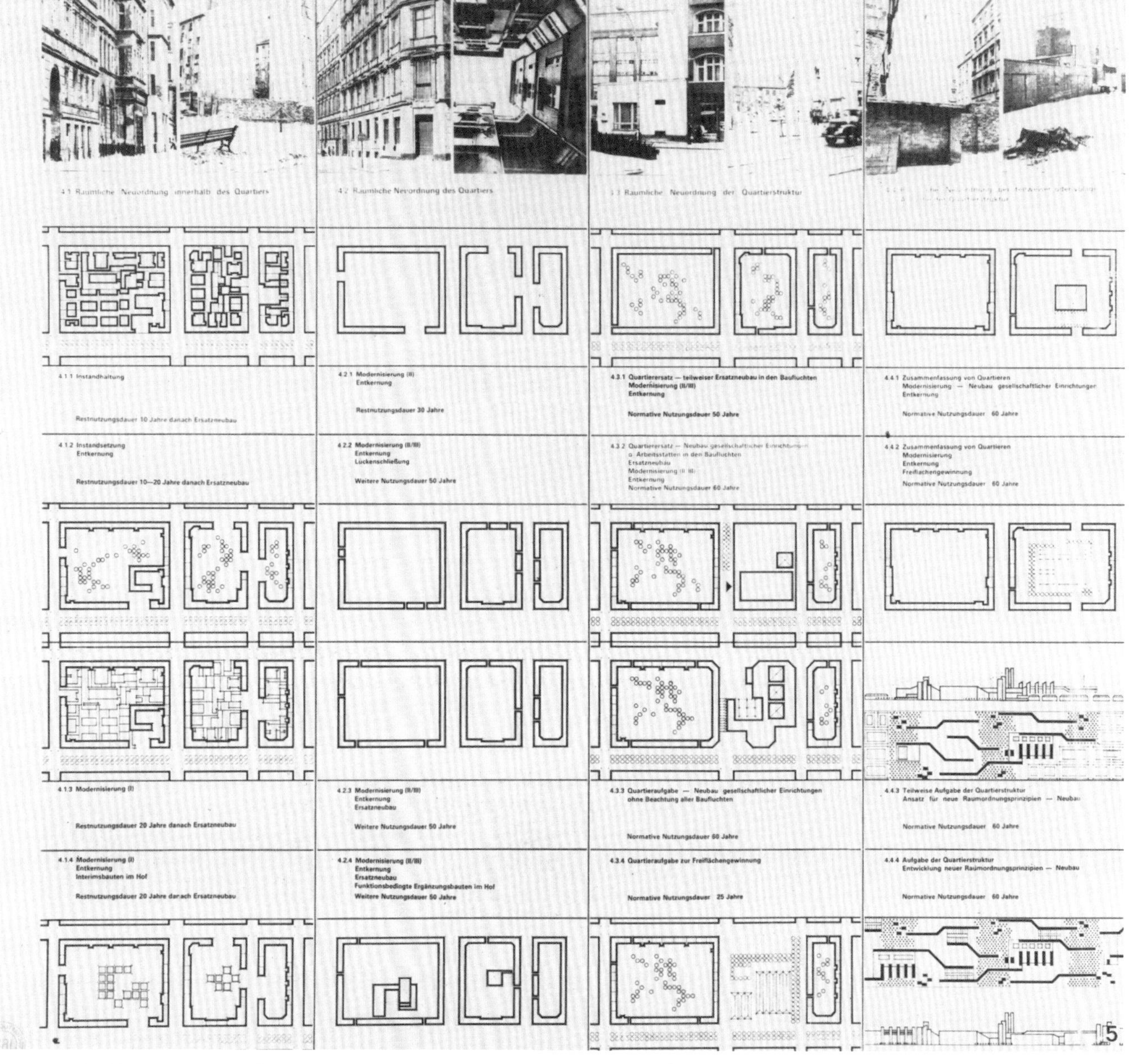

Fig. 2 The “Aufgabenstellung Grundlagenforschung zur Planung der Umgestaltung” (Task List for Basic Research on Planning the Redesign) prepared at the Bauakademie in 1976, in many parameters previously unknown, was an experiment in a complex methodology for dealing with the city. Various scenarios were worked out for the structure of neighborhoods; even new buildings were assigned a “standard duration of use.”

17 Interview with Klaus Pöschk on April 2, 2020. There was, from 1972 onward, a Bürgerbüro (citizens' office) on Arnimplatz as well. It took some convincing, at first, to get people to move back into their former apartments after renovation. Interview with Manfred Zache on May 11, 2019.

18 Work progressed from the roof downward, implemented by specialized enterprises with extensive use of prefabricated construction elements.

19 On the blurring of the distance between public and private spaces, see Holger Barth, "Mythos Prenzlauer Berg: Öffentlichkeit und Stadterneuerung in der DDR," *Wolkenkuckucksheim* 8 (September 2003), p. 1; Holger Barth, "Der öffentliche Raum in Zeiten der Schrumpfung," *Inhalt* 8, no. 1 (September 2003), www.cloud-cuckoo.net/openarchive/wolke/deu/Themen/031/Barth/barth.htm (accessed August 8, 2020).

20 Interview with Manfred Zache on May 11, 2019.

Fig. 3 In preparation for the renovation of Husemannstrasse for the celebrations held to mark the 750th anniversary of the founding of Berlin, the architect responsible for restoring façades, Brigitte Deiters, produced a series of studies of typological details. Her proposal to safeguard even the historical fabric in stairwells was rejected as too expensive.

fabric now seemed to have been overcome, the assumption was still that buildings had "remaining useful life" of thirty to forty years. Studies from the Bauakademie der DDR (Academy of Architecture of the GDR)[26] (fig. 2) and the dissertation of the director of urban development, Günter Peters, in 1972[27] noted that, although the preservation of neighborhoods built after 1900 saved money over the short term, complete rebuilding would be necessary after several decades. By contrast, the historical preservation expert Bernhard Klemm argued based on the find that the primary load-bearing structure had a long life[28]—a view that continues to be confirmed today.

Neither the aforementioned pilot projects, nor the painted façades on the "Protokollstrecke" (a protocol route for prominent state visitors) of Greifswalder Strasse, nor Husemannstrasse with its 368 modernized apartments behind twenty-four restored Gründerzeit façades[29] was able to solve broadly the problem of dilapidation. On Kollwitzplatz, between 1984 and 1987, a homage to the old days intended to be attractive to tourists—with lovingly arranged stores, historical street fixtures, and a "museum of working-class life in Berlin around 1900" (fig. 3). In an echo of how Prussia was seen at the time,[30] the Gründerzeit-era city seemed to be "sublated" dialectically in the self-image of the GDR—though this perspective was not shared by everyone. The emotional connection to the existing city seemed important even to those who analyzed the architectural culture of the neighborhood critically, such as the sociologist Fred Staufenbiel, in a special issue of the journal *form + zweck* in January 1983 (one that had serious consequences for the careers of the editorial staff).[31] Staufenbiel's co-contributor, Wolfgang Kil, who countered the holistic design concepts with the perspective of the residents, summed up the tenor in retrospect: "Against this superficial cult of images, the real processes had to be rehabilitated: local identity was to be achieved through the diverse practices of everyday life today."[32]

"ODERBERGER IS NOT JUST ANY OLD STREET IN PRENZLAUER BERG"[33]

A direct view of the "antifascist protective wall" substantially altered the quotidian atmosphere on Oderberger Strasse after the Berlin Wall was built. But stories of failed and successful escapes and the sadness and resignation of the late 1960s faded when the residents changed almost completely over the years, as some moved away and others moved in. Whereas for many tenants an apartment in a rundown old building was merely a stopover in urban anonymity during college or apprenticeship years, new neighborhoods came together in the 1970s.[34] Everyday coexistence was marked by small favors; a readiness to help, conversations in the streets, courtyards, and bars. But nevertheless, the (un)pleasant background noise of clattering mopeds, private visits, and musical excesses resounded in the crowded rear courtyards of the tenements. From the mid-1970s onward, the art scene recognized the potential of vacant buildings and rundown street façades; Oderberger Strasse, as both a cul-de-sac and an unusually broad street, offered a special kind of "open space" (fig. 4). It was largely free of traffic, offered diverse recreational attractions and legendary sites—such as the Kreiskulturhaus Prater (Prater District Cultural House, KKH), the Stadtbad (municipal swimming pool), the Jugendklub Erich Franz (Erich Franz Youth Club), and the Oderkahn bar—and formed an increasingly alternative microcosm within the neighborhood.

Inside the buildings, an atmosphere of a "new dawn" reigned: illegal squatting, partition walls knocked down, and individual, provisional redesigns of the spaces by housemates and young families were largely ignored by the

21 Rudi Spohr and Hans Esch, "Neues Wohnen am Arnimplatz," *Architektur der DDR* 28, no. 9 (1979), pp. 538–43.

22 Dorothea Krause and Manfred Zache, "Modernisierungsgebiet Arnimplatz," *Architektur der DDR* 25, no. 7 (1976), pp. 395–400, esp. p. 399. The basic idea of relaxing the unconditional separation of residential and commercial spaces is found again later in *Die Grundsätze für die sozialistische Entwicklung für Städtebau und Architektur in der Deutschen Demokratischen Republik* (resolution of 1982 by the Politburo of the SED Central Committee and the Council of Ministers of the GDR), p. 8.

23 Simone Hain, "Zwischen Arkonaplatz und Nikolaiviertel: Stadt als soziale Form versus Inszenierung; Konflikte bei der Rückkehr in die Stadt," in *Stadt der Architektur, Architektur der Stadt: Berlin, 1900–2000*, ed. Thorsten Scheer, Josef Paul Kleihues, and Paul Kahlfeldt (Berlin, 2000), pp. 336–47.

24 On this, see "Europäisches Denkmalschutzjahr 1975," *deutsche bauzeitung*, December 1, 2005, www.db-bauzeitung.de/db-themen/schwerpunkt/europaeisches-denkmalschutzjahr-1975/ (accessed August 8, 2020).

25 Krause and Zache, "Modernisierungsgebiet Arnimplatz" (see note 22), p. 398.

26 *Forschungsvorhaben Sozialistischer Städtebau im Prenzlauer Berg* and *Aufgabenstellung Grundlagenforschung zur Planung der Umgestaltung;* both viewable online at: www.digipeer.de (accessed August 8, 2020).

27 Florian Urban, *Berlin/DDR, neohistorisch: Geschichte aus Fertigteilen* (Berlin, 2007), pp. 48–54; Florian Urban, *Neo-Historical East Berlin: Architecture and Urban Design in the German Democratic Republic, 1970–1990* (Farnham, 2009), pp. 41–45.

28 Bernhard Klemm, "Die Existenz des Gebäudes als funktioneller und technologischer Prozess," *Deutsche Architektur* 2, no. 3 (1973), pp. 670–72; Andreas W. Putz, "Housing Paul and Paula: Building Repair and Urban Renewal in the German Democratic Republic," *Architectural Histories* 7, no. 1 (2019), pp. 1–23.

29 Senat von Berlin, ed., *Rundgänge durch Quartiere* 1, no. 9 (1990), fig. 13; Dorothea Krause, Uwe Klasen, and Wolfgang Penzel, "Rekonstruktion im Stil der Jahrhundertwende: Husemannstrasse in Berlin," *Architektur der DDR* 10 (1987), pp. 14–21.

Fig. 4 Life on Oderberger Strasse, June 9, 1989. The street's only flair was a result, in part, of the contradiction between the large open spaces for pedestrians and parks, on the one hand, and the unusual width of the street and the immediate proximity of the Berlin Wall, which resulted in a constant presence of state control. Photo: Gerd Danigel

KWV. After all, since the Berlin Program of 1976, the focus had been on rebuilding the prestigious center of the city and addressing the housing problem with new buildings and modernization.[35] The approach of Komplexe Rekonstruktion was therefore to see "Old and new organically combined with each other under reasonable use and design of the existing fabric ..., especially for buildings, squares, and streets that are characteristic of the history of the working people and of the German workers' movement. The architecturally valuable qualities of the past should be preserved or restored."[36] The prewar buildings on Oderberger Strasse were not included in that, as is clear from the urban development guidelines for the district of Prenzlauer Berg from 1977, according to which the majority of these buildings were to be demolished and replaced with new ones.[37]

Several Oderberger Strasse residents observed, with reactions ranging from disillusionment to outrage, that high-status thoroughfares such as neighboring Schönhauser Allee were to be renovated and modernized, but the local need for urban greenery and playgrounds seemed to play—despite studies from the Bauakademie der DDR on improving the quality of life[38]—only a secondary role in socialist urban planning.[39] A green space and playground were created in the neglected back courtyards from 1982 to 1984—on the initiative of the residents themselves and formalized by their adoption by the responsible Wohnbezirksausschuss (Residential District Committee, WBA). "The Hofspielplatz Oderberger Str. 15 / Kastanienallee 12 will be the first attempt in the RA [residential area] to create a green oasis amid the rear courtyards that was primarily intended to serve the needs of children."[40]

Inspired by such actions, which had been unfamiliar in the GDR system previously, more and more creative and nonconformist types got involved in redecorating the area. The courtyard designed by the Hofgruppe (Courtyard Group),[41] which was initiated by citizens but largely funded by the district, became famous throughout the city after 1985 as the Hirschhof, and soon became *the* meeting place for East Berlin's scene of subculture and those critical of the state. Its reputation as a political free zone derived above all from

30 After the rediscovery of Friedrich II, Otto von Bismarck and other great figures of the nineteenth century who had been defamed previously were reevaluated. See "Fahndung nach Tradition: Ost-Berliner Historiker suchen nach den Wurzeln einer nationalen Identität der DDR," *Der Spiegel* 37, no. 10 (1983), pp. 208–11.

31 "Innerstädtische Rekonstruktion: Beispiel Prenzlauer Berg," special issue, *form+zweck* 15, no. 1 (1983), especially Fred Staufenbiel, "Von sozialen Prozessen ausgehen," pp. 4–7, and Wolfgang Kil, "Kunstwerk Schönhauser," pp. 23–28.

32 Wolfgang Kil, "Kaum Konfrontation, eher Unterwanderung," www.wolfgang-kil.de/thema.php?id=21 (accessed August 8, 2020).

33 "Wir haben den Abriss verhindert: Unser Recht: Wir bleiben alle!," *Berliner Abendblatt*, April 1, 1992.

34 Bernt Roder and Bettina Tacke, *Prenzlauer Berg im Wandel der Geschichte: Leben rund um den Helmholtzplatz* (Berlin, 2004).

35 XII. SED-Bezirksdelegiertenkonferenz der Hauptstadt, "Zur weiteren Entwicklung der Hauptstadt der DDR, Berlin," *Berliner Zeitung*, March 27–28, 1976.

36 Ibid., p. 1.

37 Bauakademie der DDR and Institut für Städtebau und Architektur: Forschungsvorhaben Sozialistischer Städtebau im Prenzlauer Berg, *Städtebauliche Leitplanung bis 1990: Stadtbezirk Prenzlauer Berg, Teilgebiet Teutoburger Platz*, June 1977.

38 Bauakademie der DDR, Institut für Städtebau und Architektur, and Peter Gerlach, *Arbeiterwohngebiet Berlin Prenzlauer Berg: Ein Beitrag zur Planung und Umgestaltung* (Berlin, 1976).

39 Nadja Klier and Freya Klier, *Die Oderberger Strasse*, from the series *Berliner Orte* (Berlin, 2017).

40 On this, see Bernd Holtfreter, *Notizheft*, in Estate of B. Holtfreter (BHo 15), Archiv der DDR-Opposition, Robert-Havemann-Gesellschaft, Berlin.

41 On this, see "Diskussionsprotokolle der Kulturkommission der WBA-Sitzungen vom 23.10.1986 und 6.11.1986," in Estate of B. Holtfreter (BHo 15, see note 40).

42 On this, see ibid.

43 Klier and Klier, *Die Oderberger Strasse* (see note 39), p. 81.

Fig. 5 Everyday life in the Hirschhof: children playing on the façades made of rubble and on the Prussian eagle. The "thrown-together" design of the courtyard is evident. Photo: Gabriele Stolze, 1987–88

performances by artists who did not have permits, and even by those who had been banned from performing, and from its casual atmosphere. In order to conform with the official approval process, events were organized under the cloak of the cultural commission for WBA 55 and 56. Sensational and unique cultural events attracted not only an alternative audience but also, frequently, the state security service.[42]

The nonconformity of the Hirschhof was also evident in its architectural design: "A concrete seating group in the form of fruit and vegetables and a totem pole, … tiles …, a ping-pong table"[43] were joined by the deer sculpture of junk parts that gave the courtyard its name. An amphitheater provided a stage for theatrical performances, puppet shows for children, and politically touchy readings, film screenings, and concerts. Famous artists' groups such as Zinnober (Cinnabar) were among the regular guests on its program. This diverse cultural program was reflected in the Hirschhof aesthetic. The playground integrated fragments of historical buildings, such as a Prussian eagle and blocks of rubble, supposedly from the demolished Berliner Stadtschloss (Berlin City Palace), which encouraged a popular cult of ruins.[44]

The credo of the program of the Sozialistische Einheitspartei Deutschlands (Socialist Unity Party of Germany, SED) from 1976—namely, "Old and new [must be] organically combined with each other under reasonable use and design of the existing fabric"[45]—was thus satisfied. The Hirschhof free zone was representative, in its aesthetic of ruins and appropriation by neighborhood initiative, of the specific sense of a new era in the culture of the late 1980s. In the immediate vicinity of the Berlin Wall, on the one hand, and of socialist institutions and prominent sites, such as the Kreiskulturhaus Prater and the spiffed-up thoroughfares, on the other, the Hirschhof represented a "green oasis"[46] in the daily life of Prenzlauer Berg (fig. 5). It served as a playground for families with many children, as a green space and substitute for a garden for residents, as a place for community interaction, and as an "institution" for the subculture and those critical of the state—and for those reasons it was, like Oderberger Strasse, not just "any old" place in the city.

Fig. 6 Model drawing of Rykestrasse looking toward the water tower; produced in the Innerstädtischer Wohnungsbau und Weiterentwicklung der Wohnbauserie Berlin (Inner-City Housing Construction and Development of the Residential Housing Series in Berlin) drawing class at the Bauhaus Dessau in May 1988. The plan to replace the old building fabric with urban concrete-slab buildings is clearly evident.

"YOU DON'T BLOW UP GASOMETERS"

One of the "most beautiful centrally located sites of new construction ... of the capital"[47] was planned for the site of the former gas facility on Dimitroffstrasse (now Danziger Strasse). The Central Committee of the SED had passed a resolution to do so in February 1981. With the help of the technology of prefabricated panel construction, the Ernst-Thälmann-Park residential and recreational facility would be built, with more than 1,300 new centrally located apartments.[48] The closing of the gas facility, which had begun operation in 1873, had been welcomed by residents. They had had to put up with its dust, soot, and odors for many decades. Visually, however, the building had been integrated into the image of the district: the three brick gasometers were popular landmarks that were visible from afar and had been added to the historic preservation register.[49] The original plan had been to integrate these structures into the Thälmann-Park, and the Kunsthochschule Berlin in Weissensee had already presented proposals for their use.[50] They were, however, not included in later plans. In July 1984, the newspaper *Neues Deutschland* wrote that there was no longer "any certainty about the stability of the old buildings"[51]—the official justification for demolition.

This trigged an unusually broad response from residents, who advocated that the landmark be preserved (→ p. 44). Many of them took the official route and contacted the state offices.[52] The Ministerium für Staatssicherheit (Ministry of State Security, MfS, aka Stasi) counted around 160 such complaints.[53] Some also made their disagreement visible in the cityscape. The MfS recorded around 200 cases of handmade posters, banners, stickers, and photomontages with messages such as "You don't blow up gasometers" or "Denk Mal" (monument / think about it), distributed in bars and displayed in building corridors or on windows.[54] In addition to figures from the art and culture scene and the environmental and peace movements, people from diverse areas of society participated—a protest supported by the residents of Prenzlauer Berg.[55] This diverse commitment was, however, unsuccessful. The gasometers were demolished in the early afternoon of July 28, 1984.

APPROPRIATING THE RESIDENTIAL DISTRICT COMMITTEES

Around the same time, barely 2 kilometers away, the aforementioned Hirschhof was being created by the residents of Oderberger Strasse.[56] Because such strong commitment was not permitted to exist outside of the state structures, it was integrated into the already existing and responsible WBA.[57] As part of the Nationale Front der Deutschen Demokratischen Republik (National Front of the German Democratic Republic) and of selected special interest groups of residents, this represented the opportunity to have a say in and even have control over one's residential district.[58] The WBA was not just permitted to organize events; it also influenced the allocation of apartments.[59] In order to operate with even greater autonomy, the Hirschhof supporters soon organized their own WBA on the opposite side of the street.[60] This integration into the structures of the state had other advantages as well: in 1987–88, when there were rumors making the rounds that the dilapidated Gründerzeit buildings on Oderberger Strasse were to be demolished and replaced by new structures, a building committee was formed in the WBA. It collected information, tried to contact the urban planners involved, and organized a meeting of residents.[61] At that meeting, there was massive opposition to the planned demolitions: "The butcher Dufft made no secret of the fact that these plans could be realized only over his dead body. Many elderly people raised a real ruckus as well—that was unheard of."[62]

44 Daniela Dahn, *Prenzlauer Berg-Tour* (Halle and Leipzig, 1987); A. Kömmler, "Vergammelt der Adler vom Stadtschloss im Hinterhof?," *Berliner Morgenpost*, n.d.

45 XII. SED-Bezirksdelegiertenkonferenz, "Zur weiteren Entwicklung" (see note 35), p. 1.

46 "Oase vor der Haustür: Die grosse Berliner Hofaktion," *Neue Berliner Illustrierte* 42, no. 22 (1986), pp. 12–17.

47 Hans Rehfeldt, "Mit Tempo und Qualität errichten die Bauleute das neue Wohngebiet," *Neues Deutschland* 39, no. 164 (July 13, 1984), p. 3.

48 Bettina Tacke, "Sozialistische Stadtplanung: Der Ernst-Thälmann-Park; oder, Das Beglückungsprogramm des Staates," in *Gegenentwürfe: Der Prenzlauer Berg vor, während und nach dem Mauerfall*, ed. Bernt Roder and Bettina Tacke (Berlin, 2011), pp. 114–26, esp. pp. 120–21.

49 Ibid., p. 118.

50 "Auf dem Gelände," *Neue Zeit* 39, no. 9 (January 12, 1983), p. 8; Tacke, "Sozialistische Stadtplanung" (see note 48), pp. 117–18.

51 Rehfeldt, "Mit Tempo und Qualität" (see note 47).

52 On this, see Bundesbeauftragter für die Stasi-Unterlagen (hereafter BStU), MfS, BV Berlin, AKG, no. 1813; BStU, MfS, BV Berlin, Abt. XX, no. 5241, vol. 4; BStU, MfS, BV Berlin, AKG, no. 4601.

53 On this, see BStU, MfS, AKG, no. 1843, fols. 1–9.

54 On this, see BStU, MfS, AKG, no. 1843, fols. 1–9; BStU, MfS, BV Bln, Abt. XX, no. 3520, vol. 2, fol. 444.

55 The MfS concluded after the demolition of the gasometers that "people from very diverse social spheres who have a loyal attitude to the GDR and thought about the gasometers with upstanding intention" had participated in the protests. On this, see BStU, MfS, BV Berlin, AKG, no. 3216, fols. 28–30.

56 Bernd Holtfreter, "Die ganze Oderberger Strasse in einem Hochhaus der Michelangelostrasse," in Felsmann and Gröschner, *Durchgangszimmer Prenzlauer Berg* (see note 7), pp. 125–38, esp. p. 129.

57 Ibid.

58 Peter Nowak, "Vom WBA zu 'Wir Bleiben Alle': Mieterselbstorganisation in Ost-Berlin," in *Mieterkämpfe: Vom Kaiserreich bis*

heute; Das Beispiel Berlin, ed. Philipp Mattern, vol. 3: *Realität der Utopie* (Berlin, 2018), pp. 132–47, esp. pp. 132–33.

59 Holtfreter "Die ganze Oderberger Strasse" (see note 56), pp. 130–31.

60 Ibid., pp. 129–30; M. K. and B. H., "Einladung zur ersten Versammlung unseres neuen WBA," n.d., in Estate of B. Holtfreter (BHo 11), Archiv der DDR-Opposition, Robert-Havemann-Gesellschaft, Berlin.

61 Matthias Bernt, *Rübergeklappt: Die "Behutsame Stadterneuerung" im Berlin der 90er Jahre* (Berlin, 2003), p. 96; WBA 65/WBA 56: invitation, January 19, 1989, in Estate of B. Holtfreter (BHo 12), Archiv der DDR-Opposition, Robert-Havemann-Gesellschaft, Berlin.

62 Holtfreter, "Die ganze Oderberger Strasse" (see note 56), p. 132.

63 Bernt, *Rübergeklappt* (see note 61), pp. 96–97.

64 Dorothee Dubrau, "Bürgerbewegung und Stadterneuerung," in *Städtebau-Debatten in der DDR: Verborgene Reformdiskurse*, ed. Christoph Bernhardt, Thomas Flierl, and Max Welch Guerra (Berlin, 2012), pp. 200–17, esp. p. 208.

65 Holtfreter, "Die ganze Oderberger Strasse" (see note 56), pp. 133–34.

66 Tanja Blankenburg, "Stadterneuerung im Konflikt: Das Modellvorhaben Rykestrasse in Berlin," in *Grammatik sozialistischer Architekturen: Lesarten historischer Städtebauforschung zur DDR*, ed. Holger Barth (Berlin, 2001), pp. 253–63, esp. pp. 259–61.

67 Autorenkollektiv Wolfgang Kil, Harry Lüttger, Jürgen Raue, Kurt-Heinz Rudolf, and Veronika Wagner, *Stadtgestaltung im Prenzlauer Berg: Konzeption für die komplexe Gestaltung der Modernisierungskomplexe zwischen Prenzlauer Allee, Schönhauser Allee, Wisbyer Strasse und Saarbrücker Strasse, Berlin, Hauptstadt der DDR, Bearbeitungszeitraum Okt. 1982–März 1983*, ed. Büro für architekturbezogene Kunst Berlin (Berlin, 1983), p. 8.

The district leaders of the SED then canceled their planning for Oderberger Strasse; they turned instead further east to Rykestrasse for their renovation plans.[63] The interior area of this Gründerzeit block, in turn, was to be demolished completely and replaced by new concrete-slab buildings (fig. 6).[64] The WBA for Oderberger Strasse immediately contacted the residents of Rykestrasse. The tried-and-true concept of a special interest group was employed here again. Because there was an existing residential committee, however, a building committee was formed within the existing WBA.[65] With help from urban planners and architects, it organized a study of the existing buildings and disproved the state's argument that they were in a dilapidated state. The building committee worked out an alternative proposal that aimed to largely preserve the existing buildings. With a great deal of commitment and specialist knowledge, it managed to change the course of the district leaders. Future planning would involve the building committee. Before that could happen, however, the events of the autumn of 1989 occurred.[66]

On both Oderberger Strasse and Rykestrasse, residents were able to prevent demolition of Gründerzeit buildings. Strategically organizing as a WBA enabled them to hold meetings, use the premises, and argue and act from an official position. That provided them with an opportunity to approach communal politicians and administrators and, as in the case of Rykestrasse, even to take part in the planning.

PRENZLAUER BERG, THE EXCEPTION AS RULE?

Impetus to revitalize the center of the city and to preserve older buildings came from very different social strata in Prenzlauer Berg. As early as 1982–83, a collective of architects around Wolfgang Kil, which had a say in the complex plans to modernize the district, pointed to the changing makeup of the residents, "who are not only demanding more cultural value from their immediate living environment but should also be recognized as having important potential to participate in the redesign of the district."[67] They turned out to be right about this, as the course of the 1980s would show: the built environment concealed fuel for opposition, and protest was ultimately triggered by the state's plans for demolition. Cooperative projects of residents and planners articulated their positions in diverse ways—from the constructive to the subversive. The resulting protests and actions contributed more (Oderberger, Rykestrasse) and less (gasometers) successfully to the preservation of older buildings, but above all they revealed the unique identity of these neighborhoods and their strong solidarity. The debates over the demolition or preservation of living spaces in Prenzlauer Berg of the 1980s reflect the influence on society of individual rights and of collective "self-will" versus the socialist standardized idyll.

THE CITY AS A WHOLE

Werner Rösler, design for the Akademie der Künste (Academy of the Arts), Platz der Akademie (now Gendarmenmarkt), 1980, unbuilt
Postmodernism tempted with daring formal ideas. In this design sketch, Rösler marked the (fictive) new building for the Akademie der Künste with a brute "classical quotation."

Ehrhardt Gisske, Manfred Prasser, with Peter Weiss, Michael Ulbrich, Ernst Wallis, Dieter Bankert, Günter Boy, and others, residential and commercial buildings on Gendarmenmarkt, 1979–84, photo: Gerhard Zwickert, 2003

The middle one of the three “houses” on Markgrafenstrasse with mosaics inspired by the Gründerzeit (late nineteenth century) nonchalantly reveals the aesthetic reserves of a traditional concrete-slab façade.
Several of the buildings consist of steel skeletons with sculptural elements as curtain walls. A field factory in situ made it possible to achieve the intricacy of this façade decoration. Photo: Gerhard Zwickert, 2003

Walter Schwarz, Manfred Prasser, Dieter Bankert, Friedrichstadtpalast, shortly after its opening in 1984

Manfred Prasser, Peter Weiss, Passagen Friedrichstadt (Friedrichstadt Arcades), Friedrichstrasse, partially built from 1987 onward, demolished in 1991, model construction: Werkstatt IHB, Betrieb Projektierung, ca. 1987
Frank Dölle, cafeteria in the Passagen Friedrichstadt, view from the north, 1988, unbuilt

Iris Grund, Thorleif Neuer, Peter Schweizer, Kaulsdorf Nord residential complex, Rostock type, Lion-Feuchtwanger-Strasse, from 1984 onward, photo: Dorothea Dutschmann

Peter Meyer, new residential and commercial building, Friedrichstrasse, 1987–89. The art by Horst Bartnig (below), no longer extant, alluded to the currency exchange in the building.

Harald Metzkes, *Aufbau von Marzahn* (Building of Marzahn), oil on canvas, 1984

Marzahner Promenade, ca. 1988

The storefronts were built as infrastructure for the WBS70 residential blocks.

Thomas Weber, Michael Kny, Sabine Bondzin, main post office of Marzahn in the center of the third residential section of Berlin-Marzahn, 1981–86, photo: Gerhard Zwickert, 1991 and 2003

Wolf-Rüdiger Eisentraut, Michael Kny, Thomas Weber, Heidrun Senz, center of the third residential section of Marzahn with Marzahn S-Bahn (commuter rail) station ("Reception Building," top), central wing of the department store with cafés and dance bar (center), and patio in the Haus der Dienste (House of Services) (bottom), photos: Gerhard Zwickert, 2003

THE SMALL AND THE LARGE ALTERNATIVE

Architects at a Crossroads: Between Downtown and Marzahn

Wolfgang Kil

The industrialization of construction sector in the German Democratic Republic (GDR) was not exclusively an invention of technocrats. Among architects, it certainly had features of a question of faith; principles of a rigorous morality were part of its justification. According to the doctrine of "National Traditions,"[1] which had been imported from Moscow, all discourses on architecture were concerned with presenting advantageously "the clear, simple, and uniform tectonics of industrial construction."[2] However, twenty years later, the concept of industrial construction had run aground in the rigid dictates of prefabricated slab construction. In their massive spread, the unwieldy "products" of construction combines (*Baukombinate*) had become simply unbearable. Even in East Berlin, which as the capital of the GDR was still achieving in its central areas buildings of stature that went beyond the schematized catalogues of building types, it turned out that the potential of design repertoire of an "Eastern modernism"[3] based on constructional integrity had clearly been largely exhausted after the completion of Alexanderplatz and Rathausstrasse, and of the Fischerinsel and Leipziger Strasse.

From that point forward, there was an increasingly enthusiastic search for ways to create distinctive places that would help to create identity while retaining the principles of industrially manufactured, prefabricated parts. Whereas economists and technologists coldly continued to urge "rationalization," that is, increasingly effective production processes for increasingly reduced housing types, first sociologists and cultural historians and soon politicians as well began to call on architects to individualize "faceless" serial products. And another problem began to emerge: whereas normal construction projects, including housing construction, were to be directed from the "greenfield" back to the center of the city, the abstract forms of industrial modernism had to be harmonized with existing surroundings, which were often of premodern design. Something that had never been a concern in an open field suddenly became enormously relevant for inner-city architecture: the context.[4]

While in West Berlin from the mid-1970s onward, the actors and networks began to set up the Internationale Bauausstellung Berlin (with its programmatic division into old and new buildings), another shift in trends in the architectural activity of East Berlin was taking place as well.[5] The year 1976 can be identified as a clear turning point, and, more precisely, the completion of the Palast der Republik (Palace of the Republic). In retrospect, that building can be seen as the last beacon of Eastern modernism in Berlin, less because of its geometrically clear and tolerably undecorated outer form than because of its unprecedented diversity of urban space and use. In addition, there was the refined engineering feat of its Grosser Saal (Great Hall), featuring a variability that set international standards. The remarkable building had been erected by the state-owned construction and assembly collective Ingenieurhochbau Berlin (Berlin Architectural Engineering, IHB), based on plans by a team of experienced designers whose names and signatures would leave a decided mark on the production of architecture In East Berlin in the decade after that gigantic project on the Spreeinsel (Spree Island) had been completed. In contrast to the majority of their colleagues in the country,[6] the planners of IHB managed to be exempted from some of the restrictions of standardized planning for various special projects. This awakened in the participating designers the ambition to leave, genuinely and for the long term, the thoroughly standardized serial buildings and to once again to create memorable and popular destinations by architectural means—both within the structures of new buildings on the periphery and in locations in the inner city, where areas of ruins still awaited rebuilding even thirty years after the end of World War II.

1 The stylistic phase of Stalinist eclecticism ended abruptly in 1955 after a legendary speech by Nikita Khrushchev to architects in Moscow. The subsequent return to modernism was obediently followed in the GDR, with a heavy emphasis on aspects of industrialization.

2 This was the urgent recommendation of the Swiss architect and CIAM cofounder Hans Schmidt, who from 1956 to 1969 was head of the Department of Theory and History at the Bauakademie (Academy of Architecture) in East Berlin.

3 The term that has since gained currency can be traced back to a book that measures the architectural production of the socialist countries (in this case the GDR) against the canon of the International Style. See Andreas Butter and Ulrich Hartung, *Ostmoderne: Architektur in Berlin, 1945–1965* (Berlin, 2004).

4 For her pioneering discussions of the "contextualist leap in typologies," I am grateful to Simone Hain; for a detailed account, see Simone Hain, "Between *Arkonaplatz* and the *Nikolaiviertel*: The City as a Social Form versus the City as Mise-en-Scène; Conflicts Raised by the Return of the City," in *City of Architecture, Architecture of the City*, ed. Thorsten Scheer, Josef Paul Kleihues, and Paul Kahlfeldt (Berlin, 2000), pp. 337–48; see also Simone Hain, "Konfigurationen der Urbanität: Ein Lernprozess im sozialen Raum," in *Archäologie und Aneignung: Ideen, Pläne und Stadtfigurationen; Aufsätze zur Ostberliner Stadtentwicklung nach 1945*, vol. 10: *REGIO: Beiträge des IRS* (Erkner, 1996), pp. 110–16.

5 The explicit focus on East Berlin is important, because trends to a contextualization of standardized projects can be seen in many places in the GDR, with clearly different results. For historical comparisons, the flourishing developments in Rostock and Halle an der Saale would be of particular interest here.

6 The construction combines of the GDR had large planning departments in which staff architects worked with all of the specialist planners under one roof.

Fig. 1 Lots containing ruins that still awaited reconstruction more than twenty years after the end of the war: Platz der Akademie, photo: Klaus Lehnartz, 1968

Fig. 2 Kollektiv Manfred Prasser, Platz der Akademie. The high architectural stature of Schinkel's Schauspielhaus and Gontard's churches called for a suitable frame in which the remembered images of the prewar city would resonate. Model: IHB workshop, planning operation, 1987

EXIT 1: CONFESSED HISTORICISTS

In 1976, the decision to reconstruct Schinkel's Schauspielhaus (Theater) was made.[7] This magnum opus of the great Prussian architect dominated, with its forceful presence, the historical Gendarmenmarkt between the two churches designed by Carl von Gontard. After suffering heavy damage during the war, the theater's ruins were not cleared away but rather preserved for later reconstruction. The ultimate fulfillment of this landmark preservation promise was set in motion not least thanks to the Europäisches Denkmalschutzjahr (European Architectural Heritage Year) of 1975, which had led to a greater appreciation of old towns and historical buildings in the GDR as well. In addition, the ambitious renovation projects (1979–84) on the urban space that had been renamed Platz der Akademie (Academy Square)[8] can be interpreted retrospectively as a signal that the relationship of GDR cultural policy toward Prussian history was gradually relaxing.

The art-historical stature and architectural appeal of the incunabula of Prussian architectural culture that were now being resurrected called for a suitable framework, for the streets surrounding the square still had expansive vacant lots in the mid-1970s. Only a few prewar buildings were still standing, such as the former Preussische Staatsbank (Prussian State Bank), which became the headquarters of the Akademie der Wissenschaften (Academy of Sciences)—and hence the occasion for renaming the square. That the cumbersome apparatus of the GDR's construction industry was now supposed to march into such a core area of the city's history caused discomfort among politicians and planners in equal measure. The GDR was striving for political recognition worldwide, and imposing-looking architecture was intended to provide a reputation. In the international context, postmodernism was just then raising awareness of the value and essence of the historical city in a new way. Architects who wanted to build here in the Friedrichstadt were therefore meant to refer to remembered images of a prewar city that, after thirty years of ruins and provisional measures, was to be visible only in outlines (fig. 1).

The Platz der Akademie had a key role not only stylistically but also technologically, since on this building site one of two strategies was exemplarily presented in order to overcome models of industrial construction that were regarded as worn out. If the aesthetic privation of standardized serial construction could only be surmounted by individualization, then the world of forms of the city's historical center posed an unavoidable problem: How could one introduce "context" into abstract systems of assembly? On this question, even those personalities who had recently worked together on the Palast der Republik were divided. Whereas the convinced adherents of industrial building rejected the postmodern "game with retrospective semantics" (Simone Hain) as weak *embellissement*, Ehrhardt Gisske's Aufbaustab Sonderbauten[9] (Reconstruction Staff for Special Buildings) brought together architects who wanted to restore the old masters' term for architecture, *Baukunst*, or the "art of building." Directly opposite the magnificent buildings of Schinkel and Gontard, experienced designers such as Manfred Prasser, Matthias Borner, and Roland Steiger, but also untamed fabulists such as Dieter Bankert and Werner Rösler[10] (→ pp. 78–79), had finally decided to view once again their buildings as objects of proficiency in aesthetics and the crafts (fig. 2).

Work on the buildings along the perimeter of the new Platz der Akademie began in 1979. The buildings on the western façade of the plaza were completed first: the Hochschule für Musik Hanns Eisler (Hanns Eisler School of Music) with an interior arcade leading to Taubenstrasse and the so-called *Funktionsgebäude* (functional building) with a tunnel connecting to the

7 The building, only the exterior of which was reconstructed faithfully to the original, has been called the Konzerthaus Berlin since 1984.

8 The Gendarmenmarkt was renamed Platz der Akademie in 1950. All of the plans for the reconstruction described here and the contemporaneous publications are listed under that GDR name, which is why it is also used throughout this essay. In 1991, the original name of the square was reinstated. On this, see the essay by Gerd Zimmermann in this volume.

9 The architect and experienced construction manager Ehrhardt Gisske (1924–1993) was director general of the Aufbauleitung Sondervorhaben der Hauptstadt Berlin (Special Projects Building Department of the Capital Berlin), and later head of the Baudirektion Berlin (Berlin Building Department). In the latter function, he gradually took over responsibility for all of the prestige buildings of East Berlin. The planners' collectives for various locations all reported to his Aufbaustab Sonderbauten.

10 "The spiritus rector behind everything was Werner Rösler, albeit annoyingly difficult. He was employed in the collective with Prasser. Back then, we were constantly discussing what was allowed and what wasn't—we 'time-conscious architects.' We were familiar with postmodernism in the West from architecture magazines. But we did not want to become part of it, because we wanted to continue thinking by starting out from our prefabricated construction." Dieter Bankert, e-mail to the author, May 14, 2020.

Fig. 3 Dankwart Kühn, façade facing the square of the historical residential buildings on Markgrafenstrasse, 1975. Although historical preservationists wanted "authentic" recreations, the idea did not prevail on the Platz der Akademie.

Konzerthaus, followed by the headquarters of the then bloc party Christlich-Demokratische Union Deutschlands (Christian Democratic Union, CDU) (on the corner of Jägerstrasse) and a hotel above the popular Arkade restaurant (corner of Französische Strasse)—all steel-skeleton constructions with a curtain wall of concrete façade elements. Surfaces decorated in diverse styles were the most striking innovation of this architecture, its "authenticity" often being fiercely mocked in professional circles. By contrast, even contemporaneous publications rarely appreciated that, deep inside the buildings, diverse qualities of the interior that were unprecedented at the time were created with arcades, courtyards, and terraced roof gardens.

Such a clear turn away from the "industrial principle of the series"—and in essence toward nothing but classical individual projects—could not be sustained on the east side of the square. In the case of the section of buildings between Französische Strasse and Jägerstrasse, which was divided into three lots, it was in fact a single, contiguous residential building constructed using the traditional prefabricated concrete-slab systems of the WBS 70 housing construction series built over monolithic commercial floors—the views from the courtyard reveal that clearly. In addition to several quite luxurious special floor plans, the reference to the historical square is expressed here only in the decorated façades. Whereas the middle one of the three "buildings," with mosaics inspired by the Gründerzeit (late nineteenth century), quite uninhibitedly addresses the theme of the aesthetic reserves of a concrete-slab façade, the organically formed bay windows of the Französischer Hof restaurant in particular point to the perfection that had since been achieved in producing decorative elements: the most complicated geometries, even completely circular columns, could now be ordered as ready-to-assemble concrete parts in any quantity desired. This playing with arcades,

11 The small private company Letsch ran the concrete works on the construction site; its manufacturing size was an ideal fit for the elemental needs of the special projects. At the construction combines, such mini batches would have gotten lost if only for logistical reasons.

12 On this, see the essay by Florian Urban in this volume.

13 Florian Urban, *Berlin/DDR, neo-historisch: Geschichte aus Fertigteilen* (Berlin, 2007). In this source, the Platz der Akademie is the subject of an extensive chapter, pp. 193–206.

14 See ibid., p. 207. This kind of "somehow-historical" style also characterizes Prasser's associatively conceived creations for the interior of the Konzerthaus.

15 The chief proponents of a theoretically grounded critique of postmodernism were Bruno Flierl, Bernd Grönwald, Karin and Heinz Hirdina, Lothar Kühne, and the international circle of authors around the journal *form+zweck*.

16 Hain, "Between *Arkonaplatz* and the *Nikolaiviertel*," in Scheer et al., *City of Architecture, Architecture of the City* (see note 4), p. 346.

Fig. 4 Ricardo Bofill, L'espaces d'Abraxas housing complex, near Paris, 1982, which was carefully studied by the architects Prasser and Gisske on a business trip, photo: Christian Kloss, 2010

Fig. 5 Colonnade from prefabricated elements, building at the corner of Jägerstrasse and Charlottenstrasse, 2006

bay windows, balustrades, and reliefs was made possible by a small concrete factory on site that Gisske, as building director, had set up right next to the construction area.[11] Any desired architectural detail could be made in concrete from a plaster model relatively easily. The elements were sometimes so small that they were installed by hand or by using block and tackle (fig. 5) (→ pp. 80–81).

In an attempt to outwit clumsy and anonymous large-scale technology by employing a diversity of visual detail, the "prefabricated concrete principle" was thus crossed with the "mason's guild" principle. But the more playful the individual concrete façades seemed, the clearer it became that the compromises had been achieved at a cost. For if something was lacking here, it was lightness and elegance. It did not achieve the formal matter-of-factness of old stonemason or plaster façades, and if architectural quality also means plausible tectonic structures, then the planar mosaic tapestry on Markgrafenstrasse—the prettified concrete-slab building—offers the most convincing picture. On the Platz der Akademie, confessed historicists were at work who were searching for the art of building but found only the art of cladding. They would not have the opportunity to advance to a completely new kind of metropolitan architecture: their pet project—a labyrinthine, nested residential and commercial district on the south side of the square, which had already made considerable headway—fell victim, while still in the planning stage, to the sedate conservatism of the Domhotel (now Hilton); and its gigantic-looking successor plan, the precursor to today's Passagen Friedrichstadt, which did not shy from kitsch, was demolished while still a shell after the political "turning point" (*Wende*) following the fall of the Berlin Wall.[12]

In his fundamental study of the neohistoricism of the late GDR years,[13] Florian Urban uncovered a serious debate over principles: between "copiers" (who wanted exact reproductions) (fig. 3) and freely interpreting "adapters." In that conflict, Manfred Prasser prevailed with his *al gusto* stylistic gestures. Claims about historical preservation no longer played any role after that; the path to the city as an adventure zone with "somehow-historical design" had been chosen.[14]

Views in the professional world were very divided in the country during this period. Whereas younger architects, who found postmodernism very tempting at the time, envied the creative latitude (and the preference for construction technology and materials), proponents of modernism distanced themselves from the "unserious" playing with forms of the façade tinkerers. Something that probably few people knew at the time: in May 1980, Manfred Prasser and his direct superior, Ehrhardt Gisske, traveled to Paris, where they were also able to inspect buildings under construction at the time by Ricardo Bofill, who also employed individually formed concrete elements for his picturesque, creative buildings (fig. 4). This privileged experience in the West perhaps makes it easier to understand why the architects of Gisske's Aufbaustab were so unwavering and, even in their other projects, such as the Friedrichstadtpalast (Dieter Bankert, 1981–84) and the Nikolaiviertel (Günter Stahn, 1980–87), were able to ignore all the mockery and bitter criticism of their colleagues.

A real barrage of fire at the "Postmodernism à la DDR" that was emerging here came from the ranks of academic specialists.[15] No one denied that prefabricated elements which had been designed for mass construction in green-spaces were not suited for use on the vacant lots and crowded open areas of the inner cities. But critics of the formalism of façades that was imposed under Gisske's direction focused on another conflict: individualization did not mean simply cladding the tectonically untamed products of large series, but rather changing the system.[16] Whereas more and more renowned buildings around Friedrichstrasse served a puffed-up staging of the city, the more urgent call

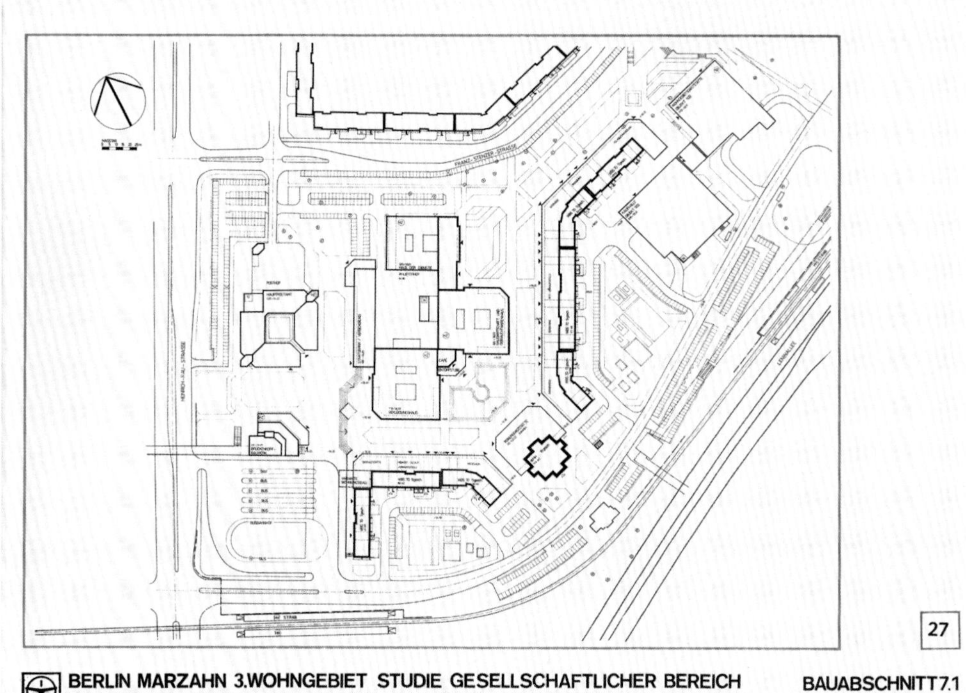

Fig. 6 Eisentraut, Kny und Kollektiv, study for the Gesellschaftlicher Bereich Marzahn (Marzahn Social Area), May 1983. Individual buildings form a coherent spatial figure and are also recognizable architecturally as a unified ensemble. This early design plan corresponds in essence to the building as ultimately constructed.

Fig. 7 Heinz Graffunder, Rolf Rühle, Geissenweide restaurant complex, 1978, standard project from the IHB catalogue of types for facilities in residential areas. The set of elements used here for the SK construction system was also based on the individual solutions of the Marzahner Promenade.

for architectural approaches to nonplaces came primarily from the "outside," from housing construction for the masses. And once again for the true believers in modernism this meant a turn to the social: not historicism in the Mitte district of Berlin, but rather a living center for the residents of Marzahn.

EXIT 2: URBAN CENTER FOR MARZAHN

Immediately after the opening of the Palast der Republik (1976), all of the energies of the construction industry in the capital were mobilized for the new district of Marzahn. The tasks were strictly separated between Berlin's two construction combines: the Wohnungsbaukombinat (Housing Construction Combine, WBK) was responsible for the housing construction proper, as well as daycare centers, schools, retirement homes, and health centers. The other standard functions in residential areas, that is, department stores, restaurants, youth clubs, service centers, and also swimming pools—all standardized projects as well—were entrusted to the IHB. This division was dependent on the construction systems available to each. Whereas the WBK built its residential blocks using the large panel building system ("slabs") exclusively, the IHB, which had originally been founded for industrial projects, could also employ the SK Berlin technology using prefabricated parts, a reinforced-concrete system that facilitated structures that were far more variable than those of simple slab technology.[17]

The first plans for Marzahn still provided for three residential areas for around 100,000 residents, but the requirement grew steadily in the early 1980s, reaching nearly 170,000, which necessitated an additional, third construction phase, the future Marzahn-Nord. As a result, Marzahn was not only the numerically largest residential area of new construction in the GDR; it also grew into an autonomous metropolis, its identity calling for an urban center. In the usual fashion, the plan for the "main social center" at the Marzahn S-Bahnhof (commuter rail) station was based on a number of individual buildings from the usual assortment of the IHB, which was to be supplemented by several additional buildings that other GDR districts would have contributed from their palette of types. However, once the Springpfuhl district center (now Helene-Weigel-Platz), which was built first, had successfully employed an experimental stacking and combining of various infrastructure buildings, the director of the IHB planning department[18] submitted an offer to the Magistrat (City Council) to have the entire main center of Marzahn planned and built by one hand—namely, his IHB! This complete offer, which was far removed from the usual practice,[19] was accepted and subsequently led to two competitions within the department,[20] in which the collective around Wolf-Rüdiger Eisentraut[21] and Michael Kny prevailed, with a pedestrian zone flanked by eleven-story residential slab buildings between two widened public squares. The boulevard, which was ultimately called the Marzahner Promenade, obtained its final form in 1983, when the striking individual buildings—post office, reception building, services building, department store, and art gallery—were arranged into flowing urban spaces and then gradually planned to completion by the same planning collective.[22] At the same time, under Eisentraut's management, a cultural, sports, and entertainment center in the same formal idiom was built on the eastern end of the promenade (fig. 6).

In a detailed analysis of the planning of Marzahn, the Swiss urban historian Simon Hubacher emphasized how decisive these two competition choices were. In contrast to the visionary sketches of city crowns in several competition entries,[23] the designs of the Eisentraut and Kny collective nevertheless revealed, according to Hubacher, for all their will to foster

17 For its daycare centers, schools, and retirement homes, the WBK also used the SK-Bauweise, but its effectiveness was debatable.

18 Dr.-Ing. Manfred Barg, whom his coworkers characterized as "a passionate engineer with a corresponding professional ethos" (see note 25).

19 In retrospect, Barg's initiative resembles the bold slogan of the president of Neue Heimat (New Homeland), Albert Vietor: "Wir liefern Ihnen eine ganze Stadt!" (We will deliver a whole city to you!). See Ulrich Schwarz and Hartmut Frank, eds., *neue heimat: Das Gesicht der Bundesrepublik; Bauten und Projekte, 1947–1985* (Hamburg, 2019).

20 Peer review process in 1977, design competition in 1978, with five collectives participating in each.

21 Wolf-Rüdiger Eisentraut had been project leader for the central foyer of the Palast der Republik. Then he became the Generalprojektant Gesellschaftsbauten (General Planner of Social Building) for all areas of new buildings, experimented with on-site combinations of buildings, and was responsible for planning and building the Marzahner Promenade until 1988.

22 Michael Kny and Thomas Weber (post office and overall direction of the Marzahn Gate), Sabine Bondzin (post office / Haus der Dienste / Galerie M), Heidrun Senz (reception building), Ralf Effenberger (intermediate building for food services), Ricarda Gehrke (bank/savings bank), and Klaus Schmieder and Heidrun Tippmann (department store).

23 The most striking alternative had been offered by the Kollektiv Bankert in the peer review process of 1977. Its Stern (Star) variation for the design sought to achieve urban density by means of a metabolic basic form—that is, a final dream of the city as a big machine. See Simon Hubacher, "Berlin-Marzahn: The Would-Be Town," in Scheer et al., *City of Architecture, Architecture of the City* (see note 4).

Fig. 8 Michael Kny, Thomas Weber, façade of the Marzahn department store, 1987. The concision of the ensemble is reinforced by the strong color scheme of white, yellow, red, and brown, which distinguished the interior and exterior of all the buildings. Photo: 1991

Fig. 9 Michael Kny, Thomas Weber, Marzahner Promenade, 1987. Thanks to a new 135-degree corner, the rigid rectangularity of the skeleton system could be overcome; the sloping forms were now permitted make the individual building volumes look like a coherent ensemble. Photo: 1991

Fig. 10 Michael Kny, Thomas Weber, Kunst-Galerie M (M Art Gallery), 1987. Final stand-alone building from the original plan, demolished in 2014. Photo: 1991

24 Ibid., p. 353.

25 I am grateful to Michael Kny and Thomas Weber for detailed information on the planning practices of the time, from an interview held on February 11, 2020. Both experiences in Marzahn provided material for the film *Die Architekten* (The Architects) by Thomas Knauf and Peter Kahane (DEFA, 1990).

26 It was true of nearly all of the building collectives that the planners had "no place on building sites."

27 Michael Kny in an interview (see note 25).

28 The Marzahn main post office became a model building for the GDR postal service and was even featured on a stamp. On this, see the essay by Gerd Zimmermann in this volume.

striking form, recognition above all of economic considerations and the heavy weighting given to aspects of building technology. Their design excelled in this respect with a skeleton construction system expanded into a modular system.[24] Indeed, it was scarcely evident from looking at the surprisingly different built forms that they were almost entirely composed of the same prefabricated elements as the otherwise ordinary standard products using the SK Berlin construction system (fig. 7), at most augmented by new surfaces (ceramic tiles, textured concrete) and a signal-like color concept of bright red, yellow, white, and brown (figs. 8–10).

In the retrospective reports of those involved, the constant battles over expanding the design latitudes take up the most space.[25] With great effort, the architects managed to overcome the rigid rectangularity of the skeleton system and to introduce corners of 135 degrees with an additional solution for the joint. That permitted not only the original diagonal floor plan of the post office but above all the memorable sloping forms that cause the individual buildings to grow together into a coherent ensemble—the very unmistakable "place for all the residents of Marzahn" that had been sought (→ pp. 87–89). Every other deviation from the strictly limited catalogue of construction parts required protracted negotiations and not infrequently was thwarted by the so-called Elemente-Gericht (Elements Court), a committee composed largely of technologists and economists who made decisions about whether prefabricated parts that deviated from the system were permitted internally. To safeguard their many "special requests," Thomas Weber often had himself transferred from the planning office to the construction sites—which was by no means a common step in those years.[26] Even bigger obstacles arose when suppliers that did not belong to the collective had to be persuaded to deviate from their standard solutions (which guaranteed easy satisfaction of the plan) and produced individually developed constructions parts—for example, skylights with shed glazing. Such ambitious independent initiatives could only be expected to succeed if the partners had the personal ambition to improve the reputation of their own operation with such exceptional solutions.

This constant dependence on the good will and the bold risk-taking of individual managers at the powerhouses of broadly ramified construction entities ultimately moved the project leader at the time to express this sobering conclusion in an interview: "Our attempt to fundamentally open up the modular system failed. The structural ossified construction industry of the GDR was able to respond to the ambitions of individual architects only in response to extraordinary efforts. That would not have been economically feasible for every other normal case."[27]

Even with such small deviations from the guidelines of the SK-Bauweise system, the original buildings of the Marzahner Promenade only somewhat managed to become prototypes for a new, richer prefabricated architecture. To develop it further would have required profound changes in the whole state construction industry, yet the GDR of the late 1980s had neither the political will nor sufficient economic resources to achieve that.

Nevertheless, the success of the enervating and exhausting commitment of all those involved in the Marzahn project was notable. The post office, which was finished first, was celebrated as a key building of a new stage in the evolution of architecture in the GDR.[28] More technical innovations, such as energy-efficient direct ventilation in the department store or experiments with greened roofs, were noticed less by the public—to say nothing of the unprecedented invention of the "reception building," a hybrid urban building block that combined an S-Bahn station, a bus station, a late-night market, a snack bar, a floral shop, a local information center, and a sales point for lottery tickets within the up and down of an atrium decorated with palm trees.

29 The demolition of all service buildings at the Mahrzahn S-Bahn station began in 2003 to make room for the Eastgate shopping mall. The Galerie M, the only cultural address in Marzahn with appeal outside the area, was the last to be closed and demolished.

There is no trace left today of the urban center "for all the residents of Marzahn" planned during the final decade of the GDR,[29] because most of its functions were designed for that era. A supermarket without rooftop parking, an entire building just for repairs, a post office in its own official building, or a multifunctional train station no longer have much to do with today's showy shopping malls or ruthlessly efficient service economy. Nevertheless, or for that very reason, its disappearance without a trace is a lamentable loss for the history of the city and the culture of architecture.

POSTSCRIPT: A LATER EXCHANGE OF LETTERS

Berlin, March 26, 2003
Landesdenkmalamt Berlin, Attn.: Landeskonservator Dr. Haspel

Dear Dr. Haspel,
We learned from the *Berliner Zeitung* of March 13, 2003, that the Hauptzentrum [Main Center] at the Berlin-Marzahn station is to be demolished and rebuilt with an Eastgate Shopping Center. As the principal authors of its design, we were involved from 1980 to 1990 in the planning and realization of this part of the Hauptzentrum for the new-building residential area Berlin-Marzahn. Under the direction of the general planner for social buildings of the new-building residential areas of Berlin, Prof. Dr. Eisentraut, we were responsible for the urban-planning proposal, the planning of all buildings (except residential buildings), the design of the open spaces, and the artistic and promotional concept for the subsection at the Marzahn station. Though we harbor no illusions that we will be able to prevent the planned demolition, we are nevertheless upset to see a work that took circa ten years to create and that marked an important part of our professional biography simply disappear so thoughtlessly and silently. Although it is not protected as a historical landmark, we nevertheless regard it as an important ensemble of German architecture from the final era of the GDR.
To our knowledge, the Hauptzentrum Marzahn is the only realized attempt to do justice to the lifeworld requirements of identity of place, originality, and quality of environment using existing prefabricated systems modified for this project. In terms of urban planning, the space-shaping possibilities of industrial construction were demonstrated.... The space-shaping new buildings are unique objects based on a consistent design concept ... with a certain degree of subjective acuity. In our view, their particular significance lies in overcoming exclusively technological determination and hence a standardized architecture—a unique process on this scale within the complex residential architecture of the GDR in that period. Under the keyword "individualization," the Hauptzentrum Berlin-Marzahn was the subject of an exhibition planned by the Institut für Auslandsbeziehungen: *Zwei deutsche Architekturen, 1949–1989* [Two German Architectures, 1949–1989].... It is probably an irony of history that the buildings of Marzahn's center will be presented in many countries as part of this large exhibition beginning in the summer of this year and at the same time disappear with the demolition of this ensemble.

We would be very pleased to receive a reply.
Sincerely yours, Kny & Weber Architekten

Reply from the Landeskonservator, April 8, 2003

Dear Mr. Kny and Mr. Weber,
Thank you very much for your message about the latest development at the Hauptzentrum at the Berlin-Marzahn station. I can very well imagine that you two, as the principal authors of the design, but also Prof. Dr. Eisentraut as the representative of the overall planning, are very much upset by our plans, which once again call into question a showcase urban planning and architectural project that is just ten or twenty years old.
Such fast-moving plans for change can be cause for reflection, even for those who do not associate part of their own biography or their own oeuvre with them. The planning for the center of Marzahn or "Eastgate" does indeed reveal how difficult it can be for the urban planning and architecture, of recent decades in particular, to preserve or claim for oneself continuity with the past in their planning and results. Similar developments—I am thinking of the Sport- und Erholungszentrum [Sports and Recreation Center, SEZ] and also specific results of IBA-Neubau—can also be seen elsewhere, after all, and stand in a strange contradiction with current goals for an architectural culture focused on sustainability, conserving resources, and preserving the existing fabric. The vexation at such processes is that much greater because not only the authors of the design are affected, as the artistic creators, so to speak. What also seems to have survived along with the products of architecture at issue here, in an incredibly brief span, are the intellectual, cultural, and social requirements for which architecture is, after all, always seeking a satisfactory response.
To keep to the example of Marzahn: it is not just the architects involved who are affected by the process, but also all of those people to whom the center was supposed to offer and convey a bit of identity, even a built homeland. The prospect that today's plans and building projects can once again turn out to be obsolete in ten or twenty years, that is, in less than a generation, is disturbing. This is true both of the practical use value of the architecture and of its schematic, secondary function which one would like to see have more durability and permanence. I can only hope that the replacement for "your" recent architectural structures will enjoy a longer half-life in its substance and significance than the buildings they will soon replace, as those responsible would have it—exactly as if it were only a matter of changing scenery.

I am very grateful for your testimony as eyewitnesses of the planning of Marzahn.
Sincerely yours, Prof. Dr. Jörg Haspel

A SOCIALIST TEMPLE TO CONSUMERISM

The Passagen Friedrichstadt and the Unrealized Plans for Friedrichstrasse

Florian Urban

> On its southern end, the gallery level in the arcade feeds into an atrium-like shopping center, topped by a skylight dome.... In the central section, the palm garden and the night bar are accessed from this level.[1]

Reading such descriptions, one thinks of a West Berlin shopping mall such as the Spandau Arcaden or the Europa-Center. And yet it is a design by the state-owned East German construction company VEB Ingenieurhochbau. The Passagen Friedrichstadt (Friedrichstadt Arcades), designed by a team headed by the architects Manfred Prasser and Peter Weiss, begun in 1985 and never completed, was intended to be the first combined shopping and entertainment center in the German Democratic Republic (GDR) (fig. 1). It was planned on three blocks between Friedrichstrasse and Gendarmenmarkt (then the Platz der Akademie), where the Galeries Lafayette, Quartier 206, and Quartier 205 shopping centers now stand (which are often also called the Friedrichstadt-Passagen). The Passagen Friedrichstadt were the heart of a planned redesign of Friedrichstrasse into a vibrant entertainment district.[2] Already at the time, the project seemed light years removed from daily life under real socialism, with its crumbling old building façades, monotonous prefab concrete-slab buildings, and comparatively empty streets smelling of heating coal and two-cylinder engines. And it was a sharp contrast to the Friedrichstrasse of the time, which was characterized by vacant lots and wartime damage, and where only individual buildings, such as the Admiralspalast, reminded one that this had once been the most famous entertainment strip of the Weimar Republic.

The plans for Friedrichstrasse reveal astonishing parallels to postmodern urbanism in the West.[3] They are evidence of how far those in power in the GDR had by then already distanced themselves from the ideological principles of socialist urban planning; and also evidence of how much—within the framework of the political and economic possibilities available to them—they adopted, for their prestige projects, themes from the postmodern and neoliberal urban development of capitalist countries. In that spirit, they called for, in the "Capital of the GDR" as well, the return of privileged classes to the center of the city; the renaissance of the dense, mixed-use city; the marketing of history to natives and foreigners; and above all the redesign of inner-city neighborhoods for commerce and amusement. Competition with its rival West Berlin, the special position of East Berlin as the "shop window of the Eastern Bloc," and the hunger of GDR leadership for hard currency reinforced these motivations in the Friedrichstrasse project especially.

The idea was to create a glittering entertainment district according to the capitalist model, with stores, restaurants, and music bars.[4] The plan was for 105 stores and 44 restaurants in the Passagen Friedrichstadt: for example, a jeweler's, porcelain store, jeans store, fashion boutique (City Tex), discotheque, and "night bar."[5] The project was supposed to connect to the idea of the "roaring twenties" and be completed in 1992. For economic reasons, it was repeatedly delayed and finally canceled after German reunification; its partially finished shell was demolished in 1992.[6]

A model from 1987 shows three building volumes linked by footbridges that cross over Jägerstrasse (then Otto-Nuschke-Strasse) and Taubenstrasse (then Johannes-Dieckmann-Strasse). The complex stands out for its extravagant, Gothic-inspired, fantastic façade, with pointed arches and hive-like, interwoven window forms (fig. 2) (→ p. 83). Drawings of the interiors, with their glass domes, are suggestive of atriums (fig. 3) (→ p. 83). The description is also impressive:

1 VEB Ingenieurhochbau Berlin, "Entwurf für die Passagen Friedrichstadt," commissioned by the Ministry of Construction in June 1986 and completed on March 31, 1987, Bundesarchiv Berlin (cited in the following as: BArch) DH1/36355, p. 5.

2 Urban, *Berlin/DDR, neo-historisch: Geschichte aus Fertigteilen* (Berlin, 2007), pp. 181–214.

3 On the principles of postmodern urbanism, see Nan Ellin, *Postmodern Urbanism* (New York, 1996); David Harvey, *The Condition of Postmodernity* (Oxford, 1989).

4 On this, see the plan "Information zur weiteren Durchführung des Investitionskomplexes Friedrichstrasse/Otto-Grotewohl-Strasse in der Hauptstadt Berlin, insbesondere für den Zeitraum bis 1990," August 18, 1988, which was submitted to the Politburo. It was produced by a team in the Ministry of Construction under the direction of Secretary of State Karl-Heinz Martini, BArch DY 30/2847, pp. 170–87.

5 Ibid., p. 176.

6 Ibid.

Fig. 1 Manfred Prasser, Peter Weiss, Passagen Friedrichstadt (Friedrichstadt Arcades), central section of the building between Jägerstrasse und Taubenstrasse. The photograph shows the shell of the building shortly before its demolition, 1991.

Fig. 2 Passagen Friedrichstadt, model by the Werkstatt IHB, Betrieb Projektierung, 1987

Fig. 3 Manfred Prasser, Peter Weiss, Passagen Friedrichstadt, view of the interior, ca. 1986

> While walking through this level of experiences [the second floor], the viewer is repeatedly surprised by the impressions of the space resulting from the different spatial geometries of the arcade articulated by covered and open bridges in the gallery area. There are also views into the halls, which, owing to their varied location within the building, offer lines of sight to the interior and exterior spaces that lend them their specific charm.[7]

From the outside, the socialist decision makers were suppressing the question of how the weakening GDR economy was meant to produce all of the goods they wanted to present here, to say nothing of guaranteeing that construction would be completed. As it began to become clear that Friedrichstrasse would not be finished by the scheduled deadline, Erich Honecker mobilized all resources, nearly doubled the budget, and even considered having military battalions work on the project.[8] Despite these efforts, workers and materials were still lacking. The recognition that the GDR economy was too weak to complete the project was, however, systematically covered up in internal documents.[9] In 1988, the plans for the Passagen Friedrichstadt were significantly cut back.[10]

Other buildings in this entertainment district were also left unfinished, such as the Haus der Unterhaltung (House of Entertainment), which was to house beer halls, wine bars, and dance clubs on the west side of Friedrichstrasse between Kronenstrasse and Leipziger Strasse; it was demolished in 1992 after being only partially completed (fig. 4). The Wintergarten, an "upmarket premiere cinema" south of the Friedrichstrasse train station, which was designed to be reminiscent of the famous variety theater on that site from before the war, was never even begun—it was also to have housed the border checkpoint (fig. 5).[11]

Buildings that were completed include the historicist Grand-Hotel, a hard-currency hotel on the southwest corner of Friedrichstrasse and Unter den Linden (1985–87, now Westin Grand Hotel), the Haus der sowjetischen Wissenschaft und Kultur three blocks further south (House of Soviet Science and Culture, 1981–84, architect: Karl-Ernst Swora, now Russisches Haus der Wissenschaft und Kultur), and the Spreeterrassen (Spree Terraces) residential and restaurant complex north of the Weidendammer Brücke (Weidendamm Bridge, 1985–89, architects: Karl-Ernst Swora et al., now Hotel Neuer Fritz). Also realized was the rebuilding of the Gendarmenmarkt with historical reconstructions of the Schauspielhaus (as the Konzerthaus), the Deutsche Kirche (German Church) and the Französische Kirche (French Church),[12] and the surrounding neohistorical buildings, as proposed in 1979 and implemented together with the redesign of Friedrichstrasse.[13]

The most famous of the buildings completed as part of these plans was the Friedrichstadtpalast (Friedrichstadt Palace) (→ p. 82).[14] The building that preceded it, which was world famous between the wars, was located on the street Am Zirkus next to the Berliner Ensemble theater and was closed because of disrepair and demolished in 1980. The new Friedrichstadtpalast was built on the east side of Friedrichstrasse, a good hundred meters away (1981–84, architects: Manfred Prasser, Walter Schwarz, and Dieter Bankert).[15] It was given a façade of concrete parts, with ornaments that were intended to "reflect the cheerfulness and joie de vivre of its function."[16] After the fall of the Berlin Wall, the building was renovated and is still a popular events location for musicals, variety theater, and other performances.

7 VEB Ingenieurhochbau Berlin, "Entwurf für die Passagen Friedrichstadt" (see note 1), p. 5.

8 Gerhard Trölitzsch to Günter Mittag, August 23, 1988; BArch DY 30/2847, p. 193. Information from the Minister of Building Wolfgang Junker, July 3, 1986, BArch DH 1/36305.

9 See, for example, the celebratory article by Ehrhardt Gisske, "Historisch, lebendig und weltoffen—die Friedrichstrasse erhält ein neues Gesicht," *Neue Zeit*, January 14, 1987.

10 Gerhard Trölitzsch to the office of Günter Mittag, April 21, 1987, BArch DY 30/2846, p. 270.

11 Construction was completed in 1985. See "Festlegungsprotokoll zur Beratung des Politbüros mit Erich Honecker 'über die weiteren Vorbereitungen ... Friedrichstrasse/Otto-Grotewohl-Strasse,'" February 5, 1985, BArch DH 1/35670, p. 2.

12 The widely known names "Deutscher Dom" and "Französischer Dom" actually only refer to the two cupolas built by Carl von Gontard in 1780–85, which are adjacent to the two churches but have no actual sacral meaning.

13 "Vorschlag für die Rekonstruktion des Platzes," March 1979, BArch DY 30/2850, pp. 62–63. See the essay by Wolfgang Kil in this volume.

14 Minutes of a meeting of Erich Honecker, Günter Mittag, Konrad Naumann, Wolfgang Junker, Ehrhardt Gisske, and Gerhard Trölitzsch on May 2, 1980 in Honecker's office, BArch, DY 30/2851, p. 53.

15 On this, see the essay by Gerd Zimmermann in this volume.

16 Berlin City Council, Department of Culture, *Friedrichstadtpalast: Dokumentation zur Investitionsvorbereitung* (East Berlin, 1980), p. 7.

1
Quartier 302 (1985, realized with “Dreispitz-passage” (tricorn passage)

2
Cinema Wintergarten, border crossing point and shopping center (unbuilt)

3
Grand-Hotel (1985)

4
Quartier 113, mixed use (unbuilt)

5
Quartier 112 (1984)

6
Russian House of Science and Culture (1981)

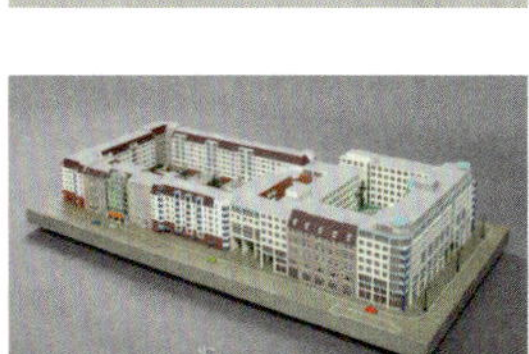

7
Mixed use (unbuilt)

8
Haus der Unter-haltung (House of Entertainment), mixed use (un-finished building, dem. after 1992)

9
Quartier 107, mixed use (1984)

10
Quartier 404 (unbuilt)

11
Friedrich-stadtpalast (1981)

12
Spreeterrassen (Spree Terraces, 1985)

13
Internationales Handelszentrum (International Trade Center, 1976)

14
Lindencorso (1963, demolished in the 1990s)

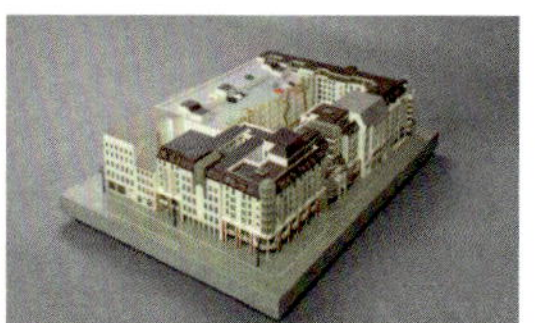

15
Youth hotel and multistory parking lot (unbuilt)

16
Passagen Friedrich-stadt (Friedrichstadt Arcades, 1985, unfinished building, demolished in 1992)

17
Quartier 204 (unbuilt)

18
Quartier 203, old buildings, mixed use (unbuilt)

19
Quartier 202, old buildings, mixed use (1984)

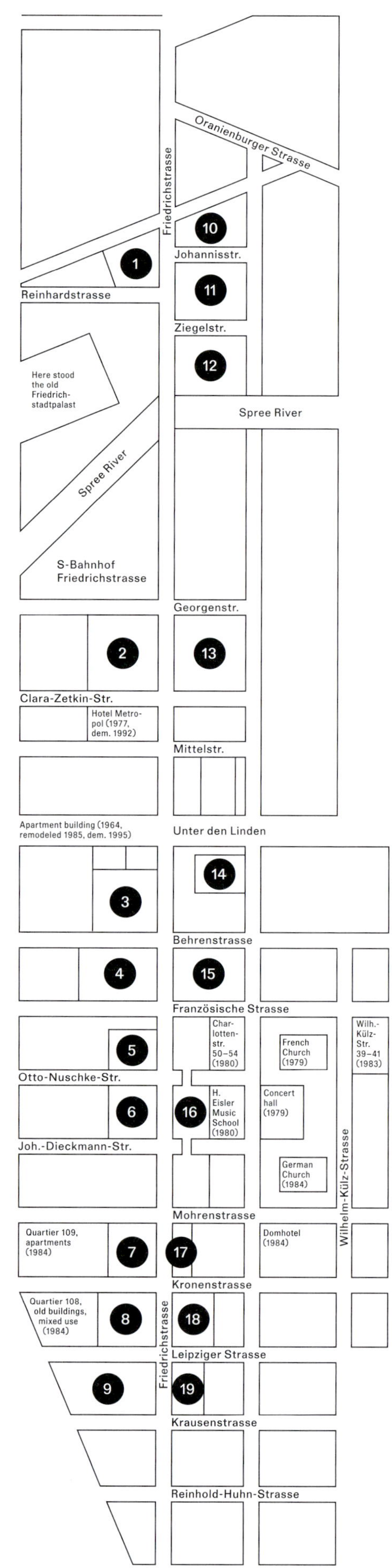

Fig. 4 Florian Urban, plans for Friedrichstrasse in 1987

17 Urban, *Berlin/DDR, neo-historisch* (see note 2); Florian Urban, *Neo-Historical East Berlin: Architecture and Urban Design in the German Democratic Republic, 1970–1990* (Farnham, 2009).

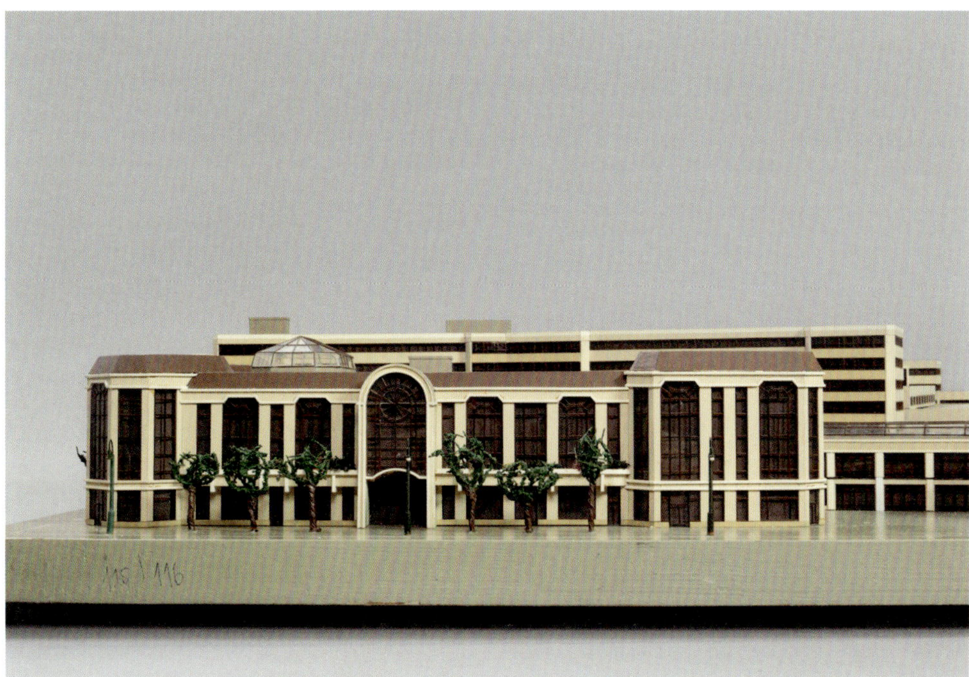

Fig.5 Premierenkino Wintergarten (Winter Garden Premier Cinema) with border control office, model by the Werkstatt IHB, Betrieb Projektierung, 1987, unbuilt

POSTMODERN URBAN RENEWAL IN THE GDR

Friedrichstrasse was not a personal idea of the chairman of the State Council, even though Erich Honecker had indeed formally announced supreme authority over it and was informed in detail about all of the steps. Unlike his predecessor, Walter Ulbricht, however, he was rather uninterested in issues of architectural details. He therefore delegated authority over the design of the center of East Berlin to the responsible government offices. This involved, in particular, the Abteilung Sondervorhaben (Special Projects Department), later renamed the Baudirektion (Building Direction), of the GDR Ministry of Construction under its influential director, Ehrhardt Gisske, who was responsible for all of the prestigious projects in the GDR; and the Büro für Städtebau (Urban Development Office) of the Berlin city council, with its director, Heinz Willumat, and its head architect, Solweig Steller.

At the same time, Honecker supported every form of image marketing, to his own citizens and to the West. One special opportunity for that was the 750th anniversary of Berlin in 1987. On the occasion, unusually, East Berlin could undisputedly present itself as the more important part of the city—after all, its historical center was located there. Friedrichstrasse was to have been the most important project for that occasion. The GDR leadership was pushing a number of other construction projects, such as the historical old town district of the Nikolaiviertel and the renovation of the historical blocks on Husemannstrasse and Sophienstrasse.[17] Just like Friedrichstrasse, these projects were characterized by the principle of postmodern urbanism. They were neighborhoods of small structures of mixed function that were ostentatiously historical and presented the center of the city as a place of consumerism and entertainment for residents and tourists alike, combined with designs for housing on the waterfront and for modernizing historical buildings.

The fundamental decision to rebuild Friedrichstrasse and the neighboring streets, as well as the Gendarmenmarkt, had been made by the Politburo in 1976, in the same meeting in which it was planned to redesign

18 "Aufgaben zur Entwicklung der Hauptstadt der DDR, Berlin," minutes of the meeting of the Politburo, February 3, 1976, fair copy, BArch DY30/JIV 2/21602.

19 Minutes of the meeting of the Politburo, January 17, 1984, fair copy, BArch DY30/JIV 2/2 2037; Minutes of the meeting of the Politburo, January 22, 1985, fair copy, BArch DY30/JIV 2/2 2095; Minutes of the meeting of the Politburo, February 5, 1985, fair copy, BArch DY30/JIV 2/2 2097.

20 There are photographs from both competitions in the archives of the Berlinische Galerie, BG-AS1436-002888, but the architects are not identified.

21 Minutes of the meeting of the Politburo, February 5, 1985, fair copy, BArch DY30/J IV 2/2 2097, p. 44; BArch DH1/35670, p. 7.

22 Ehrhardt Gisske, ed., *Berlin Friedrichstrasse, Otto-Grotewohl-Strasse gestern und heute: Konzeption und Baumassnahmen bis 1987* (East Berlin, 1987), p. 42.

23 Günter Stahn, *Probleme der räumlichen Umgestaltung grossstädtischer Zentrumsbereiche im Prozess der Herausbildung der sozialistischen Lebensweise, dargestellt am Beispiel der Friedrichstrasse in Berlin*, PhD dissertation A, Deutsche Bauakademie, Abteilung Architektur (East Berlin, 1971).

24 Ibid., pp. 20–22.

other central areas—for example, the aforementioned Nikolaiviertel, which was intended to become an "organic connection of old and new."[18] The plans were detailed in three further Politburo meetings in 1984 and 1985, but the fundamental concept did not change.[19] In addition, an architectural competition was announced in two phases in 1979–80, but its designs were not realized directly.[20] In 1985, Honecker officially granted Gisske's Abteilung Sondervorhaben authority over the project.[21] The final designs are by various teams of architects, coordinated by, among others, Solweig Steller, the head architect in the Büro für Städtebau.[22] Friedrichstrasse was thus not the work of a charismatic individual, but a collaboration of numerous decision makers.

The ideological backgrounds are especially interesting. Until that time, consumerism and the design of leisure time had not been among the highest priorities of the social regime. In accordance with the Marxist principle that "being determines consciousness," for decades the GDR leadership concentrated, more or less successfully, on improving the material basis for the livelihood of its citizens—through housing construction and low rents, universal health care, and providing the working class with food that had previously been unaffordable, such as meat.

The new projects, with their focus on consumerism and entertainment, were an expression of growing prosperity: in the early 1970s, the GDR—just like the Federal Republic—experienced its most economically successful period. The projects were also a response to the increasingly colorful life in the West and the vanishing loyalty of its own citizens. And they reflected international developments in cultural theory, especially in the fields of architectural psychology, semiotics, and communication theory.

This can be seen, for example, in the theories of the architect Günter Stahn, who, a decade later, became famous as the head architect for the Nikolaiviertel and was also employed by the state building company VEB Ingenieurhochbau on the construction of Friedrichstrasse. In his dissertation, submitted in 1971 to the Bauakademie in East Berlin, Stahn presented a design for that street as a thoroughly organized communication system.[23] He analyzed the distribution of aesthetic appeal and urban functions in order to generate "stimulating and characterful" ensembles with optimal urban activity. Friedrichstrasse should "produce and stimulate forms of behavior," for example, by means of carefully positioned storefronts or significant forms and images. One important model was the London market hall Covent Garden, whose conversion into a historically inspired place for commercial entertainment was being discussed at the time and would be implemented a decade later. At the same time, however, Stahn explicitly distanced himself from any orientation around profit and consumerism. He considered his proposals to be a response to the basic human need for culture and personal development—and indirectly to a self-determined individual's desire for knowledge, experience, and social contacts.[24]

This approach not only reveals the horizon of a young East German architect who had no experience with the elaborate systems for controlling the space of a capitalist shopping mall designed to maximize profit. It also testifies to the influence of an international discourse that criticized functional urban planning and relied on emotion and individual experience as a way out of the monotony of modern urban spaces. Like many of his colleagues in both the East and the West, Stahn was therefore influenced by the standard texts of international postmodernism: Christopher Alexander's critique of the hierarchically planned modern city; Christian Norberg-Schulz's call for sensitivity to local features; and the ideas of the West German philosopher and art theorist Max Bense, according to which urban surroundings are habitable only if conveying meaning to their users.[25] In the years that followed, the renaissance of symbolism and meaning continued to be discussed by such theorists as Charles Jencks and Heinrich Klotz and put into practice by a whole generation of postmodern architects.[26]

LIGHTING INSTALLATIONS AND LARGE-SCALE PROJECTIONS

The Friedrichstrasse project features approaches from semiotics and communication theory—in the planning of the lighting installations, for example—that outshine everything known in the GDR before then. There was a plan for a sophisticated lighting design to reinforce the "characteristic atmosphere" by means of carefully harmonized streetlamps, shop signs, and neon advertising. The submission for the plan reads like the stage directions for a Broadway musical:

> The qualities that create space and convey an experience, resulting both from the lighting and from the lighting fixtures, are designed in differentiated ways in accordance with the intended overall impression. A special Friedrichstrasse lighting dramaturgy has been developed for that purpose and lamps designed in a forward-looking style with high aesthetic visual appeal. Large-scale projection, freestanding LED marquees, timer-switched lighting elements, light designs using effects of motion, designs combining light and sound, lighting advertising spanning the full width of the street for special occasions and holidays [will be installed], [as well as] zones of changing intensity, color, and temperature of the lighting ..., bands of light, light rings for culture, shops, restaurants, floor lights that orient and subdivide, gas-discharge lamps for lighting advertisements that meet international standards, optical information systems, light-and-water displays as sculptures, light-and-sound projections, for example, in combination with displaying the time or for advertising purposes.[27]

In general, Friedrichstrasse was to be transformed into a meticulously designed special installation full of visual and acoustic effects.

The goal was to create *Erlebnis* (a complex German term with a long history in philosophy and psychology, which, depending on the context, can be translated as "individual perception," "experience," or "adventure"). This concept is omnipresent already in Günter Stahn's dissertation. The Politburo resolution of 1984 also promises "diverse areas for *Erlebnisse*."[28] The same tone dominates the documents of the construction company: in the Passagen Friedrichstadt, the connection between the buildings and the street should create "a large spectrum of *Erlebnisse*."[29] Visitors were intended to wander through the building on different "*Erlebnis* levels," which would open up for them "*Erlebnis* zones" and an "*Erlebnis* world."[30] The lighting design was meant to transform Friedrichstrasse into the "street with the most *Erlebnisse* in the capital" and hence into an "optimally functioning main street for commerce and *Erlebnisse*" with an "unmistakable look and *Erlebnis*."[31] To that end, there were plans for, among other things, "*Erlebnis*-providing ... qualities both of the light and of the lighting fixtures," which would have in turn illuminated "*Erlebnis* high points" such as entrances to arcades and restaurants.[32] Here, too, one sees a silent turn away from Marxist principles and toward an urban policy that was no longer aimed at improving the material bases of residents but rather focused on entertainment and facilitating individual experiences.

25 Ibid., p. 33. See also Christopher Alexander, "A City Is Not a Tree," *Architectural Forum* 122, no. 1 (April 1965), pp. 58–60; Christian Norberg-Schulz, *Intentions in Architecture* (New York, 1965); Max Bense, *Ästhetik und Zivilisation* (Krefeld, 1958).

26 Charles Jencks, *The Language of Postmodern Architecture* (New York, 1977); Heinrich Klotz, *Die Revision der Moderne* (Munich, 1984).

27 "Beschlussvorlage für die Lichtgestaltung in der Friedrichstrasse," signed by "Herrmann" [the director of the Abteilung Vorhaben Industrie und Stadttechnik (Department of Industrial and Urban Technology Projects) in the Ministry of Construction], November 1985, BArch DH 1/35504, pp. 1–4.

28 Minutes of the meeting of the Politburo, January 17, 1984, fair copy, BArch DY 30/J IV 2/2 2037, pp. 166–67.

29 VEB Ingenieurhochbau Berlin, "Entwurf für die Passagen Friedrichstadt" (see note 1).

30 Ibid., pp. 5–6.

31 "Beschlussvorlage für die Lichtgestaltung in der Friedrichstrasse" (see note 27), p. 4.

32 Ibid.

33 Harvey, *The Condition of Postmodernity* (see note 3), pp. 3–120; Michael Sorkin, ed., *Variations on a Theme Park* (New York, 1992).

The concept of *Erlebnis* in the modern history of culture was influenced by philosophers such as Wilhelm Dilthey, for whom it represented the possibility of knowledge through empathy. "*Erlebnis* spaces" were, however, attractive to the urban planners of the later twentieth century in both Eastern and Western Europe, primarily because of their potential for effective indirect influence. By means of sophisticated design, different individuals would experience stimuli in the same way and respond similarly to them, yet nevertheless preserve an awareness of their own freedom to choose.

It is obvious that such controlled *Erlebnisse* could be used for play and entertainment as well as for manipulation and control. Theorists of the postmodern city have repeatedly pointed out that, in a postindustrial society, power can be exerted more effectively by channeling individual perceptions and experiences than by surveillance and force.[33] In the GDR, too, the controlled mass society built on Fordist mass production also came under fire increasingly from the 1970s onward: the growing criticism of prefab concrete-slab buildings, which were perceived as monotonous, is a good example of that. Planning for postmodern "*Erlebnis* spaces" therefore also represents an attempt to control from above the increasing individualization and diversification, and to make them useful for the authoritarian socialist system.

CONSUMER FREEDOM AND EXPERIENCE CONTROL UNDER SOCIALISM

The unfinished Friedrichstrasse reveals in a contradictory way how much the GDR leadership in the 1980s was taking the lead from international developments. The focus on *Erlebnis*, entertainment, and consumerism proves that urban planning policy, at least in the case of prestigious projects, had largely abandoned Marxist principles and that decision makers in East Berlin were prepared to sustain the principles of postmodern, capitalist urbanism. That was done, on the one hand, in order to permit at least some of their own citizens to satisfy the desire for glitter and superficial luxury and to feel on a part with their rivals in the West and, on the other hand, because the potential of staged *Erlebnisse* for control could also be used in the authoritarian system of socialism.

In the planning documents of the 1980s, there were no discussions of the possibilities for financing the project through the market economy. It can, however, be assumed that the entertainment and consumer spaces on Friedrichstrasse, had they ever been finished, would have functioned at least in part on the basis of hard currency, analogously to the Intershops, where, since the 1970s, GDR citizens could also purchase imported consumer goods with Western currency, or to the hard-currency hotels such as the Grand-Hotel on Friedrichstrasse, which had been designed for visitors from the West and to which citizens of the GDR had no access. It is therefore reasonable to assume that the "Friedrichstrasse *Erlebnis* center," much like the most commercialized city centers of Western European metropolises, would have led to further divisions within the economically comparatively homogeneous GDR society—both local party elites and wealthy tourists from the West would surely have numbered among the privileged. This, too, reveals parallels to developments in Western societies, where the disparity between poor and rich grew again for the first time in the postwar era and subsequently further reinforced economic inequality.

At the same time, the plans for a "socialist adventure park" were based on international criticism of modern urbanism. The goal of the designs was to create spaces that would have been as thoroughly systematized as the housing complexes on the outskirts of the city, but at least more colorful, imaginative, and aesthetically appealing. Moreover, the focus on individual experiences was also a response to the unsatisfied needs of many citizens of the GDR, including leading party members. *Erlebnis*—subjective, uncontrolled, and in some cases extreme experience—was something clearly lacking in a society in which collective work, collective free time, and collective political activities were prescribed by the dominant ideology, and where for many daily life was restricted to a monotonous routine.

What would have happened if the plans had been realized? Perhaps Friedrichstrasse would have become a paradise for the secret desires of East Berlin's citizens, a place to enjoy pleasure and sensory stimulation in a relaxed environment, within the safe boundaries of effective control and without the risks of a capitalist social order. Perhaps, however, it would have instead become a postmodern version of the Orwellian nightmare in which an authoritarian system controls not only the thoughts and actions of its citizens but also their experiences and feelings. Probably both approaches would have mixed in a way not unsimilar to the shopping centers and entertainment complexes in the West: colorful and gaudy spaces, strictly controlled and at the same time soberingly trivial.

URBAN DIVERSITY

113 Rob Krier, Rauchstrasse, Berlin, perspective, competition entry, August 29, 1980

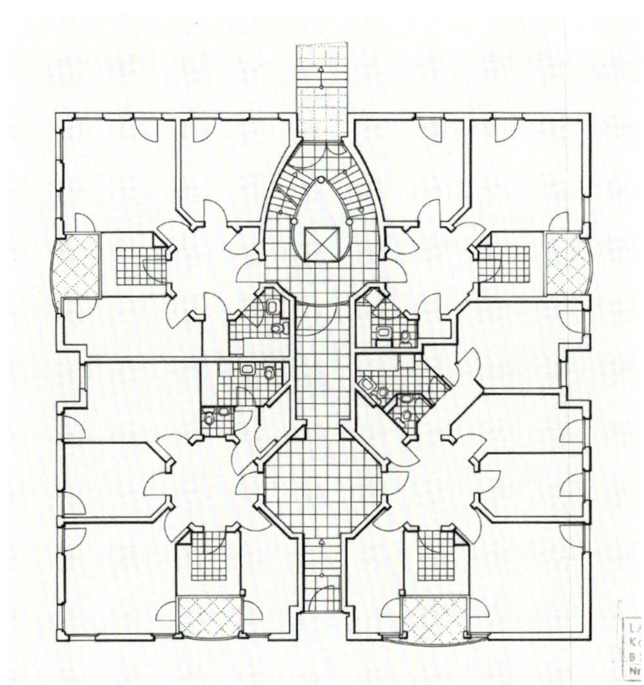

Rob Krier, urban villa, Rauchstrasse 6, plan of ground floor, ca.1980, photo: “Krier_Rauchstr,” Thomas Bomm, 2018

Aldo Rossi, Gianni Braghieri, residential and commercial building at the corner of Kochstrasse 1–4 and Wilhelmstrasse 36–38, 1980–87

Werner Kreis, Ulrich Schaad, Peter Schaad, Wohnpark am Berlin Museum (Residential Park at the Berlin Museum), Lindenstrasse 15–17, 1984–86, photo: Dieter Leistner, 1987
Vittorio Gregotti, Torhäuser (Gate Houses), Lützowstrasse 43–51, 1984–86, photo: Dieter Leistner, 1987

John Hejduk, *Victims,* sketch, design competition project for the former Prinz-Albrecht-Palais, 1984

John Hejduk, residential complex with studio tower, Charlottenstrasse 96–98, photo: Hélène Binet, 1988

Office for Metropolitan Architecture (OMA) / Elia Zenghelis, Zoe Zenghelis, apartment building at Checkpoint Charlie, 1987

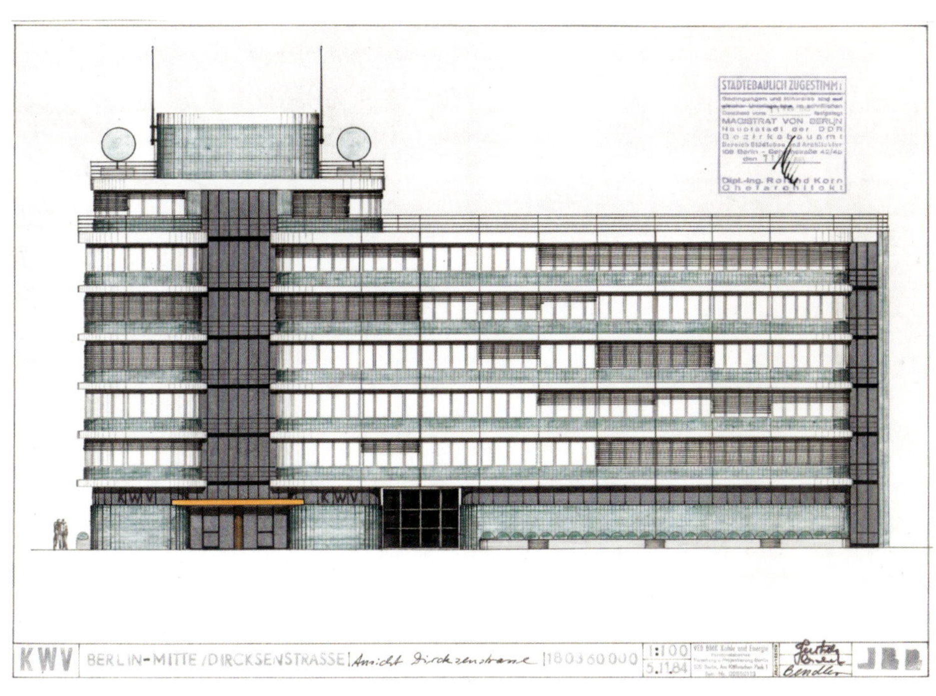

Peter Meyer, industrial complex for the NARVA lightbulb factory, Berlin, view from the south, 1985, unbuilt
Jochen Jentsch, Bernhard Brabetz, Klaus Bendler, administration building of the Wohnungsbaugesellschaft Mitte, Dircksenstrasse 38, 1984–87

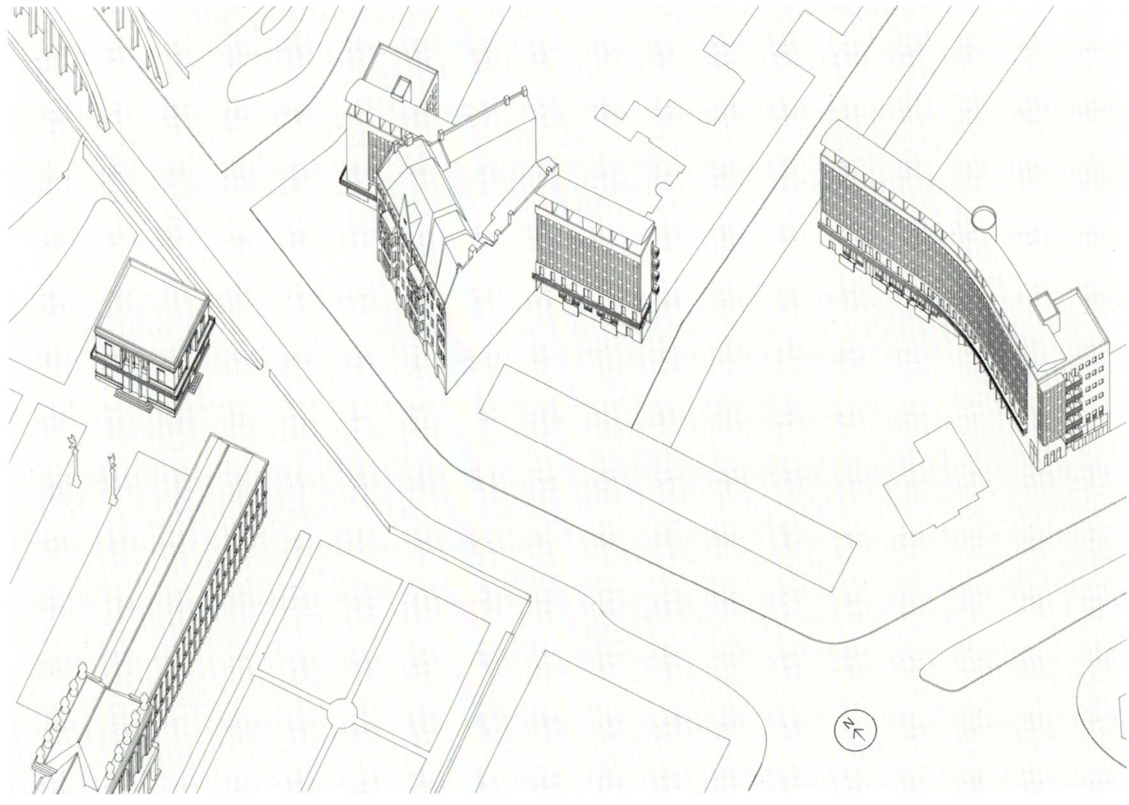

Hans Kollhoff, residential complex on Luisenplatz, view from the north, photo: Ivan Nemec, 1987, and urban design, 1982

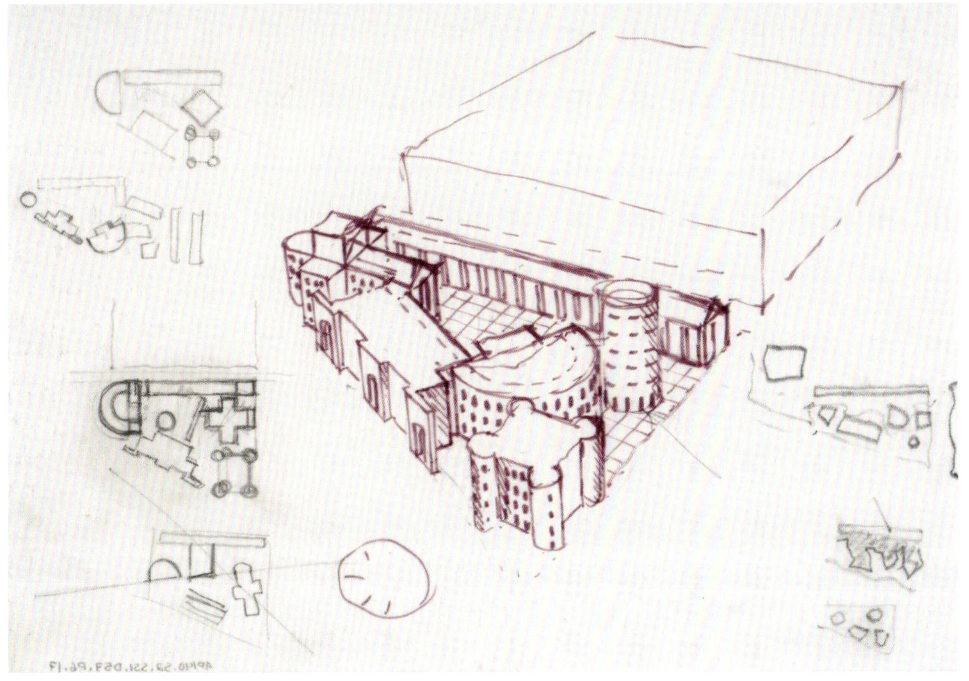

James Stirling, Michael Wilford and Associates, Wissenschaftszentrum Berlin, 1979–94, photo: Robert Göllner, ca. 1994, sketch for urban design, prior to 1987

Hans Hollein, presentation model for the Internationale Gutachterverfahren Kulturforum (International Peer-Review Process for the Kulturforum), Berlin, 1983, unbuilt

Charles Moore, John Ruble, Buzz Yudell, residential complex at the Tegeler Hafen, model, 1980 onward, built, 1985–88

Helmut Jahn, competition for the Victoria City Areal (VCA), Kranzler-Eck, Kurfürstendamm, Joachimsthaler Strasse, Kantstrasse, 1988, unbuilt

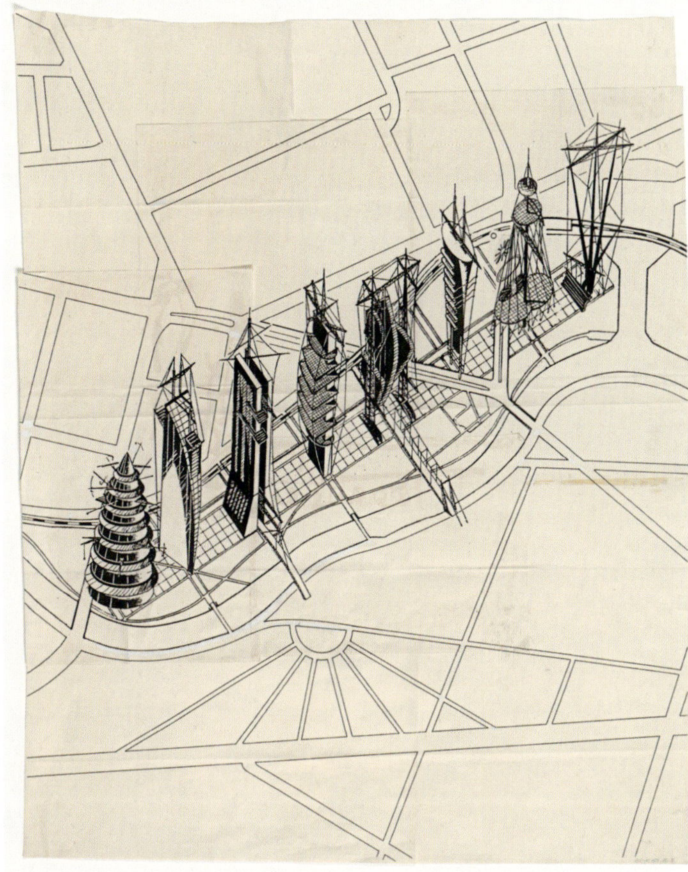

Andreas Reidemeister, Joachim Glässel, apartment building with atriums, Moabiter Werder, model, 1989, unbuilt. First prize in the urban planning competition Wohnen auf dem Moabiter Werder (Living on the Moabiter Werder), 1988. It was followed by planning for building the Atrium-Hochhaus (Atrium High-Rise). The latter had to be abandoned when the seat of the German government was moved from Bonn to Berlin.

Jasper Halfmann, Spreeufer competition, Eros Matrix 2, axonometric projection, diazotype, 1988–90, unbuilt

Daniel Libeskind, projection of Berlin psycho-cybernetics, urban concept and detail of the structure, 1988

127 Daniel Libeskind, Berlin City Edge, model, 1987, unbuilt

THE UPRISING OF THE SIGNS; OR, LEARNING FROM BERLIN

The Reinstatement of Architecture as Language

Gerd Zimmermann

Fig. 1 Robert Venturi, Denise Scott Brown, Steven Izenour, *Learning from Las Vegas*, 1972

REVOLUTIONS BEGIN WITH A CHANGE IN PERSPECTIVE

It is the moment in which the overseen, the suppressed part of reality that nevertheless unmistakably lies before us, is understood and grasped, even dragged before us. The seemingly self-contained picture forms a crack. Monarchies collapse at the moment they lose their magic. Doctrines fall with their taboos. The unconscious becomes conscious. The repressed becomes omnipresent. And precisely that, the reversal of the worldview, was from 1960 onward the mission of the postmodernists with their revocation of modernist doctrines, which—as we will be noting in a moment—first had to be construed as such by the rebels. Berlin of the 1980s was one of the capitals of this revision of modernism and Fredric Jameson one of the philosophical thinkers of the new avant-garde. With an eye to established "high modernism," he writes:

> Those formerly subversive and embattled styles—Abstract Expressionism; the great modernist poetry of Pound, Eliot, or Wallace Stevens; the International Style (Le Corbusier, Frank Lloyd Wright, Mies); Stravinsky; Joyce; Proust and Mann—felt to be scandalous or shocking by our grandparents are, for the generation which arrives at the gate in the 1960s, felt to be the establishment and the enemy—dead, stifling, canonical, the reified monuments one has to destroy to do anything new.[1]

When the architect Robert Venturi and his colleagues Denise Scott Brown and Steven Izenour published the book *Learning from Las Vegas* in 1972,[2] it was a twofold provocation. What can one learn from Las Vegas, then, this bastion of pop culture, of junk space, of kitsch, of rampant imitation, and of the banal strip of the American city? The terrain had, after all, been avoided and ignored in the established discourse of modernism. But it was what Venturi and Co. were now doing: what modernism had repressed was now becoming the subject. And what they discovered is architecture as language, as sign, as medium.

History—as the history of architecture, which Walter Gropius at the Bauhaus put a stop to—is reactivated as a powerful conveyor of meaning: Victor Hugo had, unsurprisingly for an author, described architecture as the "great book of mankind."[3] We quote from it. Complexity, which in modernism had been sacrificed to the fetish of "Less is more," returned as a commitment to plurality. With his book *Complexity and Contradiction in Architecture* of 1966,[4] Robert Venturi had kindled this discourse anew. The list of the idols of modernism who were now brought down is long. And we will have to say that its theoretical edifice was torn down step by step beginning around 1960.

There is a fundamental topos on which this postmodern revision of modernism is based. It is the reinstatement of *architecture as language*. It is about regaining its ability to express and its role as the most prominent medium of the social.

Venturi's diagnosis of Las Vegas is unambiguous: the architecture here is pure communication, a world of signs, whether it is the billboard or the types of the "duck" and the "decorated shed" (fig. 1).[5] Architecture functions as a message, indeed as a medium of persuasion, communicative and convincing. Venturi uses the didactic example of Las Vegas to reveal this semiotic nature of the architectural. Christopher Alexander speaks of "pattern language,"[6] and Charles Jencks's key text *The Language of Post-Modern Architecture* of 1977[7] already contains in its title the assumption that the overcoming of the doctrines of modernism coincides with architecture regaining the power of language that it is said to have lost in modernism. Jencks believed

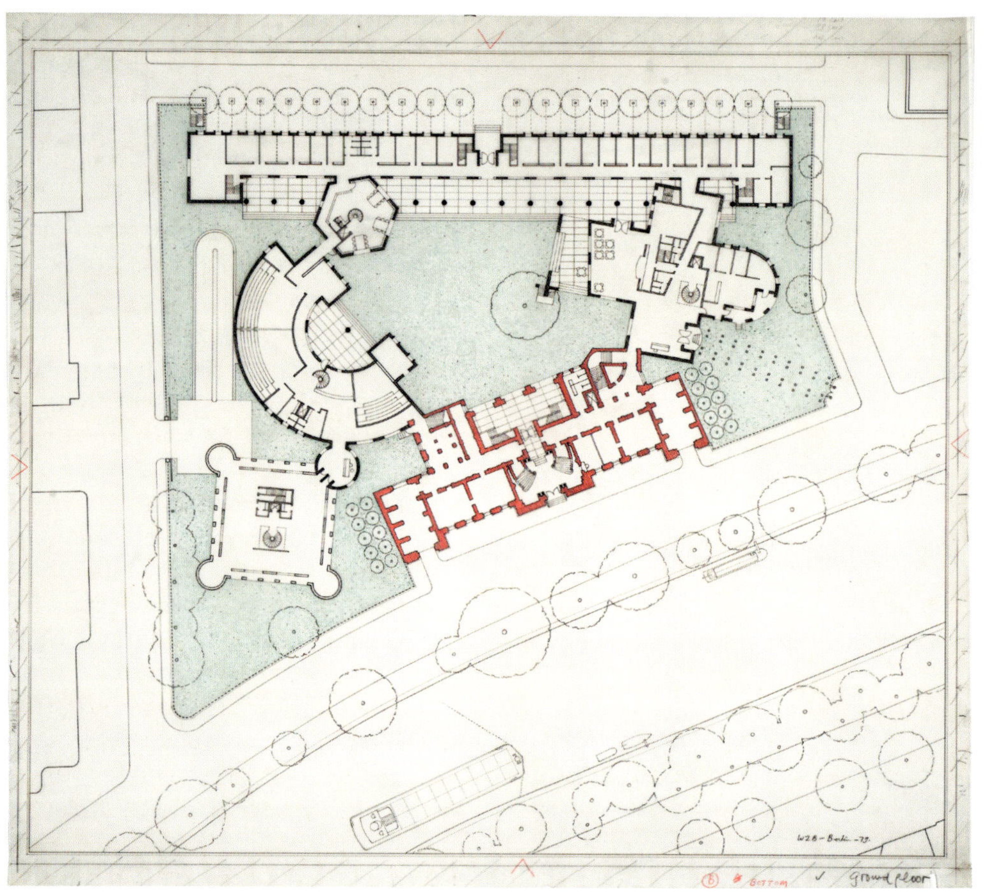

Fig. 2 James Stirling, Michael Wilford and Associates, Wissenschaftszentrum Berlin, typological study, ca. 1979

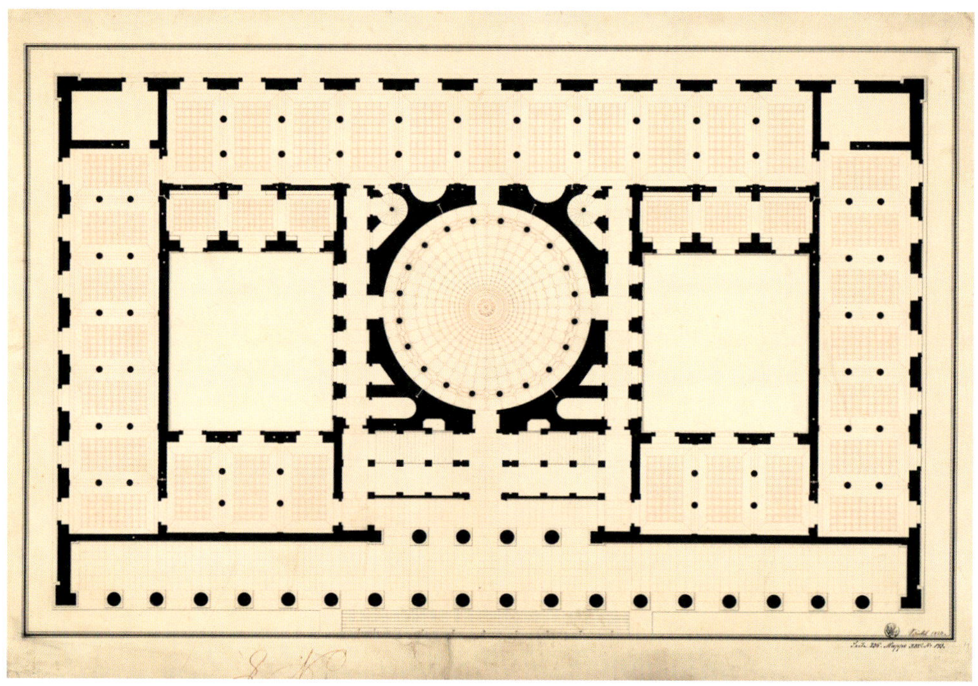

Fig. 3 Karl Friedrich Schinkel, Altes Museum am Lustgarten, floor plan of the first story, 1823

it died on July 15, 1972, at 3:32 p.m., when the Pruitt-Igoe complex in St. Louis was demolished, a once prominent neighborhood of modern social housing, which had, step by step, become rundown and was nearly vacant in the end.

The architecture of the 1980s in Berlin—in the formats of the Internationale Bauausstellung (International Architecture Exhibition, IBA) in the West and of the celebrations in the East of the 750th anniversary of the city—is one of the internationally most highly studied laboratories of this postmodern discourse. Here, too, the modernist concepts were demolished, albeit in a metaphorical sense.

The IBA in Berlin in 1987 was, of course, modeled on the format of Interbau 1957, that manifesto of the West in the divided city, but its content was clearly distanced from it. If Interbau was in part the response to Stalinallee in East Berlin, it was primarily the programmatic manifesto of the return of modern architecture to Germany, for the first time since the Nazi regime and the war. Here too, it was about signs, about language, about the interpretation of modernism as the *language of democracy*, a mode of interpretation that became established here, of course, in difference, in contrast, against the architecture of the Nazi regime and that of Stalinism—the language of politics, of the Cold War, in the medium of architecture.

Thirty years later, however, at the IBA Berlin, there were other signs standing for democracy. The concept of the city prevalent in modernity, in modernism, was replaced by turning to the old city, the existing city, and above all to its residents. The acceptance of the old city was articulated anew, also radically, at first, as a renovation, as a partial reconstruction, as participation, as practiced, for example, in the "Old IBA," but also as a "critical reconstruction" of the city, the founding concept of the "New IBA."[8] And that was based essentially on Aldo Rossi's concept of the *città analoga* (analogous city), and in a broader sense on the Venetian typological school: the new city in each case becomes the analogy of the old one. The linguistic figure of analogy is the metaphor, so that the old and the new city relate to each other as a metaphor, perhaps even reciprocally. One relies on the familiar codes of street, house, and courtyard, and even villa. But what is "critically reconstructed" here is the premodern city—more precisely, a construct of what this city is supposed to have been. History becomes, in any case, the reservoir of a new architecture, as typology and as sign.

The British architects James Stirling and Michael Wilford built, as an IBA project, the Wissenschaftszentrum Berlin für Sozialforschung (Berlin Social Science Center) from 1979 to 1988 (fig. 2) (→ p. 121). On the site of the Kulturforum, it merged several institutions with famous architecture icons like Hans Scharoun's Philharmonie and Ludwig Mies van der Rohe's Neue Nationalgalerie. What Stirling built there is as fascinating as it is shocking. The new building—attached to the old Wilhelmine-era building and in fact an office building filled with identical offices—reveals itself to be an *assemblage* of historical set pieces for the individual institutes, a collage city in miniature format.

Whereas Karl Friedrich Schinkel had once combined, in his Altes Museum (fig. 3), the Greek colonnade hall with a rotunda in the manner of the Pantheon,[9] Stirling was now reaching deep into the box of ancient models: a Greek stoa, the semicircle of a Roman theater, a Byzantine basilica with an apse, and, for the library, a hexagonal campanile. These ancient types are not really copied or reconstructed. No, the dignified forms of ancient architecture are used "merely" abstractly, as signs, as an element of an association, as a metaphor or allegory. And naturally in this refraction they bring with them the aspect of the ironic, of the unserious, even of play: form follows fiction. If, on the one hand, the semantic charge is achieved through the pathos formulas, then, on the other hand, this fundamentalist gesture is sublated in a modern

1 Fredric Jameson, "Postmodernism and Consumer Society," in *The Anti-Aesthetic: Essays on Postmodern Culture*, ed. Hal Foster (Seattle, 1983), p. 112.

2 Robert Venturi, Denise Scott Brown, and Steven Izenour, *Learning from Las Vegas: The Forgotten Symbolism of Architectural Form* (1972; repr., Cambridge, MA, 1977).

3 Victor Hugo, *Notre-Dame de Paris*, trans. Alban Krailsheimer (Oxford, 1999), p. 193. In this novel, Victor Hugo has the archdeacon say: "This will kill that, the book will kill the building." Hugo understands architecture as a medium, as a stony memory of humanity, but the new medium of the printed book is said to be far superior to architecture. It is said to convey the message with much less effort and material, appears as a swarm, as it were, and hence is far less susceptible to destruction, since several copies are always left over, and so on.

4 Robert Venturi, *Complexity and Contradiction in Architecture*, 2nd ed. (1966; repr., New York, 1977).

5 Venturi et al., *Learning from Las Vegas* (see note 2), identified in their analysis of Las Vegas two types of architectural message. First, the overall figure of a building can become a visual sign in order to refer to the use of the building; for example, in the case of a restaurant in Las Vegas that serves duck and takes on the outward form of a duck. That is the source of the name of this type of message: the "duck." In the second case, it is not the overall figure of the building but rather a meaning "façade" in front of a meaningless cube that conveys the message. Hence its name: "decorated shed."

6 Christopher Alexander, *A Pattern Language: Towns, Buildings, Construction* (New York, 1977).

7 Charles Jencks, *The Language of Post-Modern Architecture* (1977; repr., New York, 1984).

8 On this, see Harald Bodenschatz and Cordelia Polinna, *Learning from IBA: Die IBA 1987 in Berlin, Studie der Senatsverwaltung für Stadtentwicklung* (Berlin, 2010).

9 Altes Museum was, by the way, the typological model for Stirling's Staatsgalerie in Stuttgart—that icon of postmodernism, which was built at nearly the same time as the Wissenschaftszentrum Berlin.

10 Manfred Sack, "Alles Bluff," *Die Zeit*, May 6, 1988.

11 Johann Joachim Winckelmann, *Reflections on the Painting and Sculpture of the Greeks*, trans. Henry Fusseli, 2nd ed. (London, 1767), p. 1; originally published in German in 1756.

12 Hal Foster, *Recodings: Art, Spectacle, Cultural Politics* (Seattle, 1985), p. 122.

13 Ibid., p. 123.

way. But in Stirling's case it is a frivolous way: a candy-colored façade with window walls that recall Albert Speer. Clearly: anything goes. But what is the sense of these operations? Is it the reference to Berlin, to the architecture of the likes of Schinkel and Friedrich August Stüler, who indeed also found their idols in antiquity? Or is this play with forms merely sensationalism, trivial banter? After all, that is precisely what is criticized about postmodernism, its far-reaching relativism and ultimately nihilism, on the philosophical and the aesthetic level.

Manfred Sack, who had voted for Stirling's design as a judge in the competition for the Wissenschaftszentrum, wrote in a review of the opening in 1988, titled "Alles Bluff" (All Bluff):

> Nearly everything had argued against insouciant play with historical building volumes laden with meaning. Everyone saw through the juggler. What he proposed didn't belong. And yet: Was it not also seductive to see this provocation built one day? Where would we be if we no longer allowed ourselves to be ruffled up by an unconventional thinker.[10]

Stirling's maneuver did indeed practice, as paradoxical as it may sound, the avant-garde through regression. But he is in renowned company, not only of the postmodernists, since utopias are formulated in the remote, even in the remoteness of distant history. Think of Winckelmann: "To the Greek climate we owe the production of Taste, and from thence it spread at length over all the politer world."[11] Or consider the Bauhaus, which initially found its ideal, and also its name, in the medieval *Bauhütte* (masons' lodge).

UNHISTORICAL HISTORICISM AND THE DUAL NATURE OF POSTMODERNISM

Architectural history, and once again Schinkel, is the fascinating thing about one prestigious building in East Berlin that opened in 1984, in the run-up to the celebrations of the city's 750th anniversary. The former Schauspielhaus on Gendarmenmarkt, which had been heavily damaged in the war, was converted into a concert hall, and thus saved, as part of the reconstruction of the entire ensemble. Manfred Prasser, an architect working in the Baudirektion für die Hauptstadt Berlin (Building Department for the Capital Berlin), who called himself a "Romantic," took the approach (with Peter Weiss) to the hall of the Konzerthaus that a history was being constructed that had (almost) never existed. The new concert hall was built based on motifs from the small hall that Schinkel had once erected in the Schauspielhaus—but now just different and larger, in place of the theater space (figs. 4a–4b).

That is an interesting architectural operation, but it suggests that the building had always been this way and, in fact, that it had never been destroyed—an ahistorical historicism and the overture, if you will, to the new building for the Berliner Schloss (Berlin Palace). In 1985, Hal Foster wrote of this kind of culture technique in general: "This return to history, then, must first be questioned. What, first of all, is this 'history' but a reduction of historical periods of ruling-class styles that are then pastiched? A history of victors; a history, moreover, which denies the historicity of forms and materials—an *a*history, in fact." [12] And Foster continues: "The result is a history-surrogate, at once standard and schizoid. Finally, such postmodernism is less a dialectical supersession of modernism than its old ideological opponent, which then and now assumes the form of a popular front of pre- and antimodernist elements."[13]

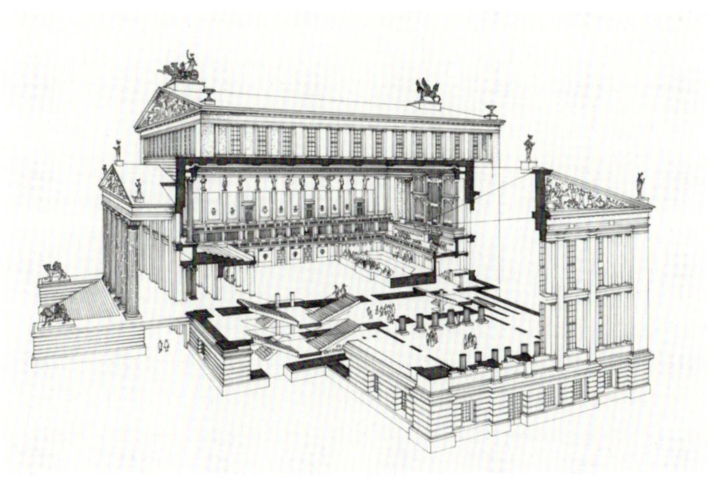

Fig. 4a Karl-Friedrich Schinkel, Schauspielhaus on Gendarmenmarkt in Berlin, 1818–21, reconstruction and conversion with a new concert hall by Manfred Prasser und Kollektiv, 1979–84, signed by Carl Krause

Fig. 4b Berliner Schauspielhaus, foyer, 1931, photo: Ernst Gränert

Fig. 5 David Chipperfield Architects, James-Simon-Galerie, Museum Island Berlin, 1999–2018, with the Neues Museum (renovation and conversion by David Chipperfield Architects, 1993–2009), originally by Friedrich August Stüler, 1841–59, photo: Ute Zscharnt

Fig. 6 Adolf Loos, *The Chicago Tribune Column*, Chicago, Michigan Avenue / Austin Avenue / St. Clair Street, façade with stone carving, signed by Bittner, 1922

Prasser's approach here is fundamentally different from, say, David Chipperfield's rebuilding of the Neues Museum years later in Berlin (1999–2009), which in a sense transforms the precise gaze of the historian into architecture in that every moment of real history, the preexisting, the destruction, and the rebuilding, is strictly distinguished and precisely articulated architectonically. One will also grant this postmodern precision to the very new and different James-Simon-Galerie by Chipperfield (2009–18), which transforms the ancient motif of the colonnaded hall, of the "Propylaea of the Acropolis" (we are speaking, after all, of the entrance building), into strictly modern syntax—three decades later as the first reappearance of the column in postmodern Berlin (fig. 5).

The column—this ancient architecture, which had varied in diverse forms and orders since Vitruvius in the first century, and had then mutated in the modern era into the "support" or into Le Corbusier's pilotis—now returns, as a sign.

In 1971, in the context of a semiology of architecture, Umberto Eco presented "A Componential Analysis of the Architectural Sign */Column/*," in which he studied the diverse denotations and connotations of this famous architectonic signet.[14] Adolf Loos submitted to the competition for the Chicago Tribune Building in 1922 a design for a high-rise in the form of a column (fig. 6). Though it had no chance in the competition, this "crazy" design received a lot of publicity in postmodernist discourse.[15] One can also recall Theodor Lipps, who used the example of a column to explain his theory of empathy, in which the viewer essentially takes its place in perceiving it and feels it bearing the weight—an anthropomorphic projection that has also been pictured in caryatids and diverse herms.[16]

As part of the IBA, Aldo Rossi inserted into the new building on Kochstrasse a monumental corner column, its function scarcely load-bearing; it could at most be confused with an advertising pillar (→ p. 115). This white column is a sign and nothing but a sign.

Another column turns out to be (probably) a pure sign. In an unrealized competition entry in 1984 for the new Akademie der Künste building on the Platz der Akademie (now Gendarmenmarkt[17]), its author, Werner Rösler, integrated a gigantically oversized sunken Ionic column into a generally modernistic architectural design (→ pp. 78–79).

As grotesque as that may be, it seems to have been an attempt to lend the Akademie der Künste a dignified form by means of an architectonic signet, especially as the motif of the sunken column presumably points not to a lack of static stability, but rather to a figure from Romanticism. It was not built, but the Platz der Akademie was, essentially under the direction of Manfred Prasser, and, because of the conditions in the German Democratic Republic (GDR), made in large part by prefabricated concrete-slab construction. Prasser, the "Romantic," sought the language of architecture not in expressing technology or the industrial in the broadest sense but by means of a historicizing ornament that covers the slabs: "slab Baroque."

The *ornament* repressed in the modern era—branded by Adolf Loos as the expression of a low stage of culture, comparable to tatooing[18]—returns.[19] In fact, there were reserves of ornament in the modern era: from the ornament of the series and of construction, say, to the elitist onyx walls of Ludwig Mies van der Rohe in the Villa Tugendhat and the Barcelona Pavilion. But what Gottfried Semper and Karl Bötticher once called for in their "Bekleidungstheorie" (theory of dressing)"[20]—namely, understanding the ornament as an art form that wraps around the core form and making it the theme of architecture—is a variation on Venturi's "decorated shed."

In the specific case of the Platz der Akademie, this is evident in the historicizing decoration, such as the Neo-Renaissance touch of the façade of

14 Umberto Eco, "A Componential Analysis of the Architectural Sign /Column/," *Semiotica* 5, no. 2 (1972), pp. 97–117; first published in French in 1971.

15 Jencks, *The Language of Post-Modern Architecture* (see note 7), p. 38.

16 Theodor Lipps, *Ästhetik: Psychologie des Schönen und der Kunst* (Leipzig, 1903).

17 On this, see the essay by Wolfgang Kil in this volume.

18 Adolf Loos, "Ornament und Verbrechen" (1908), in *Sämtliche Schriften in zwei Bänden*, vol. 1, ed. Franz Glück (Vienna, 1962), pp. 276–88; Adolf Loos, "Ornament and Crime," in *Ornament and Crime: Selected Essays*, trans. Michael Mitchell (Riverside, CA, 1998), pp. 167–76.

19 Jörg Gleiter, "Kritische Theorie des Ornaments: Zum Statuswandel der Ästhetik in der architektonischen Moderne" (PhD diss., Bauhaus-Universität Weimar, 2002).

20 Karl Bötticher, *Die Tektonik der Hellenen* (Potsdam, 1852).

21 See also Florian Urban's essay in this volume and Florian Urban, *Neo-Historical East Berlin: Architecture and Urban Design in the German Democratic Republic, 1970–1990* (Farnham, 2009).

Fig. 7 Manfred Prasser und Kollektiv, Friedrichstadtpalast Berlin, 1981–84

the headquarters of the East German Christlich-Demokratische Union Deutschlands (Christian Democratic Union of Germany, CDU), interestingly in pink, hung in front of a steel construction, or the ornamentally lined slabs (→ pp. 80–81). But the triumph of the ornamental GDR historicism in the Berlin of the 1980s, which was embedded in the conceptual change to the old city and its preservation and continuation, was the new building of the Friedrichstadtpalast, again by Manfred Prasser, who, though he was unknown even in the GDR, clearly turned out to be a secret master of this kind of historicism.[21] Dieter Bankert should also be mentioned here as its actual designer.

The Friedrichstadtpalast, which is outstanding in terms of its technology and staging, is the frivolous cultural-industrial document of this architecture, reflecting the pop culture of the pop song and of variety theater (fig. 7). Not without reason, it was popularly known in the GDR as the Grusinischer Bahnhof (Georgian Train Station) and both terms seem rather fitting: "Georgian" in this case not because of the tea, but because of the high culture of ornament there.

There were efforts to find modern alternatives for the Friedrichstadtpalast, too. That remained hopeless, since the Baudirektion Berlin (Building Direction of Berlin), which was responsible for the prestige projects in Berlin during the late years of the GDR, had essentially made this simple historicism official state policy—stately architecture without contradiction. And, consequently, the practice of architecture was divided in a way similar to the discourse on the theory of architecture. On the one hand, the "modern" industrial building of concrete-slab housing was rolling along and bringing with it the destruction of historical old towns. On the other hand, a few prestigious buildings celebrated an avowal of the historical old town, albeit only in their superficial appearance.

In one case in East Berlin, the rebuilding of the entire Nikolaiviertel (1980–87), this "double coding" of wanting to be equally modern and traditional, led in several planning steps to a strange collage: bricks and concrete slabs, Middle Ages and modernity, unique object and series represented an

22 Christian Schädlich, "Der Postmodernismus—eine alternative Architektur?," *Architektur der DDR* 31, no. 6 (1982), p. 346.

23 Claude Schnaidt, "Die Architektur der Moderne—ein unvollendetes Projekt?," in *Anders gesagt: Schriften, 1950–2001* (Weimar, 2009), p. 471.

24 See also Silke Ötsch, *Überwältigen und Schmeicheln: Der menschliche Körper im Visier der Planer* (Weimar, 2006).

archipelago of architectural treatments. The postmodern transformation here was obvious and highly popular. Notably, however, the semiofficial discourse took very different paths.

In the GDR—in Weimar, to be specific—committed scientists, above all Bernd Grönwald, succeeded in breaking through the taboo on the Bauhaus that had been ongoing since 1950. Intense research began; the first Bauhaus-Kolloquium was held, and in 1976, fifty years after its opening, the Bauhaus building in Dessau was officially reopened. This important but late official reception—indeed, the rehabilitation of the Bauhaus, which was of course also intended to legitimize the industrial architecture of the GDR—now turned out to be the moment when the international criticism broke out of the very doctrines of modernism for which the Bauhaus stands prototypically. The reflex was ideological indoctrination: postmodernism was interpreted as a phenomenon of late capitalism and rejected—with almost the same stereotypes with which the Bauhaus had been denounced as "capitalist" since 1950. In an article in the journal *Architektur der DDR* from 1982, Christian Schädlich offers a differentiated and critical overview of the scenario of postmodern architecture and then concludes: "The Modern Movement of the 1920s produced a historically important concept that was certainly capable of development. We should not allow postmodernism to blind us to the creative principles it contains."[22] The East was not alone in that criticism, however. For example, Claude Schnaidt—in a text titled "Die Architektur der Moderne – ein unvollendetes Projekt?" (Modern Architecture: An Unfinished Project?)—ended his final reckoning with the postmoderns with a passage aimed directly at the problem of language in architecture:

> As citizens—may they [the postmoderns] speak a language that people want to hear. People will be speechless with amazement, and the state will say to itself: What a joy! That will confirm once again the old rule of despots: If you want to silence the people, then let the stones speak.[23]

Fredric Jameson, too, who was also a neo-Marxist critic, saw postmodernism in the logic of late capitalism, of the unbridled market, and of consumer society. Whereas Schnaidt failed to acknowledge the dialogue with human beings in architecture's engagement with meaning and language, instead emphasizing its potential for demagogical seduction, Jameson believed that in modern society reality is reduced to images and that history is degenerated into gestures of pastiche. Both of them, though coming from different directions, meet in their criticism of the *blinding* that results from postmodern narrations and rhetorics and from tactics of overpowering.[24]

And the latter can, of course, as Friedrich Nietzsche already realized, lead to affirming power, but they can also be a medium of critique and of subversion. The uprising of the postmoderns thus has a double nature: it can become the language of neoconservatism as well as the language of an avant-garde. This ambivalence is inherent in architecture, the "most public of all the arts," in any case, also—it must be said here—in modern architecture, which was, of course, avant-garde, but at the same time, in Italy, for example, the language of Fascism.

ARCHITECTURE'S MEDIA TURN

The IBA projects, both old and new, assign new tasks to the repressed quality of modernism, for example, democratizing building with participation and

DIY—that is to say, those forms of *bricolage* that Claude Lévi-Strauss described so well with the contrast of the engineer and the *bricoleur*—and the experimental ecological alternatives such as the Ökohaus am Tiergarten by Frei Otto and others. Such approaches point to the future.

More restrained, and in a completely different context but nonetheless noteworthy, was the new building for the main post office in Marzahn, in East Berlin (competition, 1979). Michael Kny and Thomas Weber, under the direction of Wolf-Rüdiger Eisentraut, wrested from their collective planning new solutions to counter industrial monotony with articulated architecture.[25] They employed, among other things, the motif of the arcade—that nineteenth-century architectural type, which also experienced a postmodern renaissance in general.[26] And they turned supports into columns by adding "capital" to them (fig. 8).

An apartment building on Friedrichstrasse, built in 1987 by Peter Meyer in the style of "late modernism," as Charles Jencks would have called it, is another of these attempts to break out of the tristesse (→ p. 85).

But just how much architecture can become a medium of subversion, even of direct uprising, is demonstrated with great potent effect by several designs by Bernd Ettel and Christian Enzmann in East Berlin, probably most immediately by their competition entry for Bersarinplatz in 1984: Ikarusflug (Flight of Icarus) (figs. 9a–9b).[27] Their entire design—drawing, text, and model—is an architectural allegory, a parable of the repressive state of the GDR, that form of exposure that is precisely an unmasking. The signs are clear: the simulation of the Berlin Wall, the hollow protest marches across the square, the backdrop, the Potemkin village, and a high pedestal from which an Icarus can start out, who, as soon as he reaches the portal in the wall, will be shot down. Architecture could hardly tell a political story more clearly. It was scarcely less explosive in a competition entry for the Topographie des Terrors that the same authors sent to West Berlin—this, too, was, of course, "illegal." Both figures were arrested and deported to the West, which fatally underscores the accuracy of their architectural metaphor.

The concept of Critical Reconstruction, from which the IBA had set out as a response to the modernist abdication of the old town, and which became the dominant doctrine of urban renewal after 1989, had to be questioned in turn. OMA (Office for Metropolitan Architecture) in Rotterdam did so in a very nice entry to the IBA competition in 1980 for the corner of Kochstrasse and Friedrichstrasse (→ p. 118). The image looks like a collage of fragments of old blocks and a painting by Piet Mondrian and thus does not suggest in a problematic way a seamless continuation of some snapshot of the old city.

A far more radical attempt to break out of the mantra of reconstruction is doubtless Daniel Libeskind's *Berlin City Edge* project in 1987 in the context of the IBA, even before this architect won the competition for the new building for the Jüdisches Museum (Jewish Museum) (→ p. 127). The project was a fundamental architectural statement, formatted in models and computer-generated plans. A 450-meter-long, oblique slab cuts through the neighborhood. It is not an attempt to rebuild, reconstruct, or repair the destroyed city—the "urban fabric" or "urban "grid." Rather, the fragments, the traces of the war and of destruction, are deliberately left open. The scars remain visible; they are not supposed to be handed over to oblivion, but rather be made to speak.

The key concept here is "difference": the rift between, say, the existing city and the new structure. The philosopher Jacques Derrida had, starting out from the thesis that things (objects, concepts, texts) are defined only in their difference from others, developed the method of the deconstruction of texts,[28] and, at the invitation of Bernard Tschumi, he had already translated it into architecture—in the design for the Parc de la Villette in Paris in 1983.[29]

25 Michael Kny and Thomas Weber, "Erinnerungen an die Planung und Errichtung des 'gesellschaftlichen Hauptbereiches' Berlin-Marzahn in der Zeit von 1979–1990," in *Fachtagung 40 Jahre Wohnstadt Marzahn: Vom Neubaugebiet zur grünen Wohnstadt, 1977–2017*, ed. Bezirksamt Marzahn-Hellersdorf von Berlin (Berlin, 2017).

26 See also Bernd Grönwald and Gerd Zimmermann, *Passagen: Analysen und Entwürfe für Leipzig*, vol. 67: *Schriften der Hochschule für Architektur und Bauwesen Weimar* (Weimar, 1988).

27 Bernd Ettel and Christian Enzmann, *"Ikarusflug": Wettbewerb Bersarinplatz* (Berlin, 1984), www.enzmann-ettel.de/seite01.html (accessed May 5, 2020).

28 Jacques Derrida, *Writing and Difference*, trans. Alan Bass (Chicago, 1978).

29 Michaela Gugeler, "Der Parc de la Villette: Würfelwurf der Architektur; Das Zusammenwirken von Bernard Tschumi und Jacques Derrida beim Parc de la Villette in Paris," *Kritische Berichte* 33, no. 2 (2005), pp. 45–57.

Fig. 8 Michael Kny, Thomas Weber, main post office in Marzahn, interior (competition, 1979)

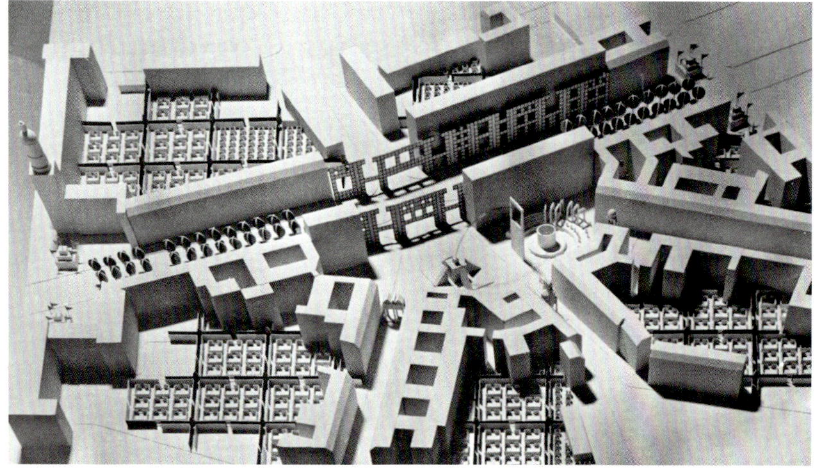

Fig. 9a Bernd Ettel, Christian Enzmann, *Ikarusflug* (Flight of Icarus), competition entry for Bersarinplatz Berlin, 1984, model

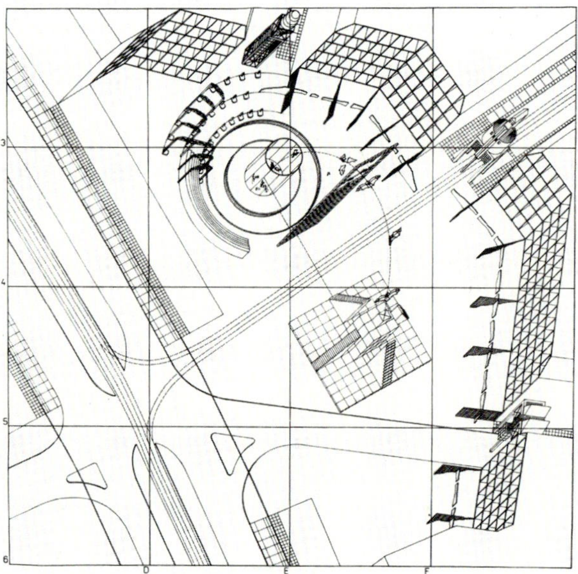

Fig. 9b Bernd Ettel, Christian Enzmann, *Ikarusflug* (Flight of Icarus), competition entry for Bersarinplatz, Berlin, 1984, isometric drawing

That is the point of departure in the philosophy of language for the poststructuralist—one could also say the postmodern—method for formulating new grammars of architecture that then became public under the label *deconstructivism*.[30] Berlin was also one of the creative places for this avant-garde, with Daniel Libeskind, but also with an early, very beautiful design by Zaha Hadid in a competition as part of the IBA for a building on Kurfürstendamm on a lot just 2.7 meters wide (fig.10).

What we now find is actually a kind of schizoid double movement. On the one hand, there is the *reconstruction* of represented patterns and linguistic models of the old city; on the other, the *deconstruction*, its grammars and architectures recalling, not coincidentally, the avant-garde of the Russian Constructivists. It was precisely this connection between the Deconstructivists and the Constructivists, such as El Lissitzky, Vladimir Tatlin, and others, that was already being explored in the exhibition *Deconstructivist Architecture*, curated by Philip Johnson and Mark Wigley at The Museum of Modern Art in New York in 1988; Libeskind's *Berlin City Edge* was also included in it.[31]

Both uprisings, as Ulf Jonak has described them,[32] manifest the idea of the end of grand narratives, the "broken scaffolding of the world," if you will. What unites the two of them is the break with convention; to put it another way, what uses them is *modernity*. And that is what needs to be discussed, since the discourse of modernity enables us to understand postmodernism neither as a beginning nor as an ending phenomenon, but rather as one outstanding station in the unfolding of modernity. Naturally, the uprising came at the beginning: the attack on the modern era in its ossified form, congealed into an ideology—a state that can perhaps be grasped with the term "modernism." The very concept of postmodernity, however, has not at all abandoned the link to modernity, after all, not in Stirling's Wissenschaftszentrum, not in the work of Oswald Mathias Ungers, not in the work of Josef Paul Kleihues, or that of others.[33] It is the fundamental break with convention that connects the rebels of postmodernity with those of modernity. And this break is also what wrests the things from silence.

Clearly, the language of architecture oscillates between the construction and the deconstruction of meaning. Only forms that have been forgotten, or repressed and their meanings therefore lost or faded, or forced into the unconscious, can then be—in a process of interpretation—connected to new content, new expression, new life as such, until they perhaps sink back into routine again. Viktor Shklovsky, for example, had already seen art's method as breaking through the routines of reception by means of enstrangement ("de-automatizing perception").[34] And, much later, Umberto Eco saw the "open work" in his eponymous book as, in a sense, a matrix that not only permits ever-new readings, interpretations, but that also challenges by means of a poetics of suggestion, of ambiguity, and so on.[35]

The key concept here is interpretation, or *reflection*. For Anthony Giddens, too, reflexivity is the true feature of modernity, precisely where tradition, history, is concerned.[36] Modernity breaks with tradition, indeed with all traditions; it can take possession of history at all only reflexively, as an intellectual operation—just as Schinkel needed an idea of Hellenism, the Bauhaus the Middle Ages, and James Stirling everything all at once: Athens, Rome, Byzantium. Giddens remarks on this: "The 'use of history to make history' is substantially a phenomenon of modernity and not a generalised principle that can be applied to all eras—it is one version of modernity's reflexivity."[37]

This reflexivity, however, occurs in languages, signs, and media, and we will be able to say that postmodernism since 1960, with its insistence on the linguistic and semiotic quality of architecture, can be read as a launch

30 Mark Wigley, *The Architecture of Deconstruction: Derrida's Haunt* (London, 1993).

31 Philip Johnson and Mark Wigley, *Deconstructivist Architecture* (New York, 1988).

32 Ulf Jonak, *Sturz und Riss: Über den Anlass zu architektonischer Subversion* (Braunschweig, 1989).

33 In 1990, Wolfgang Welsch formulated this, with reference to art, in the clear title of a short essay, which alludes to Nietzsche: "Die Geburt der postmodernen Philosophie aus dem Geist der modernen Kunst" (The Birth of Postmodern Philosophy from the Spirit of Modern Art). He examines this spiritual relationship in five points: (a) decomposition, (b) reflection, (c) the sublime, (d) experiment, and (e) plurality. And after examining these points, Welsch sees a "homology" between modern art and postmodern philosophy: "Postmodern philosophy articulates discursively what modern art previously demonstrated artistically." Wolfgang Welsch, "Die Geburt der postmodernen Philosophie aus dem Geist der modernen Kunst," in Welsch, *Ästhetisches Denken* (1990; repr., Stuttgart, 2017).

34 Viktor Shklovsky, "Art as Device," in *Viktor Shklovsky: A Reader*, ed. and trans. Alexandra Berlina (New York, 2017), pp. 73–96.

35 Umberto Eco, *The Open Work*, trans. Anna Cancogni (Cambridge, MA, 1989); originally published in Italian as *Opera aperta* (Milan, 1962).

36 Anthony Giddens, *The Consequences of Modernity* (Cambridge, 1996).

37 Ibid., p. 50.

Fig. 10 Zaha Hadid, office building Kurfürstendamm 70, competition design as part of IBA Berlin, 1986

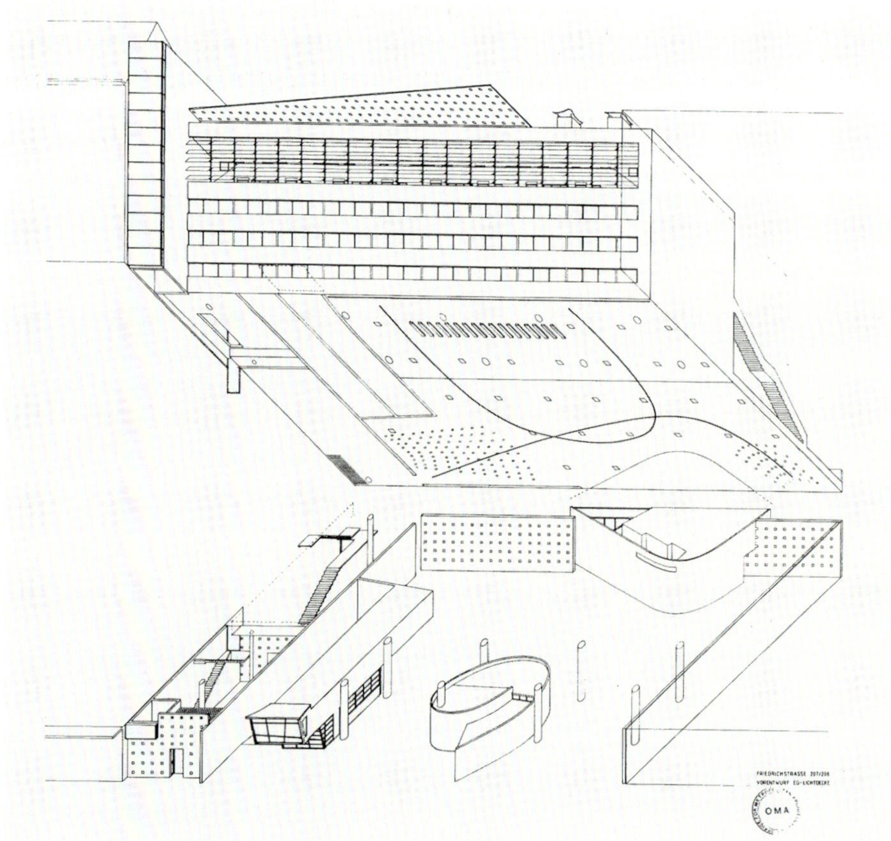

Fig. 11 Office for Metropolitan Architecture (OMA), Elia Zenghelis, residential building at Checkpoint Charlie, Friedrichstrasse 207–208, preliminary design, light ceiling on ground floor, 1981

pad for today's global and digital media society. The postmodern discourse came out of the linguistic turn; the city was understood as a text; architecture as sign and language. That was followed, driven by the development of digital visual techniques, by the iconic turn. Architecture is once again understood as an image, and the Berlin of the 1980s, which was already the showcase on the seam of two systems, leaves no doubt about that. The iconicity becomes a crucial vehicle of attraction in the global economy of attention.[38] Finally, this is followed by what we can call the media turn: the fact that architecture is a medium that is now playing out its nature as a moment of universal mediatization. *Architecture is what its media are.*

Drawing, too, has its language—as the folded-open isometric drawing of the building at Checkpoint Charlie by OMA shows—making visible the landscape of forms of the ground floor, and also the broadly projecting roof as a gesture toward the checkpoint—it, too, a sign (fig. 11).

Jean-François Lyotard, in his *La condition postmoderne* of 1979,[39] had already indicated that language and its associated sciences and technologies were positioned in the cradle of the postmodern uprising—that is, communication theory, information theory, cybernetics, and so on. The system of architectural thought that becomes manifest in the Berlin of the 1980s is also based on the transformations of this knowledge and leads to the conditions of digital culture, at the threshold of which we now stand. In that sense, the IBA is highly topical. Its avowal of the old city as a place for living is an extremely explosive subject right now; its avowal of a new urban architecture leads to the digital city, the smart city; its insistence on and *architecture parlante* raises the question of today's codes. And they are based on the linguistic patterns of the digital, for example, those of the digital image. A line leads from poststructuralist methods to computer-aided design. From the early "deconstructionist" designs of Zaha Hadid, in Hong Kong and Berlin, to her digital, parametric design techniques in which her office partner and now successor, Patrik Schumacher, claims to see the new epochal linguistic figure of the digital world after the International Style of modernity. That would be a hot subject—but not here and now.

38 Charles Jencks, *Iconic Building: The Power of Enigma* (London, 2005).

39 Jean-François Lyotard, *The Postmodern Condition: A Report on Knowledge*, trans. Geoff Bennington and Brian Massumi (Minneapolis, 1984); originally published in French as: *La condition postmoderne* (Paris, 1979).

MIGRANT BERLIN AND MULTIPLYING THE VOICES OF ARCHITECTURE

Esra Akcan

1 For more discussion and the related bibliography, see Esra Akcan, *Open Architecture: Migration, Citizenship and the Urban Renewal of Berlin-Kreuzberg by IBA-1984/87* (Berlin, 2018).

Berlinische Galerie's catalogue on the architecture of Berlin in the 1980s can shed light on the little acknowledged contribution of immigrants in building some of the most sought after neighborhoods of unified Berlin. Even though there were additional smaller sites, the main location for the Internationale Bauausstellung (IBA) of 1984/87 in West Berlin was the immigrant neighborhood of Kreuzberg. IBA 1984/87 also functioned as the urban renewal of this borough in the 1980s. However, the 1984/87 exhibition took place in the context of the discriminatory housing laws and regulations instituted by the Berlin Senate, such as the ban on entry and settlement, and the moving quota. Justified as "integration" of "guest workers" (or "foreigners" in daily parlance), the Senate's laws prohibited the movement of additional migrant families to Kreuzberg, Wedding, and Tiergarten, and mandated that only 10 percent of residential units be rented to noncitizens all over West Berlin. These laws were transposed into the functional program of new buildings during Kreuzberg's urban renewal, in the form of the low percentage of large flats which would have been fitting for the migrant families. Namely, this program would either diminish noncitizen families' chances of moving into new public housing or welcome the migrants only after they had changed their lives to fit the German family size standards. For this reason, I find some of the themes in my recently published book *Open Architecture* relevant to the projects included in the Berlinische Galerie's new exhibition. This book discloses how policymakers used architecture as a mechanism of social control and displacement. At the same time, it discusses how architects responded with varying degrees of complicity, irony, or subversion to these discriminatory housing regulations. The book also analyzes how immigrants appropriated the results in a creative way once they were given a chance to move in.[1] For instance, a group of architects in the Altbau team directed by Hardt-Waltherr Hämer mobilized tenant organizations, squatter demonstrations, and refugee and guest worker participation to carry out a radically democratic urban renewal, so that not a single migrant family was unwillingly displaced. Thus, the Senate's 10 percent mandate and discriminatory laws were subverted by a group of professionals employed by the Senate itself. However, the same was not true for most of the remaining areas affected by IBA; but these sections had other lessons or cautionary remarks for the relevance of immigration on architecture, and by extension for the definition of open architecture.

A related historiographical theme is multiplying the voices that speak for the built environment. In addition to underrepresented architects from around the world, this also means including habitants' stories in historical narratives. I gave weight to the voices of immigrants through a genre inspired by oral history and storytelling. An oral historian refrains from representing an entire ethnicity or group, and adds the name of the underrepresented individual into history; and a storyteller acknowledges that the fabric of everyday life unfolding in an individual's experience of a space is also part of a building's history. When this approach is applied to the study of architecture, history does not end when the building leaves the hand of the architect. Opening the definition of architecture to resident appropriation is also a feminist gesture to write more women into architectural history. By honoring the stories of resident-architects as much as those of the architects, it is possible to stop seeing architecture as an occupation historically practiced by men.

And indeed, residents of Kreuzberg appropriated many apartments designed by high-end architects: bridges were repurposed as bedrooms; voids were mechanized as kitchens; unfunctional winter gardens were turned into playrooms; additional rooms were integrated into apartments from next-door buildings that were on higher levels. These oral histories and archi-

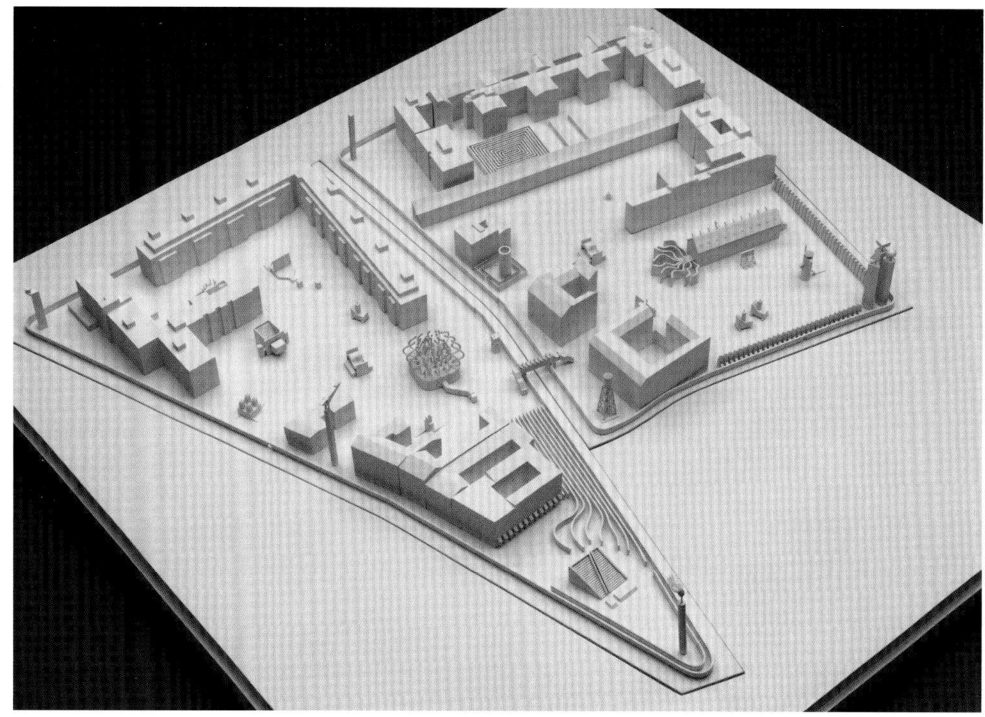

Fig. 1 John Hejduk, *Berlin Masque*, model, 1981, Wilhelmstrasse competition project, IBA 1984/87

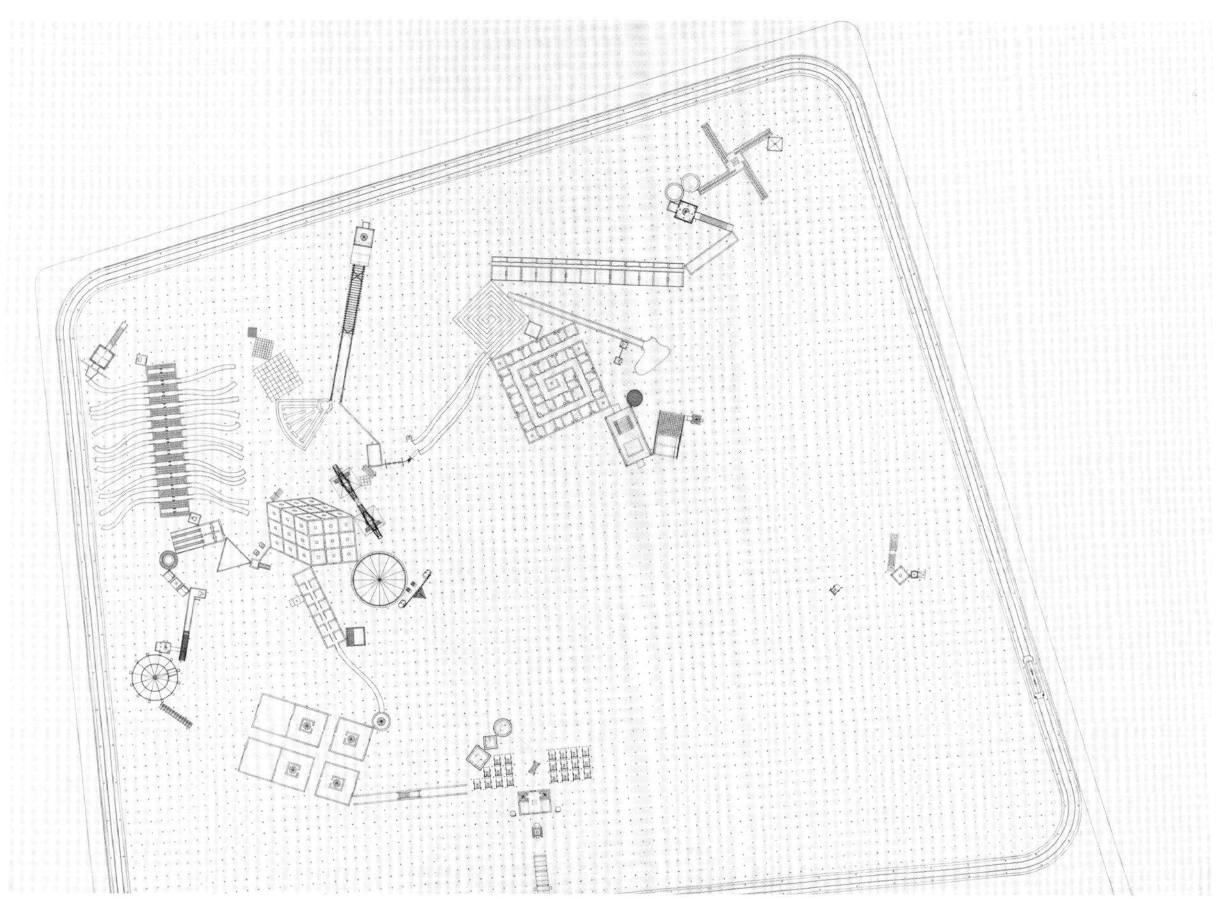

Fig. 2 John Hejduk, *Victims*, partial site plan, 1984, competition project for the design of the Prinz-Albrecht-Palais, IBA 1984/87

tectural analyses reveal the agency of immigrants who rightfully take credit for the success of urban renewal back then, and for Kreuzberg's special place in the global imagination today.

While learning the stories of immigrant habitants is rewarding in itself, these stories should also motivate architects to reevaluate their own assumptions and values. What would happen if architecture were shaped by a new ethic of hospitality toward the immigrant? I call the answer open architecture. While architects have not paid much attention to the challenge of international migration, which would have involved the expansion of political rights and social citizenship through space, there are nonetheless some latent modes of open architecture in history that one could build on. Such modes include formal, procedural, and programmatic ways of designing open architecture, such as the flexibility and adaptability of form, collaboration and collectivity during the design process, participation and radical democracy in decision-making, anticipation of the multiplicity of meaning, open-sourceable design, and so on.

BERLIN MASQUES AND OPEN ARCHITECTURE

Among the different ways of openness in architecture, John Hejduk's work holds a special place. Each of Hejduk's two competition projects for IBA 1984/87, the Wilhelmstrasse and the Prinz Albrecht Palais competitions, suggested a *Berlin Masque*—an enigmatic concept where freestanding sculpture-like objects were scattered within a hedge-enclosed site (figs. 1–2). In the Wilhelmstrasse competition, the list of proposed ritualistic structures included a reading theater, a pantomime theater, a public theater, a house for the eldest inhabitant, an observation tower, a clock tower, a conciliator, a crossover bridge, bell, watch, and wind towers, a book market, a lottery kiosk, and so on. The Prinz Albrecht Palais competition project, which Hejduk named *Victims*, was located on the site that had been used for torture by the Nazis. The sixty-seven objects for that many characters—each with a name, a picture, and a story—would have been located within the borders of the site, to activate the emerging Holocaust memory debate in Germany.[2] Hejduk continued to prepare many more *masques,* with intertextual relations between them, until he passed away in 2000.[3] The designed objects and their assigned characters moved in between different *masques,* just as actors could embody different characters in multiple plays. After a while, they even inherited wheels as if to travel freely (figs. 3–4).

Of the many possible interpretations that Hejduk's work calls for, I suggested the idea of an adventure game, as one form of open architecture, to delineate a rapport that opens self to a stranger on the one hand, and a happening that evolves over time on the other hand. A *masque* is a theatrical form that emerged in the sixteenth and seventeenth centuries, usually with no beginning, end, or fixed plot. It could involve singing, dancing, acting, pantomime, and improvisation in an elaborate stage design, where spectators could join in. If Hejduk's *masques* had been built in Berlin, then a visitor could have seen the site/stage, circled around the structures without any predefined order, entered the houses, climbed the towers, crossed the bridges, shopped at booths and kiosks, and engaged with the structures that stimulated one's imagination in search of metaphors: theaters with tails, façades with eyes, towers like umbrellas, bridges like geometrized caterpillars, kiosks like medusa heads with bad-hair days, booths like tents, houses like robots on wheels, and so forth.[4] Reading Hejduk's accompanying texts, the visitor could have joined the dots in multiple directions, both within and across writing

2 Drawings can be found in the John Hejduk Archives at the Canadian Centre for Architecture; IBA Prinz Albrecht Palais competition holdings in the Landesarchiv, Berlin. Also see John Hejduk, *Victims: A Work by John Hejduk* (London, 1986).

3 For instance, see John Hejduk, *Lancaster/Hanover Masque* (London and Montreal, 1992); John Hejduk, *Berlin Night* (Rotterdam, 1993); John Hejduk, *Vladivostok: A Work by John Hejduk*, ed. Kim Shkapich (New York, 1989); John Hejduk, "Evening in Llano," *A+U* 91, no. 1 (1991), pp. 127–28; John Hejduk, "Oslo Fall Night," *Columbia Documents of Architecture and Theory* 2 (1993), pp. 7–35; John Hejduk, *Adjusting Foundations*, ed. Kim Shkapich (New York, 1995).

4 The "Berlin Masque Sketchbook" represented these objects with poems, stories, sketches of Medusa heads, and drawings of fallen angels. "Berlin Masque Sketchbook," John Hejduk Archives at the Canadian Centre for Architecture, DR 1998: 0098:001.

Fig. 3 John Hejduk, *Berlin Masque*, elevations and plans for guest towers and shopping booths, 1981, Wilhelmstrasse competition project, IBA 1984/87

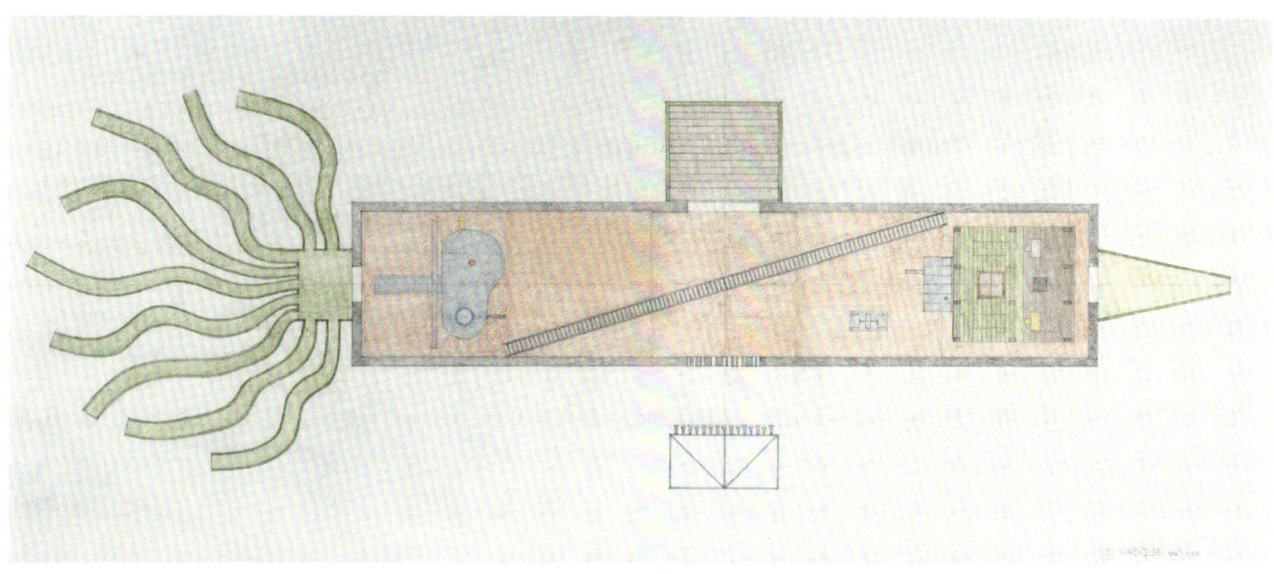

Fig. 4 John Hejduk, *Berlin Masque*, plan for a *masque*, 1981, Wilhelmstrasse competition project, IBA 1984/87

and physical space. A set of characters allegorized in built structures could have generated an indefinite number of stories in each visitor's imagination.

In an adventure game, players transport themselves into a new world that is free from existing memories. They must look around for clues in an environment totally new to them, as if waking up to a world of which they remember nothing. Unlike their daily routines, they open every drawer, lift every book, check every corner, and collect every possible clue in the hope of solving the mystery of the game. Players are asked to engage with the artifacts of this artificial universe by agreeing to enter a state of amnesia, leaving behind the symbolic system and know-how of their daily lives. The decoding of Hejduk's intertextual *masques* is a similar experience. While they invite us to a world without memories, they are not meant to make us forget permanently. On the contrary, they offer an alternate way of remembering something—as in *Victims*—that is beyond representation with one's familiar symbolic system. Overall, the oeuvre of the late Hejduk is like an adventure game, where players wander physically or mentally in between the objects, from one *masque* to another, from one character's life to another, decoding messages, finding a clue in each step and following it to find other clues, until stories are revealed and his universe makes a bit more sense, even if each one of us might interpret things differently. The whole process seems like a puzzle-solving and empathic exploration, an adventure game that is predicated on an intersubjective experience.

Hejduk's self-naming of his work as *masque* invites us to discuss architecture through the lens of theater and performance studies. The objects of Hejduk's projects are highly personal, but they simultaneously invite the participation of a second mind and confirm the meaning-construing reader. Unlike classical stages that put the theatrical play in a separated frame in front of the audience, Hejduk's objects invite their participation in the theater, just like the historical *masques.* The architectural work here is conceived less as a finished building than as an evolving, performative stage; the architect less as an all-defining author than as a co-producer of a play; and the habitant less as a user who is expected to live the life determined by the all-knowing architect than as an active, participating audience. This intersubjective experience in the adventure game may involve a one-on-one relationship between the architect and the viewer (just like in interactive art), or it may inspire many people to activate a social practice (just like in participatory art). In *Victims*, for example, the city habitants would have decided the placement of each of the sixty-seven objects in a span of sixty years.

In this scenario, there is something similar to what Umberto Eco identified as "openness." Eco compared Luciano Berio's and Karlheinz Stockhausen's musical compositions to "the components of a construction kit" that the composer hands on to the performer, as if he were "unconcerned about the manner of their eventual deployment."[5] The concept of the emancipated reader in an open work has retroactively inspired scholars to understand the ability of the visual arts to construct a communal space, a space of collective and political engagement.[6] Today, the idea of an emancipated spectator continues to motivate thinkers as a model for an apposite relation between aesthetics and politics. In his book *Emancipated Spectator*, for instance, Jacques Rancière spoke about the possibility of realizing a "theater without spectators," and of challenging the separation between viewing and acting, seeing and doing, so that a spectator is not simply seduced by images but becomes an active participant.[7]

5 Umberto Eco, "The Poetics of the Open Work," in *The Open Work*, trans. Anna Cancogni (1962; repr., Cambridge, MA, 1989), p. 4. Translated from *Opera Aperta* (Milan, 2000). During the peaks of post-structuralist thinking, Umberto Eco and Roland Barthes explained the "Open Work" (1962) and the "Death of the Author" (1968) respectively as a historical necessity rather than as a random choice. Several chronological markers, including the emergence of the modern subject, brought the "sharpening awareness of the concept of the work susceptible to many different interpretations" in Eco's words, and "the birth of the reader at the cost of the death of the author" in Barthes's words. See Roland Barthes, "The Death of the Author," in *Image Music Text*, trans. Stephen Heath (1968; repr., New York, 1977), p. 148.

6 For example, rereading the history of modern and avant-garde art from the perspective of performance studies, Claire Bishop pointed out in 2013 that the "desire to activate the audience in participatory art is at the same time the drive to emancipate it from a state of alienation induced by the dominant ideological order." Claire Bishop, *Artificial Hells: Participatory Art and the Politics of Spectatorship* (London and New York, 2012), p. 275.

7 "The less the playwright knows what he wants the collective of spectator to do, the more he knows that they should, at any rate, act as a collective, transform their aggregation into community." Jacques Rancière, *The Emancipated Spectator*, trans. Gregory Elliot (2008; repr., London, 2014), p. 16.

8 The drawings can be found in the John Hejduk Archives at the Canadian Centre for Architecture.

9 Yeliz Erçakmak in conversation with Esra Akcan, spring 2012, Berlin, video and audio recording in the author's collection. Other related information in this article is also drawn from this interview, and from subsequent conversations and visits.

10 Eco, "The Poetics of the Open Work" (see note 5).

OPENING THE BUILT FORM

Despite losing both of the competitions, John Hejduk was asked to design housing complexes in ways that were appropriated into IBA's urban design principles. Hejduk designed an urban villa in Tegel, and the Berlin Tower housing and the Berlin Gatehouse (Uhrenhaus Friedrichstrasse) in Kreuzberg. The latter was built in a tiny infill plot on the Wilhelmstrasse competition site. Confirming Hejduk's inclination for self-referential intertextuality, it adopts elements from the architect's previous installations. IBA's Neubau team mandated the idea of "critical reconstruction" quite rigidly, selecting projects in competitions that stayed loyal to the idea of the perimeter block because they perceived it as the "gene" of the city, in the words of the director Josef Paul Kleihues. After the process of mutual rapprochement, the result seen in the Berlin Tower housing design was midway between Hejduk and Kleihues: not a perimeter block, but two parallel five-story buildings staging a fourteen-story tower in between, all standing out with metal-clad, bright-green balconies, awnings, and window frames against a grayish stucco surface (→ p. 117). Enclosing a green area and a playground, the compound was completely open to public access, but it was nevertheless secluded from the street due to its set-back location.[8] The adventure game was partially closed, so to speak, due to its adaptation to IBA's urban design principles. Nonetheless, once the residents moved in, Hejduk's buildings regained their life as *masques,* as the inhabitants took on extended roles in shaping their built environment in this relatively unordinary space, thereby amplifying the intended character of the project as unfinished and open architecture.

For example, Yeliz Erçakmak embraced the idiosyncratic and unfamiliar spaces in John Hejduk's design as an evolving, performative stage, and herself as a meaning-construing participant. Having grown up in Dortmund, as the daughter of two Turkish migrant teachers, Erçakmak lived in one of the duplexes in Hejduk's Berlin Tower with her husband during the time of our interview. Working at Türkische Gemeinde Deutschland (Turkish Community in Germany, TGD), she is well aware of the continuing practices of discrimination, although she acknowledges not to have been subject to it herself. "I do believe that there is a certain level of discrimination in all state buildings, such as kindergartens or public housing. The ad-hoc research also adds up to this conclusion.... In Germany, it is common that they would not rent a vacant apartment based on the name of the applicant."[9] The Erçakmaks were not insistent on living in Kreuzberg, and she had not imagined herself in Hejduk's building either. "When I saw this building from the outside, I never expected to live here. On the contrary, I told myself that this is an uninhabitable building. It is a bit gray, a bit green, it does not look like a house. I also found it weird that the building is standing in the middle of the site, without a *Hof* [courtyard]. When I walked along the street, this building always caught my eye; I found it odd ... It was rather a coincidence that I moved here, but I am really glad I did."

Her appropriation of the apartment suggests that it is perhaps not the original design itself that she likes, but her own version of it. The Erçakmaks do not use the second floor of the apartment as Hejduk had intended; in other words, it is not used as an open space for artists, but rather as a divided one with several private rooms. Hejduk's daughter and the architectural students who visited the apartment have informed her about the architect's original intention, but she still prefers the divided space to a loft, as a more appropriate setup for modern couples. She explains this as adopting the part of the empowered user, which does not necessarily diminish her respect for the

Fig. 5 View of the balcony in Yeliz Erçakmak's apartment in John Hejduk's Kreuzberg Tower for IBA 1984/87, photo: Esra Akcan, 2010

Fig. 6 Satellite dishes on John Hejduk's Kreuzberg Tower, photo: Esra Akcan, 2009

architectural community. On the contrary, she empathizes with the groups of ten to twenty architectural students who often appear on her doorstep without prior notice and expect to be invited in—a request she always accepts, even if the apartment is too messy to receive visitors.

The small, square balconies are another space of curiosity (fig. 5) (→ p. 117 right). Before moving in, she knew that the two balconies are rather unusually small, but she grew to find them quite functional and sufficient. Imagining that the man and the woman of the house would each sit on one of the balconies, her husband joked about constructing a bridge by placing a wooden platform in the air between the two balustrades. Now using only one of the balconies for outdoor activities, they are amazed that the small space can accommodate not only two chairs and a coffee table, but also their bicycle. However, they had to reserve the second balcony for their satellite dish, which hardly fits in (fig. 6). The scattered satellite dishes all around Hejduk's housing complex remind one of the architect's original *masques*. After a Turkish immigrant family won its appeal to the German Federal Constitutional Court in 1993, the residents gained legal permission to install satellite dishes as part of their constitutional right to freedom of information, so that they can watch TV channels from Turkey—something they could not do before. Germany hence started being populated with satellite dishes all around. Visual cacophony according to some, but symbols of calls for freedom to receive information according to others, these dishes are testimony to the lived forms of IBA buildings (fig. 7).

One of the most idiosyncratic features of Hejduk's tower is the set of transparent bridges that one needs to cross to reach the small towers on the sides—a feature that is similar to the bridges in the architect's Wall House in Groningen (completed posthumously). A kitchen, a bathroom, a laundry room, and a reading room are included in the Erçakmaks' place, each of which is no bigger than a mere 6 square meters. Yeliz smiles with a sense of tolerance at the unordinary decision to design a transparent bridge on the way to the bathroom. She appreciates the other three side-tower rooms much more. She can quickly finish up the household in the minimal efficient kitchen and enjoy the rest of the day; she can feel that the laundry room is conveniently detached from the rest of the house. She appreciates how she can cross the bridge to the reading room, and how that act of crossing creates the feeling of leaving the house, and how that detachment allows her to feel outside in another world if she chooses to close the door of the reading room; or how an open door instead allows her to stay informed about the inside, while still being able to read her book, and how that ability to choose to be inside or outside empowers her (fig. 8).

Hejduk himself did not comment on the immigrants' rights to the city, but his design approach opened a space for immigrant voices indirectly. As a matter of fact, Hejduk's work reminds us that architecture is by definition open, in the sense that buildings always get appropriated by their habitants, whether or not their architects have anticipated or forbidden these changes. Yet, it is not appropriatability and interpretability that distinguish an open work from a closed one, but rather its intentionally unfinished nature awaiting habitant completion. Umberto Eco emphasized a similar distinction. It is not interpretability that differentiates an open work from, say, a traffic sign or a closed work, but rather its intentional openness awaiting performer or audience completion.[10] While buildings and spaces always get activated with the life that emerges in them, open architecture takes place when designers embrace or anticipate new qualities of openness during the stage of design.

Fig. 7 Esra Akcan, *Freedom of Information,* installation at the exhibition *Open Architecture: A Book on Migration,* John Hartell Gallery, Architecture Art Planning (AAP), Cornell University, September 30 to October 9, 2019, Ithaca, New York

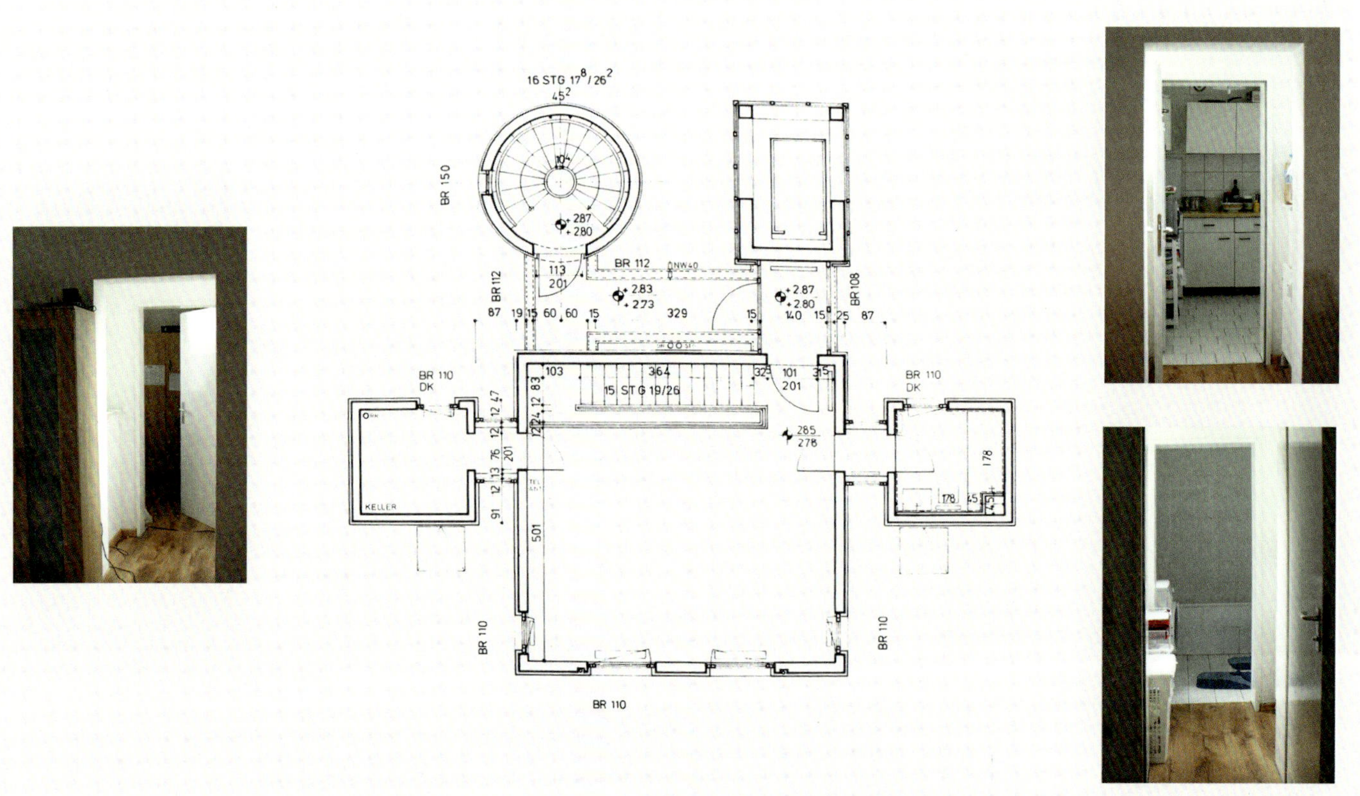

Fig. 8 Appropriations of side-tower rooms in Yeliz Erçakmak's apartment in John Hejduk's Kreuzberg Tower for IBA 1984/87, photo: Esra Akcan, 2010

ARCHITECTURE FOR THE PEOPLE

153 Hinrich and Inken Baller, apartment building on Fraenkelufer, 1979–84, view from the promenade along the riverbank

Hinrich Baller, Torhaus (Gate House) on Fraenkelufer, 1981
The new building fits in with the historical structure of the block. The gap was filled but not closed.

Detail of a Torhaus (Gate House) on Fraenkelufer, photo: Reinhard Friedrich, 1984

Frei Otto, sketch of an idea for a treehouse, 1980
Frei Otto, Hermann Kendel, Ökohaus (Eco House), 1987–91

Frei Otto, model for the Ökohäuser, design for Askanischer Platz, 1981

Myra Warhaftig, apartment building at Dessauer Strasse 38–40, view from the west, ca. 1993

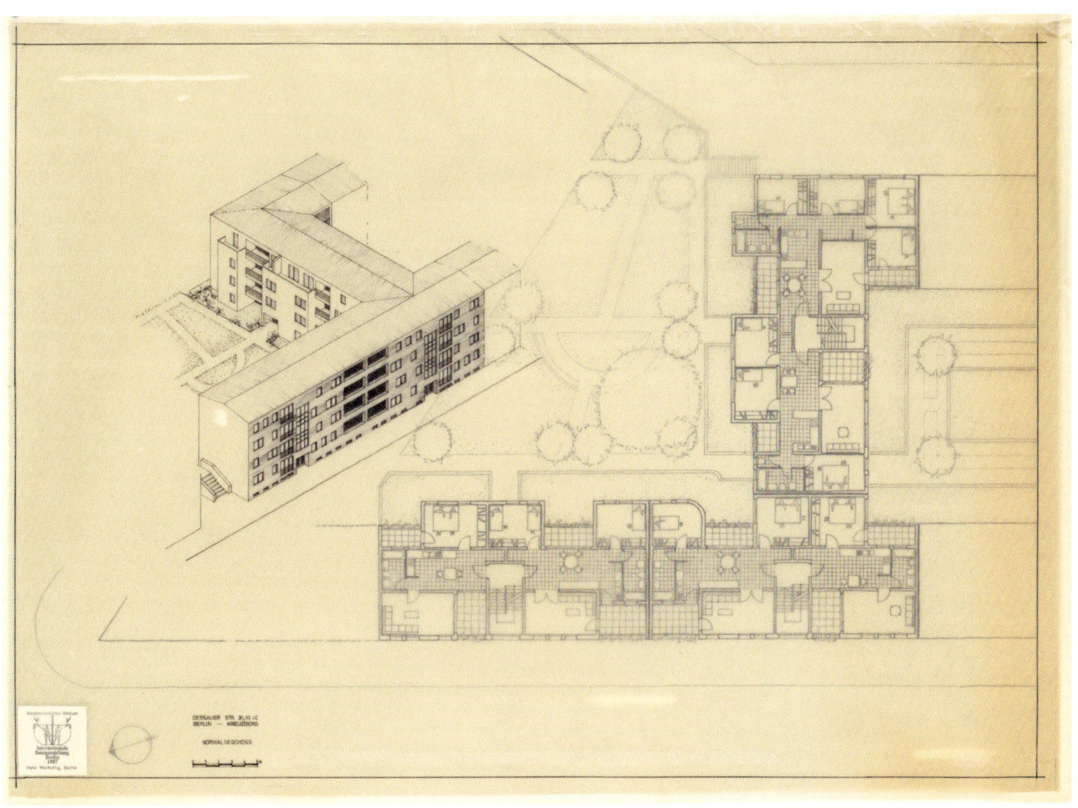

Myra Warhaftig, “Kinderorientiertes Wohnen” (Child-Oriented Housing), Dessauer Strasse 38–40, design of floor plan and isometric drawing of the building volume, 1987, and eat-in kitchen, ca. 1993

Heiner Hoffmann, ecological planning for the conversion of a former chocolate factory into the Frauen-Stadtteilzentrum (Neighborhood Center for Women), visualization, ca. 1984
Declan Kennedy, garden use of the attic in the Frauen-Stadtteilzentrum, ca. 1985

Heiner Hoffmann, hammam and café in the Frauen-Stadtteilzentrum, visualization, ca. 1985
Hammam in the Frauen-Stadtteilzentrum, 2007

Martin Küenzlen, ecological planning for the conversion of a parking garage into a daycare center, Dresdener Strasse 128, 1983
Invitation card for "Ich werf' die Autos raus ... und werd' ein Kinderhaus" (I am throwing the cars out and becoming a house for children), a citizens' gathering with children's party in the parking garage on Dresdener Strasse, Turkish version on the recto, German version on the verso, September 10, 1983

Martin Küenzlen, greenery inside the daycare center on Dresdener Strasse 128, 1983

Martin Küenzlen, Uwe Drepper, new winter garden windows, Paul-Linke-Ufer 44, exterior and interior view, 1982–83

165 Martin Küenzlen, ecological urban renewal in the center of the city, rooftop greenery of IBA Block 108, 1986

“THE CITIZENS’ VOTE COUNTS!”

Inken Baller in Conversation with Anna-Maria Nitschke

1 Ernst Bloch, *The Principle of Hope*, vol. 2, trans. Neville Plaice, Stephen Plaice, and Paul Knight (Cambridge, MA, 1995), pp. 744–45.

2 Johannes Göderitz, Roland Rainer, and Hubert Hoffmann, *Die gegliederte und aufgelockerte Stadt* (Tübingen, 1957).

> Architecture as a whole is and remains an attempt to produce a human homeland—from the sedate residential purpose to the manifestation of a more beautiful world in proportion and ornamentation.[1]

The apartment complex on Fraenkelufer (1982–84) realized by Inken Baller and her then husband and firm partner, Hinrich Baller, still gives this part of Kreuzberg an inimitable look. Developed on the basis of a new, interdisciplinary, and participatory approach, their concept emphasized direct dialogue with future residents. It resulted in unusual residential buildings that solved the social, urban planning, and ecological problems of the 1980s in a convincing way.

CONSTRUCTION BOOM

Anna-Maria Nitschke: You came to West Berlin in 1962 to study architecture. The city was in a precarious situation, politically and economically, and in an isolated situation as a result of the building of the Berlin Wall a year earlier. Why did you decided to study there?

Inken Baller: I had been fascinated by the city ever since a class trip in 1959. It became my big dream to study in Berlin. After the Wall was built, only 300 new students, including me, were admitted in the winter semester of 1962–63 to the architecture department at the Technische Universität (TU).

AMN: You completed your training successfully in 1969. At that time, Berlin was experiencing a construction boom. It was founded on an urban renewal program that was controversial with the public, which intended to destroy the old building fabric in favor of new housing. To what extent were urban planning discourses reflected in the teaching at the university?

IB: At the TU, the growing critique from citizens that would later result in a paradigm shift was palpable: away with the so-called subdivided and opened-up city,[2] in favor of increasing density and rediscovering city centers as residential areas. The large housing developments being built at that time led to another economization of housing construction. Such themes were barely touched on by professors when I was a student. Only in the final two years of my studies were there exceptions, such as a seminar by Dieter Frick on Neues Bauen (New Building) on the historical layout of the city.

This deficit of critical teaching led to student initiatives. For the group diploma on the theme "Innerstädtische Sanierung" (Inner-City Redevelopment), we formed project groups in theoretical areas such as work, leisure time, socialization, and mobility and then tested their relevance to the neighborhoods that had been declared renewal zones from 1963 onward in Kreuzberg, Neukölln, and Wedding. "Redevelopment" here was essentially understood to mean wholesale redevelopment. The housing shortage had to be created in the first place in order to move renters to the periphery, it was claimed. The developers of large housing developments on the outskirts of the city were largely identical to those responsible for renewing the zones with old buildings. These practices of building policy and urban planning were rejected by us students. For that reason, only a few of my fellow students went into design after completing their studies: in their view, society had to be changed first before building again. Hinrich Baller and I, by contrast, belonged to a group that said: We will build anyway. But we will do so in an especially beautiful and right way.

3 Herta Hammerbacher (1900–1985) was a garden and landscape architect who held the chair for garden and landscape design in the architecture department at the TU Berlin.

4 On this, see the essays by Marco De Michelis and Gerd Zimmermann in this volume.

CALL FOR DEMOCRATIZATION

AMN: In 1968, Hinrich Baller, who at the time was an assistant professor at the TU, organized with other architects and students the exhibition *Diagnose zum Bauen in West-Berlin* (Diagnosis of Building in West Berlin), in which residents of new housing developments were asked about their living conditions. What significance do you attribute to this exhibition from today's perspective?

IB: The exhibition opening in 1968 critically addressed themes related to entanglements among architects, Senate, and construction business, among urban redevelopment practice, land use policy, and lack of citizen participation, but also to the dearth of theory in education and to the job profile of architects and city planners. Renters in the Märkisches Viertel complained in interviews about the loss of their old neighborhood and about their new housing situation. The exhibition became a turning point in professional and public discussion: people discovered the good qualities of buildings from the late nineteenth century that had previously been scorned and the importance of citizen participation. The *Planer-Flugschrift* (Planners' Pamphlet) by the author collective of the architecture department resulted in a reorientation of the planning concept and initiated the development of municipal and regional planning into an autonomous university discipline.

Working on the exhibition had a big influence on us as well. Just as important was the competition announced shortly thereafter, *Freizeit 2000* (Leisure Time 2000) of 1971, in which we participated with Herta Hammerbacher[3] in the context of the Internationale Gartenbauausstellung (International Horticultural Exhibition, IGA) in 1973, and in which we reflected on the concept in an interdisciplinary way. We were planning a landscape of buildings in combination with the horticultural exhibition. The sociologist Gunther Soukup taught us a lot about listening at citizens' meetings. Two sentences that shaped my work life: You have to pick people up where they are standing. And if you want to achieve something, you have to package a thing gently.

NEW BUILDINGS AS CATALYSTS OF URBAN DEVELOPMENT

AMN: For the Internationale Bauausstellung 1987, the architect Hardt-Waltherr Hämer headed the section IBA-Alt (IBA Old Buildings).[4] After an exemplary refurbishing of prewar buildings in Wedding and Charlottenburg, he developed the planning principle of Behutsame Stadterneuerung (Cautious Urban Renewal). What significance do you attribute, in retrospect, to the integration of new buildings for Kreuzberg?

IB: In the area of IBA-Alt, there were vacant lots that could sensibly be filled in with new buildings. The situation in Kreuzberg is no longer imaginable today. The buildings that were marked for demolition had not been kept up; their technical infrastructure was poor; and anyone who could afford to do so was moving out of the neighborhood. Because labor from East Berlin was no longer available after the Berlin Wall had been built, replacements were being recruited in Turkey. Many guest workers and also students were moving into cheap apartments that had previously been abandoned. For IBA-Alt, it was important to change the image by means of high-quality new buildings. It was not enough to renovate the old buildings to the standard then current. A couple of exclamation points had to be added to show that it was worth moving to Kreuzberg again. It is important to understand that these new buildings were all built as social housing.

Fig. 1 Aerial photograph of the large IBA-Block 70 between Kohlfurter Strasse and Fraenkelufer, ca. 1979
The rear courtyards had already been gutted in preparation for area rehabilitation. By 1979, an embankment was foreseen as part of the plans for the autobahn ring road, which was to pass through this neighborhood.

Fig. 2 Álvaro Siza Vieira, design sketch for the open peer-review process of IBA 1979 at Fraenkelufer, 1979

LIVING NEXT TO THE FIRE WALL

AMN: Fraenkelufer in Kreuzberg had a nearly intact urban structure until the mid-1970s, even though the Senate declared the district a redevelopment area in 1963 and, as late as 1973, was planning to demolish it completely. A change of strategy in this policy was first demonstrated by the peer-review process announced by the IBA in 1979, in which you participated.

IB: In 1979, the district decided to preserve the buildings still standing on Fraenkelufer and on Erkelenzdamm and was trying out, in collaboration with the IBA, new concepts for developing the area inside of the block that had resulted from demolition (fig. 1). Four planning firms—Hahn, Urbanke-Maedebach-Redeleit, Siza, and Baller—were asked to submit competing reviews. In a process with a jury of experts and with citizen participation, the review by the firm Baller became the basis for further action.

AMN: The jury of experts had initially decided on the design by the architect Álvaro Siza Vieira, which pursued a different vision of urban planning on the Fraenkelufer.[5] What factors led to rethinking that?

IB: Avoiding closing the block again, Siza's design incorporated late-nineteenth-century building types from Berlin into the courtyard, so that there was no contiguous courtyard space and only a few apartments were created (fig. 2). The jury of experts liked his intellectual approach of using the existing historical traces as the point of departure for his reinterpretation of urban planning. By contrast, we pursued a more emotional engagement. The citizens felt almost provoked by Siza's design, which triggered violent aversions. Siza was the only one of the participants in the competition who had not built up the fire wall. When the residents saw the possibilities of a different construction, they argued strongly for it. The IBA coordinator Bernhard Strecker won over Hardt-Waltherr Hämer for our not-yet-finished building on Kottbusser Damm. The party responsible for the redevelopment, the GSW,[6] was unsure whether we—as young architects considered unconventional—could successfully realize such a large building. Hämer, as head of Altbau-IBA, ultimately decided: "The citizens' vote counts!"

AMN: What new ideas did you pursue in your concept for Fraenkelufer?

IB: We listened to the existing needs. The residents were helplessly subjected to the demolition of their apartment buildings. The Americans stationed in Berlin had practiced house-to-house combat in the ruins (→ p. 153). The neighborhood had to put up with all of that. No thought was given any longer to specific layouts, but instead to a fundamental improvement of the situation. That was, in fact, the main desire of the residents. On the whole, the newly built apartments were a reaction to the requirements of social housing construction in terms of furnishings, which is why the setups were similar to one another. We had to demonstrate that on Fraenkelufer, but we went beyond the direct fulfillment of functional needs. On later visits to the buildings, I was pleased to see how individually the spaces had been treated (fig. 3). Those are the opportunities for people to become creative. An especially anonymous apartment does not invite its occupants to do so. The Gründerzeit apartments of the late-nineteenth century, which at the time were still much derided, exhibit high spatial qualities combined with functional quality. We could learn from that.

5 The planning proposal by the architect Álvaro Siza Vieira did not close the gap in the block perimeter structure but instead added the new buildings inside the block. The house on the corner of Admiralstrasse and Fraenkelufer would have been built without any connection to the fire wall of the adjacent building. See Hinrich Baller and Inken Baller, *Städtebauliches Neuordnungskonzept Fraenkelufer*, ed. Internationale Bauausstellung Berlin GmbH 1984–1987 (Berlin, 1980), pp. 62–63.

6 Gemeinnützige Siedlungs- und Wohnungsbaugesellschaft (Nonprofit Development and Housing Construction Company).

7 Anonymous, "Mietshaus Fraenkelufer 44," in Landesdenkmalamt Berlin, n.d., www.stadtentwicklung.berlin.de/denkmal/liste_karte_datenbank/de/denkmaldatenbank/daobj.php?obj_dok_nr=09060153 (accessed August 8, 2020).

8 Ibid.

9 Ibid.

UNBOUNDED SPACE

AMN: The guiding idea of your design was the creation of individual interiors and exteriors. What architectonic design did you implement within the framework of social housing?

IB: Hinrich's and my understanding of how to approach space and the related choice of materials and construction method belongs to the tradition of Bernhard Hermkes, but it also stands in a dialectical interrelationship with architects from earlier times such as Francesco Borromini, Guarino Guarini, Balthasar Neumann, and Antoni Gaudí. In their works, the chosen construction method is implemented to remove the boundaries on space. In the apartment building on Fraenkelufer, a large number of sloping supports facilitates an implementation that makes supporting walls within a unit unnecessary. Openings at floor height and large, curving balconies establish a close but shielded connection to the exterior. The apartment is not a prefabricated final product but rather defined spaces for placement. The Fraenkelufer project shows that its sensibly employed constructions and techniques offer potential for savings. It was thus possible to remain within the budget for social housing at the time. For example, all of the supports are of the same diameter in order to use the smallest possible number of shuttering volumes by prefabricating them on site. Because the curved balconies were prefabricated parts from the concrete factory, they had the same curving radius, so that one casting form was enough, and it was only necessary to alter the dimensions of the terminations.

AMN: The Kreuzberg neighborhood on Fraenkelufer was in part abandoned in the 1970s. How important were ecological considerations to you in the case of the Fraenkelufer project?

IB: Herta Hammerbacher's ideas viewed the garden as a space, plants as a way to shape the space, and the house and the garden as a spatial unit. That provided us with impetus for an architecture that sought a close connection to the garden and the landscape. In the case of the Fraenkelufer, the rundown vacant lot presented a big challenge. One of the conditions of the peer review process was to create a publicly accessible space in the courtyard that could compensate for the loss of the Böcklerpark resulting from the building. We integrated the access routes required by the fire department and the open-air parking places in the courtyard, as requirements for social housing, into the concept for the garden in a way that concealed them as much as possible. The building inspectors were demanding proof of a soccer field in order to sign off on use, but that was prevented by collecting signatures from all of the renters. Instead, they wanted a sandbox, a pond, and an area for water games.

APPRECIATION

AMN: Forty years ago, there was still rioting on Fraenkelufer, but today it is a popular residential neighborhood. Your building has since been listed as a historical landmark. The justification of that emphasizes above all the uniqueness of the construction,[7] the complex layout,[8] and the incorporation of the buildings into the street façade of the neighboring historical apartment buildings.[9] Were your visions for Fraenkelufer fulfilled?

IB: The new building was intended not to conflict with the Elisabethhof, the historical promenade on Landwehrkanal with its trees, and the prewar buildings,

Fig. 3 View into the maisonette apartment on the top floor of the firewall building. The open design of the interiors made it possible to use the rooms individually.

Fig. 4 Urban life in the rear courtyard on the Elisabethhof firewall, which is more than 100 meters long and 30 meters tall. According to the guidelines of social housing, construction is not allowed in rear courtyards. It could be built only because a special permit was granted.

Fig. 5 The cornerstone ceremony on June 8, 1982, took place under police protection. Front right: Hinrich Baller

but rather to achieve a shared value with what was already there. The idea was for the fire wall of the Elisabethhof to start to flourish in the truest sense of that word; a new quality was to result from the rear courtyard, which has traditionally had a bad reputation (fig. 4). I believe we achieved these goals. But I see the danger of gentrification. The regulations for protecting the character of neighborhoods were developed as part of IBA-Alt, so that, in certain neighborhoods, buildings could not easily be converted into condominiums. Hämer was aware that a degree of gentrification could also have a positive effect. The rent ceiling makes sense, but it is too late now. The apartments and stores have to be protected by ensuring that renters can stay there while paying modest rents.

AMN: Your architectural language evolved out of a new, interdisciplinary way of working. Have interdisciplinary requirements changed the architect's profession in lasting ways?

IB: The competition in 1971 made it clear that we as architects have to learn from other disciplines. The cornerstone ceremony for the Fraenkelufer was in 1982 (fig. 5). Our interdisciplinary approach has vanished today and has been replaced by a splintering into many specialized disciplines, such as fire safety, energy consultation, project management, and so on, each with its own increasingly restrictive regulations. Architecture has become more hermetic and fragmented. A balcony is already seen as disturbing the building, which is conceived as a box, and yet there is also a conservativism specific to Berlin, for example, small neoclassical reminiscences on new buildings. I have nothing against increasing density in the city, on the contrary. Fraenkelufer and the adjacent Graefe neighborhood show how to achieve a green city with high quality of life despite density.

I miss that about some of the recent new housing developments such as Europacity or the new buildings around Mercedes-Platz.

This conversation took place on April 21, 2020, at the Berlinische Galerie.

Suggested Literature

Amann, Renate. "Hoffnung auf ein neues Bauen?: Wohnbauten von Hinrich und Inken Baller in Berlin." *archithese: Zeitschrift und Schriftenreihe für Architektur / Revue thématique d'architecture* 19, no. 3 (1989), pp. 23–29.

Anonymous. "'Behutsame Stadterneuerung' und 'Das Prinzip Hoffnung': Interview mit Inken Baller, Berlin-Neukölln, 28. April 2018." In *Berliner Portraits: Erzählungen zur Architektur der Stadt*, edited by Lukas Fink, Tobias Fink, and Ruben Bernegger, pp. 18–32. Cologne, 2019.

Anonymous. "Fraenkelufer: Neues Bauen in den Resten alter Umgebung." In *Bauen und Wohnen in alter Umgebung: Wohnen in der Innenstadt*, edited by Internationale Bauausstellung Berlin 1987, pp. 66–72. Contribution of the Berlin-Kreuzberg district to the national competition "Bürger, es geht um Deine Gemeinde" (Citizens, It's Your Community, 1983–84). Berlin, 1984.

Anonymous. "Mietshaus Fraenkelufer 44." In Landesdenkmalamt Berlin, n.d., www.stadtentwicklung.berlin.de/denkmal/liste_karte_datenbank/de/denkmaldatenbank/daobj.php?obj_dok_nr=09060153 (accessed August 8, 2020).

Anonymous. "Planung als Zuversicht." *Die Zeit*, June 8, 1984, www.zeit.de/1984/24/planung-als-zuversicht/komplettansicht (accessed August 8, 2020).

Baller, Hinrich, and Inken Baller. *Städtebauliches Neuordnungskonzept Fraenkelufer.* Edited by Internationale Bauausstellung Berlin GmbH 1984–1987. Berlin, 1980.

Bogner, Simone. "Block 70: Eckhaus, Torhäuser, Brandwandbebauung." In *Forschungsinitiative IBA 87 (F-IBA)*, n.d., http://f-iba.de/block-70-eckhaus-torhaeuser-brandwandbebauung/ (accessed August 8, 2020).

Fassbinder, Helga. "Hinrich and Inken Baller." *Architecture and Urbanism A+U* 12, no. 195 (1986), pp. 75–130.

Internationale Bauausstellung Berlin 1987, ed. *Idee, Prozess, Ergebnis: Die Reparatur und Rekonstruktion der Stadt.* Exh. cat. Martin-Gropius-Bau. Berlin, 1984.

Jäger, Dagmar. "Interview mit Inken Baller: Policy of Geometry." *jp3_ architektur + gestaltung* (February 2000), www.jp3.de/baller/intballr.htm (accessed August 8, 2020).

Nitsche, Rainer. *Internationale Bauausstellung Berlin 1987.* Project overview, pp. 278–79. Berlin, 1987.

Sontheimer, Michael. "Berliner Häuserkampf: Utopie und Krawall." *Spiegel Geschichte*, January 29, 2014, www.spiegel.de/geschichte/berliner-haeuserkampf-in-den-achtziger-jahren-a-953279.html (accessed August 8, 2020).

Ullmann, Gerhard. "Die grosse Geste: Wohnbebauung am Fraenkelufer in Berlin-Kreuzberg." *Fachzeitschrift für Architekten und Bauingenieure: Deutsche Bauzeitung* 121, no. 4 (1987), pp. 34–35.

Wunderlich, Carola, ed. *Schritt für Schritt: Behutsame Stadterneuerung in Kreuzberg; Eine Wanderausstellung.* Exh. cat. S.T.E.R.N. Gesellschaft der behutsamen Stadterneuerung. Berlin, 1990.

ARCHITECTURES OF IMPRECISION

The Eco Houses of Frei Otto

Georg Vrachliotis

1 Frei Otto, "Wohnhaus für 12 Familien," unpublished study, TU Berlin, 1951, Frei Otto Werkarchiv, saai | Archiv für Architektur und Ingenieurbau, Karlsruhe Institut für Technologie.

2 After doing construction work while a prisoner of war in France, Frei Otto resumed his studies in Berlin in 1948. His teachers included Hellmuth Bickenbach, Gerhard Jobst, and Hans Freese, among others.

Fig. 1 Frei Otto, "Das übereinandergesetzte Eigenheim" (The Stacked Single-Family Home), unpublished study, TU Berlin, 1951

> Every apartment is sold together with the accompanying part of the lot. There is, therefore, not just one owner of the whole building. Every partial owner has a total, unlimited right to ceilings or the middle of the central wall. With his architect, he builds his house as he sees fit. He has complete freedom to do so. The less the building department worries about artistic matters—it must, after all, negotiate with every individual owner and perhaps with a number of architects—the more interesting the building will become. A Le Corbusier builds the one apartment, a Wright or Bonatz the other. Everywhere different people live in different apartments. You can see it from the outside of the building. You know immediately who lives where.[1]

This quotation is from the pen of twenty-six-year-old Frei Otto, who at the time, in 1951, was just completing his studies in architecture at the Technische Universität (TU) Berlin.[2] It is a description of one of his earliest surviving student projects and consists of a series of large-format pen-and-ink drawings with short, handwritten texts. The title of the design is simple: "Das übereinandergesetzte Eigenheim" (The Stacked Single-Family Home) (fig. 1). But what at first sounds like a traditional concept for a multifamily dwelling turns out to be one of the most remarkable contributions in the recent history of experimental housing construction. The highlight of the project is concealed not in the idea of stackable apartments but in the initially ordinary-sounding term "single-family home" and the associated individual freedom in dealing with one's own property and land. Rather than giving the entire power over decisions to the architect and homogenizing the aesthetic and planning of the project in that way, Frei Otto decided to leave the future residents as much latitude to design as possible. The task of the architect is in a sense limited to designing a simple shelf system of reinforced concrete in which the individual floors function like open platforms. Each resident has the opportunity to design and build it according to her or his individual wishes, either independently or with the help of an architect. The "stacked single-family home" is thus one of the earliest examples of Frei Otto's reflections on experimental housing construction.[3]

The idea of multifamily housing based on a radical concept of participation and ecology begins with his aforementioned student project from the early 1950s, continues with an ecological housing project for Central Park in New York, and ends with the building of the so-called Ökohäuser (Eco Houses) for the Internationale Bauausstellung (International Building Exhibition, IBA) in the late 1980s.

SEARCHING FOR SOCIAL FORM

Frei Otto worked across the boundaries between disciplines. Already in the late 1950s, he was lending a distinctive look with his tent constructions to the horticultural shows of the young German republic and thus made a special contribution to reconstruction after World War II. The filigreed tent structures he designed for the Bundesgartenschau (Federal Horticultural Show) in Cologne in 1957[4] and for Interbau in West Berlin that same year[5] number among his most impressive projects from that period. His student project from 1951 in turn shows that Frei Otto was not just experimenting in the area of light construction but already at the time critically engaging with the specific issues of housing.[6] His statements from this period suggest—even if it must remain speculation—that the housing concepts of the projects built in the Tiergarten were not radical or progressive enough for him. For Frei Otto, the architecture of the future looked different. In 1955, four years after his student project, he published an essay written in a courageous style: "Bauten für morgen? Eine Kritik am deutschen Wohnungsbau" (Buildings for Tomorrow? A Critique of German Housing Construction).[7] In it, he criticized not only the "horrible schematism of the single-family home of so many construction companies"[8] but was already anticipating several aspects of the architecture exhibition that was then still in the planning stages, for example, when he wrote: "If we want to pursue genuine social housing construction, then we must organically transform fields of ruins and community gardens and not shy away from doing so because several old buildings will for a time have views of the new greening, human, living land."[9] From the outset, the young Frei Otto was searching both for new forms of construction and for new forms of social architecture.

APARTMENT BUILDINGS FOR NEW YORK

Inspired by discussions in the context of Interbau, Frei Otto began to work more intently on alternative housing concepts. In a manuscript written in 1959—which is more an open and incomplete collection of materials than a finished book[10]—Frei Otto combined under the concept of "adaptable architecture" his own notes and sketches with selected contributions, projects, and reprinted fragments of texts by other architects. This not only produced a unique sourcebook on the subject of "adaptable architecture in the postwar era," but also an experimental commentary on the situation of the housing question at the time (fig. 2). The spectrum of assembled contributions ranges from lesser-known works, such as "Flexibility in the Planning and Design of Structures" by the American architect Antony Herrey (thesis project at MIT, 1956–57), to more popular projects, such as Martin Wagner's *Das wachsende Haus / The Growing House*, Yona Friedman's *L'architecture mobile*, and Rudolf Doernach's "Die dynamische Wohn-Hülle" (Dynamic Housing Shell)

3 Frei Otto's social housing project of 1954 for the Protestant housing construction company Alexandra-Stiftung should be mentioned in this context. The residential complex lies to the west of the Tempelhofer Feld in Berlin and consists of an ensemble of seven residential slabs of four to ten stories. With the aid of a horizontal sundial that Otto had developed in 1951, the shadow falling on every individual building could be minimized depending on topography and the location of the sun. See "Alexandra-Stiftung Residential Complex," in *Frei Otto: Thinking by Modeling*, ed. Georg Vrachliotis et al., exh. cat ZKM Karlsruhe (Leipzig, 2017), pp. 292–98.

4 See Frei Otto, "Vier Zeltkonstruktionen auf der Bundesgartenschau in Köln," *Bauwelt* 48, no. 30 (1957), pp. 754–61.

5 Frei Otto was represented at Interbau by a series of experimental tents and as an advisor on roof construction for the central exhibition pavilion. See Sandra Wagner-Conzelmann, *Die Interbau 1957 in Berlin: Stadt von heute – Stadt von morgen* (Petersberg, 2007).

6 See Joachim Kleinmanns and Martin Kunz, "The Path to Light Construction: Frei Otto's Early Works," in Vrachliotis et al., *Frei Otto* (see note 3), pp. 31–41.

7 Frei Otto, "Bauten für morgen? Eine Kritik am deutschen Wohnungsbau," *bauen+ wohnen* 10, no. 3 (1955), p. 131.

8 Ibid.

9 Ibid.

10 Frei Otto, "Anpassungsfähiges Bauen / Adaptable Building," Mitteilung no. 6, Entwicklungsstätte für den Leichtbau, Berlin, June 1959. Frei Otto Werkarchiv, saai | Archiv für Architektur und Ingenieurbau, Karlsruhe Institut für Technologie.

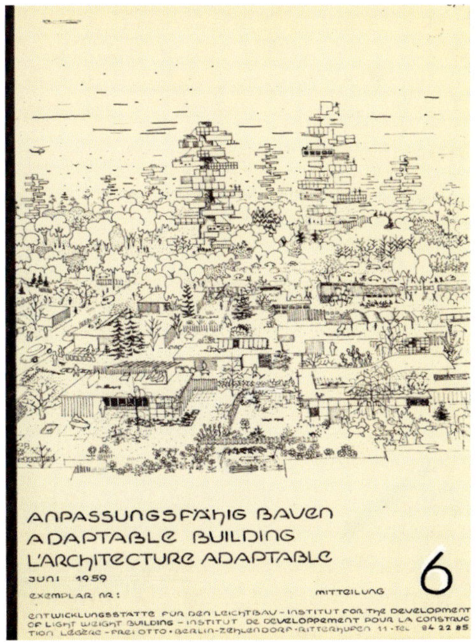

Fig. 2 Frei Otto, title page of "Anpassungsfähiges Bauen / Adaptable Architecture," Mitteilung no. 6, Entwicklungsstätte für den Leichtbau, Berlin, June 1959

Fig. 3 Frei Otto, model of the Ökohäuser (Eco Houses) with finished and greened platforms, design for Askanischer Platz, 1981

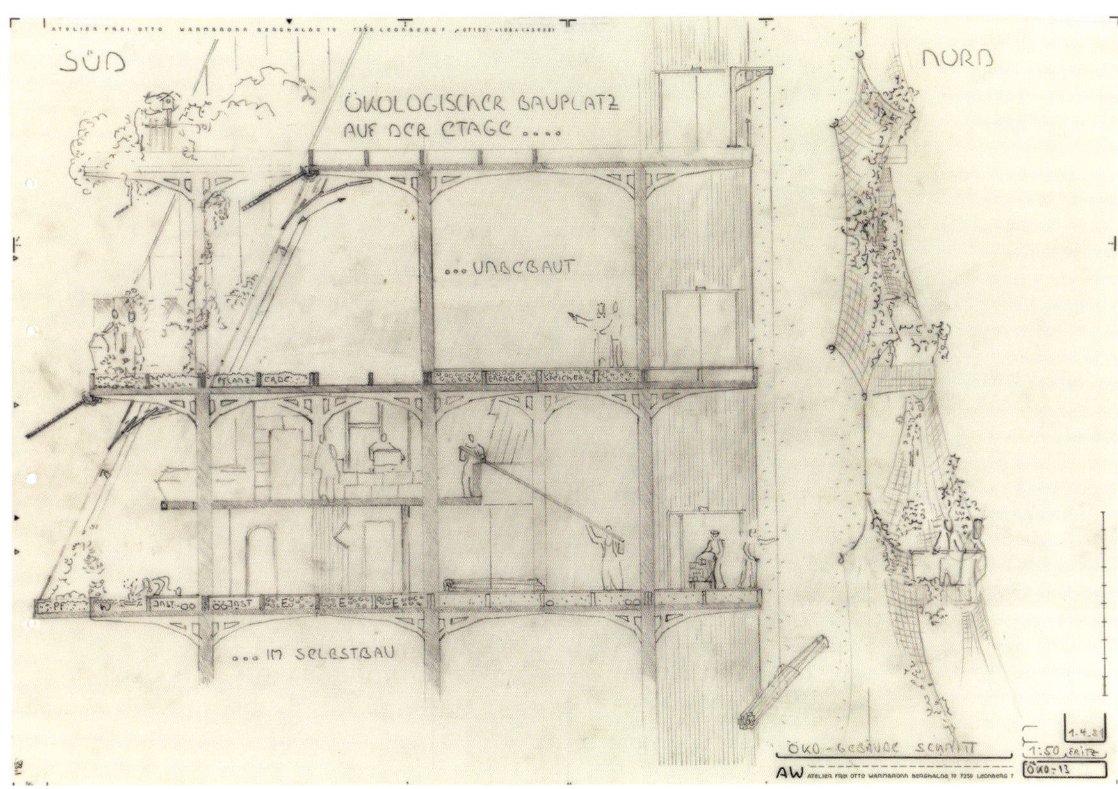

Fig. 4 Frei Otto, "Ökologischer Bauplatz auf der Etage ... umgebaut ... im Selbstbau" (Ecological Construction Site on the Floor ... DIY Conversion), section of the Ökohäuser (Eco Houses), scale: 1:50, design for Askanischer Platz, April 1, 1981

11 Frei Otto to Josef Paul Kleihues, July 30, 1980. I would like to take this opportunity to thank Fee Kyriakopoulos for calling this letter to my attention and for kindly discussing the Ökohäuser with me.

and references to industrial architecture by David Georges Emmerich or Konrad Wachsmann. Frei Otto was appearing here in separate roles: sometimes as an intellectual architect and author, sometimes as an editor. He himself wrote a series of short texts with programmatic titles such as "Die anpassungsfähige Innenstadt" (The Adaptable Inner City), "Anpassungsfähige Einfamilienhäuser auf gemeinschaftlichem Grundeigentum" (Adaptable Single-Family Homes on Shared Land), "Anpassungsfähige Bauordnungen" (Adaptable Building Codes), "Das autonome Haus" (The Autonomous House), and "Die dynamische Wohnhülle" (The Dynamic Housing Shell).

One central chapter in the manuscript is the project "Wohnhäuser für New York" (Apartment Buildings for New York). In drawings and a brief text, Frei Otto presented his design for three residential towers with greenery in Central Park. But instead of using the shelf system for their construction, as he had in his student project and for the Ökohäuser, this time Frei Otto experimented with a central master to which the separate residential floors are attached, permitting a free design of the space. "The building is oriented in all directions. There will be sunny, shady, and wind-protected places. There will be places where no one can look in, even in this densely settled city," as Frei Otto wrote, thus pointing to both the ecological dimension and the social interchange of public and private—aspects that would come up again in the Ökohäuser more than two decades later.

LIVING IN A "THREE-DIMENSIONAL GARDEN CITY"

In the run-up to the IBA, Frei Otto was hired by Josef Paul Kleihues, then director of the New Building department, to conceive and plan an ecological residential building based on the principle of "Natur und Bauen" (Nature and Building). Otto oriented it around the idea of a habitable "three-dimensional garden city." He imagined a fully greened and individually designed residential high-rise with open platforms, just like those he had developed previously in his student project and later for New York (figs. 3–4) (→ p. 157). Originally planned for a lot on Askanischer Platz in the Kreuzberg district of Berlin that had been vacant since the war, the project was moved, during later overall planning for the IBA, to a much smaller lot on the southern edge of the Tiergarten near the Landwehrkanal, where it was ultimately built in 1988. One can only speculate about the reasons why Kleihues decided to realize the project in a comparatively remote location. It is reasonable to assume, however, that, while he agreed with the ecological basic concept of the design, the informal look of the Ökohäuser seemed to him an aesthetic impertinence compared to the postmodern ordering principles of the other designs. Frei Otto's work was not about "block perimeter" and "critical reconstruction," but rather about "platform" and "nature." The project "would be a large tree and would have apartments on all its branches. I have drawn something like it often and even once studied it in detail for an apartment building on Central Park in New York.... According to today's aesthetic rules, what I am striving for is certainly not more beautiful, but it is more natural,"[11] as he wrote in a critical letter to Kleihues and thus surely touched a sore point for the planning director. It is certain, in any case, that this change in location had direct effects on the overall conception of the project.

Frei Otto had to work with Hermann Kendel to rework fundamentally the original design and adjust it to the urban planning conditions of the new property. Compared to the first concept, the second design had to be considerably reduced in height and area. Whereas the drawings and photo-

12 See "Otto and the Open System: Georg Vrachliotis in Conversation with Jean-Philippe Vassal," in "Frei Otto," special issue, *uncube magazine* 33, www.uncubemagazine.com/sixcms/detail.php?id=15508949&articleid=art-1429001789303-71c8ac75-dcca-4664-8331-3fb42d523bb0#!/page41 (accessed July 13, 2020).

Fig. 5 Frei Otto, model of the Ökohäuser as open platforms, built-ins not yet installed, 1983

graphs of models show the urban context around Askanischer Platz with high-rise-like structures of units with generous floor space and terraces with lots of greenery, Frei Otto now had to adjust to the height of the surrounding IBA buildings and the existing trees. The new site, where the Vatican's embassy once stood, was a great architectural challenge because of the uneven topography of the terrain, the irregular form of the lot, and a dense growth of trees. Frei Otto and Hermann Kendel thus decided to design an ensemble of three multistory apartment buildings as open platforms with floors 6 to 12 meters tall (fig. 5). Because the project was realized in an effort to support the construction of social housing, all of the residential floors were nearly equal in height. Every residence consists of an open reinforced concrete skeleton with a structural core, which houses which the central building services. This gave future residents as much design freedom as possible to finish their units individually based on ecological principles.

Today, nearly forty years after the IBA, the Ökohäuser are regarded as a pioneering prototype[12] in the history of experimental housing construction and as an international icon of alternative architecture of the late twentieth century.

A FUTURE FROM THE PAST

Sibylle Bergemann, from the series *Das Denkmal* (The Monument), 1986, documentation of the building of the Marx-Engels Forum on Usedom and in Berlin, 1975–86. Here, Friedrich Engels is being lifted into his Berlin location at the Palast der Republik (Palace of the Republic).

View of the historical Nikolaiviertel in East Berlin, after destruction during the war and removal of the rubble, with the ruins of the Nikolaikirche (St. Nicholas Church) and the Kurfürstenhaus (Prince Elector's House), ca. 1980
Rebuilt Nikolaiviertel, 1987

Andreas Prüstel, *Disney-Spezial*, 1988

Celebration of the 750th anniversary in East Berlin: by combining old and new in architecture, folklore and modernity, this postcard with commemorative stamp and postcard represented the capital of the GDR, 1987.

Postcard for the 750th anniversary celebration with commemorative stamp and postmark

Aldo Rossi, new building for a German historical museum, model, ca. 1987, unbuilt

Christian Enzmann and Bernd Ettel, *Diktatur* (Dictatorship), entry to the competition Gestaltung des Geländes des ehemaligen Prinz-Albrecht-Palais (Design for the Grounds of the Former Prinz-Albrecht-Palais), concertina brochure, 1983–84, unbuilt

Daniel Libeskind, Jüdisches Museum Berlin (Jewish Museum Berlin), 1989–99, photo: Hélène Binet, 1996

189 Daniel Libeskind, Jüdisches Museum Berlin, 1989–99, photo: Hélène Binet, 1996

A HIGHLY CHARGED DECADE FOR THE POLITICS OF MEMORY

The Debate over Three Projects for Museums or Memorials in West Berlin

Antonia Wolff

"A NATIONAL TASK OF EUROPEAN RANK"

In the front city of the Cold War, the question of how architecture should refer to recent history in view of the "unchanged weight of the burdens of the architectural legacy of the Third Reich"[1] and an ongoing competition between the systems of the Federal Republic of Germany and the German Democratic Republic turned the city into the site of debates over the culture of memory.

Probably the largest and most controversial museum project of the 1980s was the Deutsches Historisches Museum (German Historical Museum). Initiated in 1981 by the Senate of West Berlin, it was intended as a countermodel to the Museum für deutsche Geschichte (Museum of German History) in the Zeughaus (Arsenal) in East Berlin, which had existed since 1952, its permanent exhibition expanded and reopened in 1981.[2] In 1985, after years of complicated discussions in Berlin, Federal Chancellor Helmut Kohl took on the project and declared:

> As a birthday gift from the Federal Republic of Germany [on the 750th anniversary of the city in 1987[3]], we want to build and furnish the Deutsches Historisches Museum in Berlin.... The project itself is a national task of European rank. [T]his is at the core of our national identity and of our national and European fate.[4]

A new building was to be erected along the Spreebogen (Bend in the Spree River), opposite the Reichstag building.[5] The project was controversial if only for the chosen site: the Kroll-Oper had once stood between the Platz der Republik and the Tiergarten, and Albert Speer's giant Halle des Volkes (Hall of the People) was supposed to be located there. Critics also feared that the engagement of the federal government would force the new institution to adopt a neoconservative interpretation of history close to that of the government and had to "ensure the lost identification of the people in our country with their government."[6] Be that as it may, in August 1987 an architectural competition was announced and on October 28—as part of a ceremony for the celebration of the 750th anniversary—the plaque for its foundation was unveiled. The Italian architect Aldo Rossi took first prize in the competition with his proposal for a "museum city"[7] (→p.186). It was to be composed of four functionally connected building volumes with designs related to various buildings important to the tradition of architecture in Berlin (fig.1). For example, Rossi planned the extension of Grosse Querallee as an allusion to Karl Friedrich Schinkel's rotunda in the Altes Museum (Old Museum), a circular entrance that can be seen from afar. Adjoining it to the west was to be an "educational building," with an auditorium, a cinema, and a theater, featuring a chamberlike structure inspired by the turbine hall that Peter Behrens had built for the Allgemeine Elektricitäts-Gesellschaft. Rossi's design for the "administrative wing" facing the street alludes to Schinkel's colonnade in front of the entrance to the Altes Museum with its columned corridors—a traditional symbol of democracy—with which the architect tried to do justice to the aim of the grounds as a whole to bolster the state. The center of Rossi's complex would have been crowned by an exhibition hall with a glass roof that was to be flanked on both sides by long rows of gabled buildings. Facing the river, it would have presented itself as a "dock" with adjacent storage buildings, whereas its street façade was intended to recall a cathedral with buildings "as in the city of the Middle Ages."[8]

The urban planning expression of the museum grounds and its connections to the organic European city won over the prize jury and the museum's founding director, Christoph Stölzl:

1 Norbert Huse, *Unbequeme Baudenkmale: Entsorgen? Schützen? Pflegen?* (Munich, 1997), p. 34.

2 Andrea Brait, "Im Kampf um die Konstruktion des 'deutschen' Geschichtsbildes," in *Asymmetrisch verflochten?: Neue Forschungen zur gesamtdeutschen Nachkriegsgeschichte*, ed. Detlev Brunner, Udo Grashoff, and Andreas Kötzing (Berlin, 2013), pp. 28–29.

3 On this, see the essay by Verena Pfeiffer-Kloss in this volume.

4 Helmut Kohl, "Bericht zur Lage der Nation," February 27, 1985, in *Deutsches Historisches Museum: Ideen, Kontroversen, Perspektive*, ed. Christoph Stölzl (Frankfurt am Main, 1988), p. 641.

5 The location was changed in 1986 because the need for space in the northwest was increasing. See Hendrik Tieben, "Aldo Rossis Auseinandersetzung mit Geschichte, Erinnerung und Identität am Beispiel des Projekts des Deutschen Historischen Museums" (PhD diss., ETH Zurich, 2005), p. 64.

6 "Warum soll die deutsche Geschichte in ein Deutsches Historisches Museum eingesperrt werden?," discussion organized by the Green Party/Alternative List Grünen/AL, April 21, 1985, in Stölzl, *Deutsches Historisches Museum* (see note 4), pp. 249–77, esp. p. 250.

7 Aldo Rossi, "The Design for the German History Museum: Excerpts from the Explanatory Report for the Competition," in Aldo Rossi: Deutsches Historisches Museum 1989, trans. Miller Stevens, exh. cat. Aedes, Galerie für Architektur (Berlin, 1989), pp. 15–17, esp. p. 17. Cf. Aldo Rossi, "Das Wettbewerbsprojekt," in *Aldo Rossis Entwurf im Gefüge der Kulturforen*, ed. Alberto Ferlenga (1991), pp. 39–56, esp. p. 41.

8 Rossi, "The Design for the German History Museum" (see note 7), p. 15.

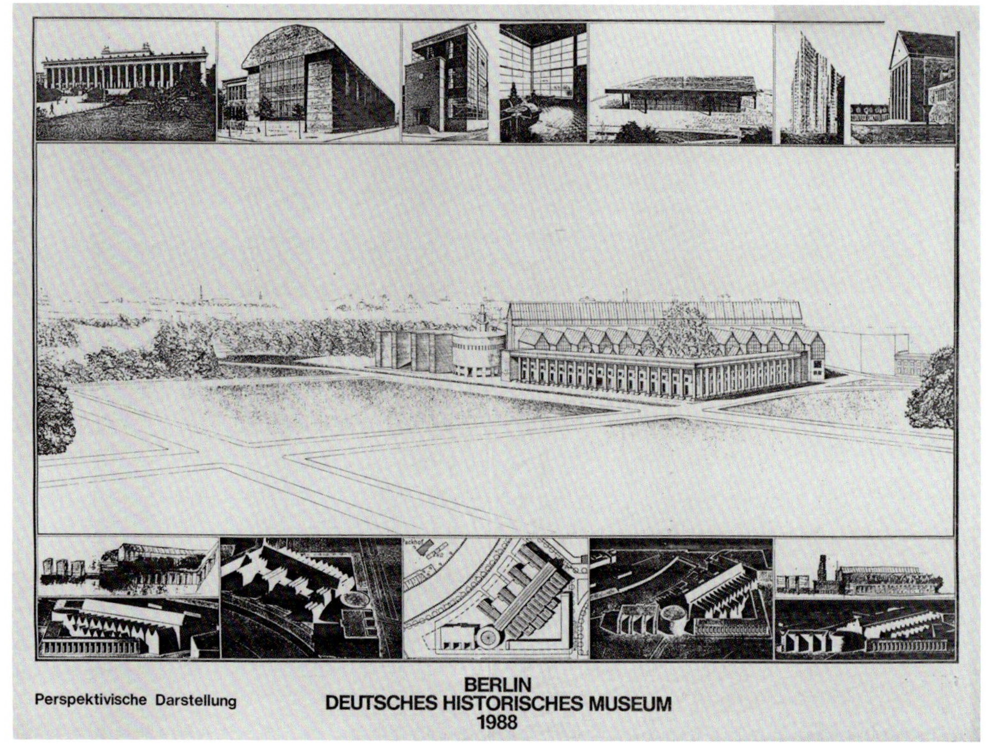

Fig. 1 Aldo Rossi, new building for a German historical museum, perspective view with reference buildings, copy, 1988

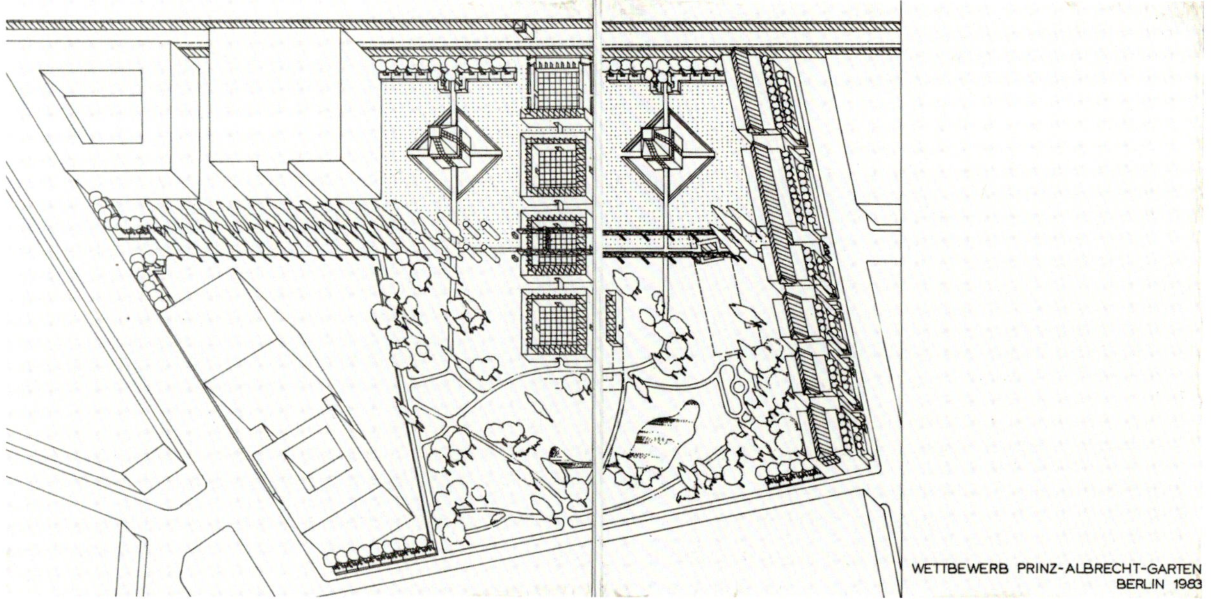

Fig. 2 Christian Enzmann and Bernd Ettel, *Diktatur* (Dictatorship), entry to the competition Gestaltung des Geländes des ehemaligen Prinz-Albrecht-Palais (Design for the Grounds of the Former Prinz-Albrecht-Palais), concertina brochure, detail, 1983–84, unbuilt

> Aldo Rossi lends convincing form to the central ideas of the museum project. With a commanding gesture, the key idea of turning to the past in an enlightened and self-confident way, while keeping out of controversies and rifts, is transformed into an architectonic image. It is an image that from the very first glance reveals itself as European.[9]

In a political tightrope walk, Rossi seems to have found for his contribution the right balance between a pluralistic image of history that is more European than national and a monumentality in support of the state. But half a year after the preliminary design was completed, the Berlin Wall fell. Now the Spreebogen was to become the government district, and in 1990 the DHM moved into the Zeughaus—to which a new building would later be added—where it replaced the Museum für Deutsche Geschichte.

A MEMORIAL FOR THE PRESENT

In 1983, the Senate of West Berlin responded to long-standing demands from engaged citizens and announced an open competition for the building of a memorial on the historically fraught site between Wilhelmstrasse, Niederkirchnerstrasse, and Kochstrasse. Until 1949, the Prinz-Albrecht-Palais had stood there, which from 1933 had been first the site of the headquarters of the Geheime Staatspolizei (Secret State Police, Gestapo) and then, from 1939, the site of the Reichssicherheitshauptamt (Reich Main Security Office). The ideas of the competition's organizers for what should be built on this site right next to the Berlin Wall ranged from a monument in a neighborhood park to a memorial site with a documentation center. The goal was to "combine harmoniously the historical profundity of the site with needs such as a park design, a playground, places for activity, and so on."[10] The vaguely defined guidelines may have been one reason that none of the designs submitted was completely convincing, and although the competition jury chose a winner, his project was never built.

The openness when setting the task for an area immediately adjacent to the border between the two Germanys inspired the East Berlin architects Bernd Ettel and Christian Enzmann to participate in the competition. Because they lacked permission from the East German Ministry of Building, however, they felt compelled to submit their contribution secretly. In the form of two handmade concertina folders (→ p. 187), they smuggled their design into West Berlin and handed it over to Ulrich Conrads, editor in chief of the architectural journal *Bauwelt*. Based solely on the topographical location next to the border, Ettel and Enzmann seem to have felt that the site for the building should be related to their idea of the present and of the past: "The grounds are located on the border, that is, not only completed history but current, unassimilated history is refracted in this place."[11] The title of their design, *Diktatur* (Dictatorship), was intended to point to a general engagement with totalitarian systems. In addition to a park, a documentation center, and two "halls of silence" meant to invite contemplation, their plan was to build a cruciform memorial in which the "chronicle of a dictatorship" was to be graphically illustrated in four phases of development (fig. 2). These stages in the development are represented by four square courtyards arranged axially on the grounds, in which staffage figures become the objects of a theatrical staging. From courtyard to courtyard, they are first walled in (Limitation) and discriminated (Selection), then separated out and destroyed (Elimination), after which the dictatorship tries to extend the sphere of its rule (Expansion).

9 Stölzl, quoted in Tieben, "Aldo Rossis Auseinandersetzung" (see note 5), p. 71.

10 Senator für Bau- und Wohnungswesen, ed., *Offener Wettbewerb Berlin, Südliche Friedrichstradt: Gestaltung des Geländes des ehemaligen Prinz-Albrecht-Palais* (Berlin, 1983), p. 25.

11 According to the explanatory report in the concertina brochure.

Fig. 3 Ernst Gisel, design for the reconstruction of and extension to the Ephraim-Palais in West Berlin, 1979, unbuilt

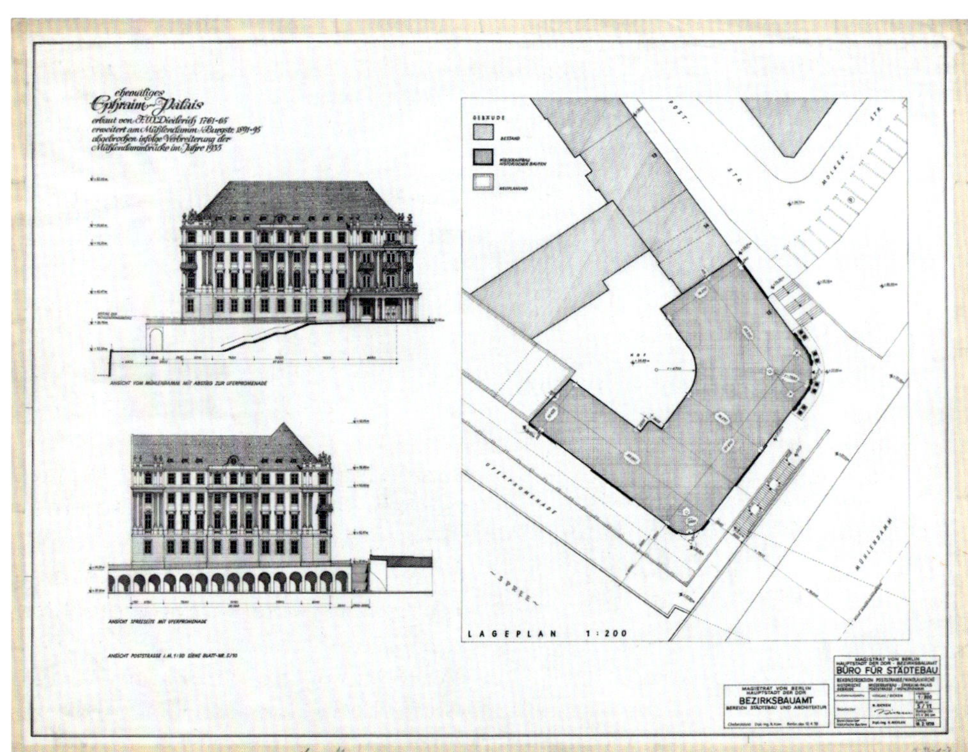

Fig. 4 Günter Stahn, Roland Korn, Heinz Mehlan, Rolf Ricken, design for the reconstruction of the Ephraim-Palais based on the historical model and using surviving construction elements, approximately 12 meters from its original location, 1978

12 Christian Enzmann and Bernd Ettel, "Diktatur," contribution to the competition Gestaltung des Geländes des ehemaligen Prinz-Albrecht-Palais, concertina brochure, 1984, BG-AS 96/2019,2.

13 "Offener Wettbewerb Gestaltung des ehemaligen Prinz-Albrecht-Palais," minutes of the meetings of the prize jury, 1984, n.p., Berlinische Galerie, BG-Hb A 3088.

14 State Secretary Karl Schmiechen to the Ministry of State Security, May 4, 1985, Stasi-Unterlagen-Archiv, MfS AU 11750-85, vol. 3.

15 Heinz Graffunder's reports, October 10, 1984, p. 6, Stasi-Unterlagen-Archiv, MfS AU 11750-85, vol. 9.

16 Criminal files, Stasi-Unterlagen-Archiv, MfS AU 11750-85, vol. 10. See also Bernd Ettel, "Internationales Dokumentations- und Begegnungszentrum Topographie des Terrors: Ein Entwurf aus Ost-Berlin und seine Folgen," in *Stadtentwicklung im doppelten Berlin: Zeitgenossenschaften und Erinnerungsorte*, ed. Günter Schlusche, Verena Pfeiffer-Kloss, and Gabi Dolff-Bonekämper (Berlin, 2014), pp. 130–35, esp. p. 134.

17 Florian von Buttlar and Stefanie Endlich, "Der Wettbewerb," in *Der umschwiegene Ort*, ed. Sabine Weissler and Neue Gesellschaft für Bildende Kunst (NGBK) (Berlin, 1986), pp. 39–48, esp. p. 42.

18 Sabine Weissler, "Der 5. Mai 1985 in Bitburg und Kreuzberg: Zwei sehr verschiedene Arten, die Vergangenheit zu nutzen," in Weissler and NGBK, *Der umschwiegene Ort* (see note 17), pp. 56–64, esp. pp. 57–58.

19 Irmgard Wirth, "Zur Wiedererrichtung des Ephraim-Palais" (1975), in *Das Jüdische Museum im Stadtmuseum Berlin: Eine Dokumentation*, ed. Martina Weinland and Kurt Winkler (Berlin, 1997), p. 99.

20 Dieter Hoffmann-Axthelm, "Architektur als Geschichtsfälschung: Zur geplanten Neuerrichtung des Ephraim-Palais," *Arch+* 11, nos. 43–44 (1979), pp. 11–14, esp. p. 13.

Because the architects wanted to integrate a piece of the actual wall into the building of their first courtyard, Limitation, their design suggested a reading critical of the German Democratic Republic (GDR). In this reading, the GDR could be understood as a dictatorship and the border grounds as its historical beginning—an interpretation also suggested by the explanatory text: "Beginning at the border, the chronic of a dictatorship is constructed."[12] It is not certain whether this clear allusion to the contemporaneous situation in the GDR contributed to the prize jury eliminating this contribution in the third round.[13] The East Berlin authorities, in any case, understood the image of history sketched by Ettel and Enzmann as criticism of their regime and concluded that "the design of the subject matter ... in terms of the identification of the term 'dictatorship' with border security facilities is apt to harm the interests of the GDR."[14] In a jury report, Heinz Graffunder described the entry as "lacking political instincts, as detrimental in its solution to the reputation and humanitarian concerns of our republic."[15] In June 1985, Ettel and Enzmann were sentenced to two years and two years and nine months, respectively, in prison "for public degradation, i.a."[16]

For West Berlin, the competition did not ultimately result in a building. The prizewinning design by Jürgen Wenzel and Nikolaus Lang, which involved plastering the grounds with cast-iron reliefs of documents, was never realized.[17] Sealing the ground also precisely contradicted symbolically the request of the Aktives Museum Faschismus und Widerstand in Berlin e. V. (Active Museum of Fascism and Resistance in Berlin) that the history of the site be studied in excavations.[18] In 1986, this idea finally got a hearing, and as a result the remnants of the walls of the Gestapo's former torture chambers were uncovered. In 1987, the *Topography of Terror* exhibition was organized, originally with the idea of being only temporary, but it evolved into the documentation center with a permanent exhibition that opened in 2010.

CONTINUITY OR RUPTURE? SPATIALIZATIONS OF JEWISH HISTORY IN BERLIN

Nearly contemporaneously with the first efforts to create a memorial site on the former Gestapo grounds, there were discussions in West Berlin about reconstructing the Ephraim-Palais, which had been demolished in 1936 (fig. 3). Since the end of the war, the parts from its façade had been in storage in the western part of the city, even though the building had stood on Mühlendamm in the city's historical center, which at the time belonged to East Berlin. By reconstructing the magnificent Baroque building, which had been renovated by the Jewish mint master Veitel Heine Ephraim from 1762 onward, the Senate hoped to find a suitable place for a Judaica collection that was being reestablished. From the outset, the project flourished under the flag of "making amends."[19]

Funding difficulties, discussions of locational factors, and public debates over whether the project made sense in terms of historical preservation delayed planning. Dieter Hoffmann-Axthelm criticized the planned reconstruction of the Ephraim-Palais on Lindenstrasse as an act of "historical forgery" and diagnosed a repression mechanism: "[W]e are building the Ephraim-Palais, which belongs somewhere else entirely, here, because we want to forget the Prinz-Albrecht-Palais."[20] Under pressure from the press, Berlin's Senate and Parliament rejected the reconstruction plan in 1982 and handed over the parts of the façade to the Magistrat (City Council) of East Berlin in 1983 after the latter had announced its desire to reconstruct the Ephraim-Palais near its original location in the Nikolaiviertel and open

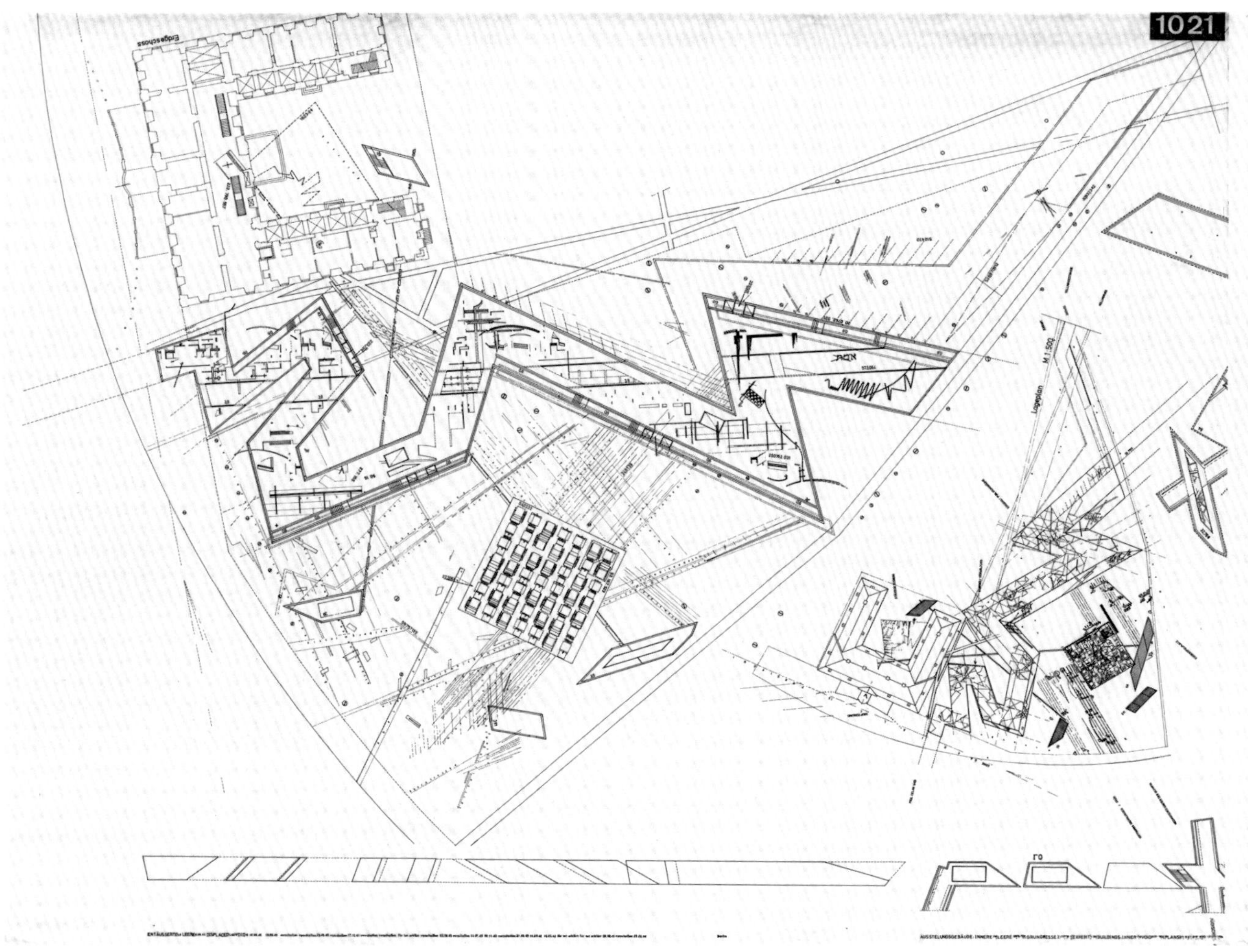

Fig. 5 Daniel Libeskind, Jüdisches Museum (Jewish Museum), site plan and floor plan, 1989–99

21 Weinland and Winkler, *Das Jüdische Museum im Stadtmuseum Berlin* (see note 19), p. 19.

22 Ibid., p. 36.

23 Daniel Libeskind, "Between the Lines," in *Erweiterung des Berlin Museums mit Abteilung Jüdisches Museum*, ed. Kristin Feireiss (Berlin, 1992), pp. 57–61, esp. p. 58.

24 Ibid., p. 61.

25 Wolfgang Schäche, quoted in Weinland and Winkler, *Das Jüdische Museum im Stadtmuseum Berlin* (see note 19), pp. 41–42.

it for the celebration of Berlin's 750th anniversary (fig. 4).[21] In the course of ideological rivalry—East Berlin was also planning to rebuild the Neue Synagoge (New Synagogue) on Oranienburger Strasse as the site for a Jewish museum to be opened on the fiftieth anniversary of the night of the November Pogrom—the establishment of a Jewish department in the Stadtmuseum (Municipal Museum) of West Berlin seemed increasingly urgent. In 1988, those ideas expanded into the planning for the "Berlin Museum—Jewish Museum";[22] that same year, a competition for a new building was announced.

The design by the American architect Daniel Libeskind took the first prize. It formed the basis for the building of the Jüdisches Museum (Jewish Museum), which opened on September 9, 2001, as an institution independent of the Stadtmuseum. The succinct floor plan of his building (fig. 5) is based on an "invisible matrix," which connects the former residences of Jewish and non-Jewish citizens of Berlin: Rahel Varnhagen von Ense, Ludwig Mies van der Rohe, Heinrich von Kleist, Heinrich Heine, and several others.[23] In this way, Libeskind was inscribing the interwovenness of Jewish life and German culture into the floor plan in a graphic way. Cutting through the zigzagging figure of the building volume is a straight line that results from a series of "voids": concrete shafts that cannot be entered and that bore through the entire height of the building (→ p. 188). The "voids" were supposed to make visible and accessible the absence of Jewish life in the city.[24]

Instead of making the sections on the history of the city and on Jewish history areas that could potentially be entered separately, Libeskind bound them inseparably together, but in doing so the void marked the deep rift in the history of the city and of the entire nation that the National Socialist genocide of the Jews of Europe had torn open. This was a reinterpretation of the brief for the planning that persuaded the prize jury.

> Against the backdrop of an inseparable Berlin and Jewish history, his museum design thus reveals the structural spatialization of this interwoven and linked historical process with all its commonalities and contradictions, approaching and distancing, leading up to the terrifying, unforgettable catastrophe.[25]

Just how radical this interpretation of history was against the background of the debates in the 1980s on museum buildings and memorials becomes especially clear if one recalls the initial history of the Jewish museum in the Ephraim-Palais. The reconstruction of the Baroque building as a place to house the Judaica collection would have built a bridge across the entire twentieth century to an era of fruitful Jewish-Berlin culture and thus suggested a continuity with which Libeskind's architecture decisively breaks. At the end of a decade highly charged with the politics of memory, West Berlin thus received a design for a building that takes into account the inner conflicts of German history.

CELEBRATION AND COUNTER-CELEBRATION

Architectural and Political Competition for the 750th Anniversary in Divided Berlin

Verena Pfeiffer-Kloss

1 Ulrich Eckhardt, ed., *750 Jahre Berlin, Stadt der Gegenwart: Lese- und Programmbuch zum Stadtjubiläum* (Berlin, 1986), p. 15.

2 Erich Honecker at the founding session of the committee; see Komitee der Deutschen Demokratischen Republik zum 750jährigen Bestehen von Berlin, ed., *750 Jahre Berlin: Das Buch zum Fest* (Berlin, 1986), pp. 10–11.

3 See Wilfried Rott, *Die Insel: Eine Geschichte West-Berlins, 1948–1990* (Munich, 2009), p. 294.

Fig. 1 Miners' band from the industrial center Karl-Marx-Stadt in the historical parade for the celebration of the 750-anniversary in East Berlin, capital of the GDR, July 4, 1987

The 750th birthday of Berlin fell in the year 1987, and the festivities were a task of political relevance that would have an effect far beyond the city. "We want," wrote Eberhard Diepgen, the governing mayor of West Berlin, in 1986, "the 750th anniversary celebration to become a historical event of its own. We are celebrating, proudly and reflectively. But that is not enough. Out of remembrance at the 750th-anniversary celebration should grow energy for the future—even beyond Berlin." The goal was to "discover the new in the old" and, "despite the wall and separation, work on the opportunities for unity."[1]

The celebration took place in both halves of the city, each with its own program, and thus became an expression of the competitions of the systems of East and West: "May the citizens of our capital and, by their side, the builders from the entire republic contribute with their exemplary contributions to Berlin continuing to flourish in the way we already experience now day after day. May the city's anniversary contribute to the further strengthening of socialism and hence to peace."[2] These words were spoken by Erich Honecker, chairman of the State Council of the German Democratic Republic (GDR), in 1986 at the founding meeting of the East Berlin festival committee, thus elevating the celebration to the rank of a state event to which all regions of the GDR were to contribute (fig. 1).

The objectives were thus set high politically on both sides, yet could at the same time not be more opposed: the manifestation of division in the East was opposed to the idea of unity in the West. There was, however, one important commonality between East and West Berlin that further enflamed the competition over the more impressive festival program: around 1980, when planning began, both Berlins found themselves in an image crisis. Both were economically weak, had lost the attention of international politics, and were searching for new guidelines for establishing identity for an increasingly dissatisfied population that in the West was even emigrating.[3] The 750th-year celebration gave politicians the opportunity to present fresh images of the city, of which both sides took advantage.

4 Akademie der Künste, Berlin, Baukunstarchiv, A 159 GV / 87: Hans Stimmann, "Vermerk 750-Jahr-Feier Ost-Berlin," December 5, 1984, p. 8.

5 Krijn Thijs, "Politische Feierkonkurrenz im Jahre 1987: Die doppelte 750-Jahr-Feier in Ost- und West-Berlin," *Revue d'Allemagne et des pays de langue allemande* 49, no. 1 (2017), p. 78, published online on June 16, 2018, https://doi.org/10.4000/allemagne.523 (accessed July 28, 2020).

6 Akademie der Künste (AdK), Berlin, Baukunstarchiv, A 159 GV / 87: Mythos Berlin Ausstellung GmbH, "Mythos Berlin: Wahrnehmungsgeschichte einer Metropole," manuscript, March 1985, p. 4.

7 On the construction projects in the Nikolaiviertel and on Friedrichstrasse and Gendarmenmarkt, see the essays by Florian Urban and Wolfgang Kil in this volume.

8 See the files of the Scientific Collections of the Leibniz Institute for Research on Society and Space (IRS), Bauausstellung der DDR.

9 *750 Jahre Berlin: Das Buch zum Fest* (see note 2), p. 78.

10 On the construction of the history of the city of Berlin as part of preparations for the anniversary, see Krijn Thijs, *Drei Geschichten, eine Stadt: Die Berliner Stadtjubiläen von 1937 und 1987*, ed. Zentrum für Zeithistorische Forschung Potsdam, vol. 49: *Zeithistorische Studien* (Cologne, 2008), p. 253.

11 See Felix Richter, *Das Neue Hoyerswerda: Ideenhaushalt, Aufbau und Diskurs der zweiten sozialistischen Stadt der DDR* (Berlin, 2020), p. 334.

12 Thijs, *Drei Geschichten, eine Stadt* (see note 10), p. 180.

13 Ibid.

14 Ibid., pp. 193–94.

15 See Thijs, "Politische Feierkonkurrenz im Jahre 1987" (see note 5), p. 77.

16 Martin Warnke, "Bau und Gegenbau," in *Architektur als politische Kultur: Philosophia Practica*, ed. Hermann Hipp and Ernst Seidl (Berlin, 1996), pp. 11–18, esp. p. 17.

POLITICAL COMPETITION AND GEOPOLITICAL ADVANTAGE

The West Berlin organizers initially tried to approach the anniversary together with East Berlin. This was also indebted to the fact that the city's historical core lay in its eastern part, and West Berlin was comparatively without a history for that reason alone. Those responsible for the festival in East Berlin used this geographic situation to their political advantage. From the outset, they categorically rejected a joint celebration and self-confidently set the tone for the festival planning (fig. 2).

West Berlin was on the defensive and felt compelled with its program "to prevent an upside-down world: 'Glamour in the otherwise gray East, tristesse in the otherwise so radiant west'."[4] Accordingly, the planners of the B-750 team did not by any means want a "celebration by decree … with military pomp,"[5] as was planned in East Berlin, with parades, state ceremonies, processions, and bugle calls. Moreover, they felt a need to distance themselves from the kinds of celebrations for the 700th anniversary that had been held fifty years earlier in National Socialist Berlin. However, those responsible in the GDR did not feel the pressure to distinguish themselves from the celebration of 1937. Concerned primarily with continuing the socialist version of its own history, East Germany proposed a program of state policy and thus forced the Western part of the city to demonstrate as well its relevance to international politics with events such as visits from Ronald Reagan and Queen Elizabeth II and a musical parade of Western allies.

COMPETING ARCHITECTURE EXHIBITIONS: A PAST FOR OUR PRESENT

In addition to political events, the central components of both 750th anniversary celebrations included building exhibitions, historical architecture exhibitions, and the opening of large-scale construction projects. They demonstrated paradigmatically the goal of providing the present, with the aid of the past, a historical confirmation and at the same time a new identity for both halves of Berlin—with each also independent of that of the other side.

Using architecture and urban planning to express the competition between the systems of East and West was not new, even at the time. Showing off contemporary architecture had been a visible means of expressing this competition since the 1950s. In the early postwar period, the measuring stick was primarily quantitative and technically outstanding achievements in building—one need only think of the pairs of antitheses that Martin Warnke called "Bau und Gegenbau" (construction and counter-construction), such as Karl-Marx-Allee versus the Hansaviertel, the television tower versus the Springer high-rise, the Palast der Republik versus the International Congress Centre (ICC), or the large-scale housing developments on each side. In comparison to this, however, both halves of the city tried in the 1980s to outdo the other by displaying a more convincing architectural connection between the present and the past. It centered on the question of which side was telling the "true" story of Berlin—in other words, which present was derived more consequently from the past. The architectural exhibitions and 750th-anniversary celebration were mutually fruitful here.

The most important architectural event of the celebration in West Berlin was the Internationale Bauausstellung 1987 (International Architecture Exhibition, IBA), which had been planned since 1975 as a response to urban planning problems and later integrated into the anniversary program. Under the slogan "Kaputte Stadt retten" (Saving the Broken City), old buildings in

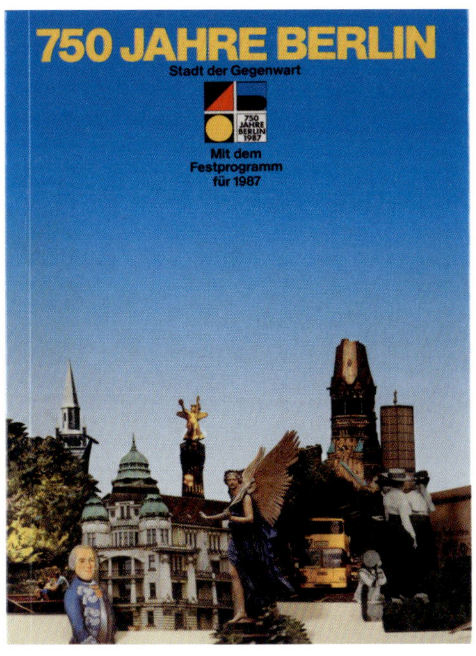

Fig. 2 The two programs for the 750th-anniversary celebration. Top: East Berlin; bottom: West Berlin

residential neighborhoods from the late-nineteenth-century Gründerzeit in Wedding and Kreuzberg were renovated (IBA-Alt or IBA Old Buildings); under the guideline of "Kritische Rekonstruktion" (Critical Reconstruction), internationally renowned architects designed projects for new buildings in Tegel and the southern Friedrichstadt (IBA-Neu or IBA New Buildings). One of the basic ideas behind this was founded on the Gründerzeit layout and elevation view of the city, which was now considered the epitome of urbanity and characteristic of Berlin. The same semantic connection was proposed by the central exhibition for the celebration in West-Berlin, *Berlin, Berlin* at the Martin-Gropius-Bau, which focused on the "interior and exterior urbanization" of the late nineteenth century, and hence on the "development of the cosmopolitan person exemplified by the Berliner."[6] The urban planning of this era and the associated urban sense of life became West Berlin's answer to the critique of the monotony of modernism and its search for a new image that would offer its citizens opportunities to identify with it. At the same time, however, this focus also created the impression that on the level of urban policy it had been accepted that the historical center was unreachably located on the other side of the Berlin Wall.

In East Berlin, architects and urban planners were trying for their part to offer a response to contemporaneous criticism of construction practices in the GDR. The historicizing new buildings of the Nikolaiviertel, the Gendarmenmarkt, and on Friedrichstrasse are examples to counter the reproach that industrial methods of construction could only produce faceless and lifeless urban neighborhoods.[7] The *Bauausstellung der DDR* (GDR Building Exhibition),[8] which took place from May 18 to August 31, 1987, on the grounds of the Dynamo-Sporthalle in Hohenschönhausen, was dedicated to current building activity. With more than 500,000 visitors over three months, it was the largest and most successful building exhibition in the GDR, and it also attracted international attention. Under the title "Bauen zum Wohl des Volkes" (Building to Benefit the People), current architectural achievements were presented in the form of exemplary new construction projects and modernizations (fig. 3). The central exhibition was a model glass apartment featuring the floor plan and furnishing program of industrial, mass-produced housing construction and hence also the country's current design practice. The new connection between the past and the socialist, industrial, and modern present was demonstrated by exhibits on the exterior grounds. A number of diverse prefabricated concrete-slab elements, some of which featured historicizing decoration and plaster variations ranging from functionalism to classicistic borrowings, were intended to demonstrate the possibilities for combining architectural traditions and industrial construction methods (fig. 4). In addition, and specifically related to Berlin, the exhibition *Unser Berlin* (Our Berlin) at the events center below the television tower showed models, plans, photographs, and drawings of "important building works and urban planning ensembles that have been created in Berlin since the founding of the GDR or are planned by 1990."[9] The program was intended to support the historical interpretation that the evolution of Berlin as the capital of the GDR should be seen as the high point of the history of the city of Berlin after centuries marked by capitalism.[10]

Both building exhibitions in East Berlin thus reduced the history of urban planning to the present day. The new buildings constructed in the historical center at the time had borrowings from the decoration of past decades, while at the same time making it unmistakably clear by whose hand and in what era they were made. These buildings, first, showed how little of the original building fabric still existed in the original core of Berlin and, moreover, overshadowed it. At the crucial historical festive procession on July 4, 1987, old and new fused into a backdrop for the presentation of the socialist

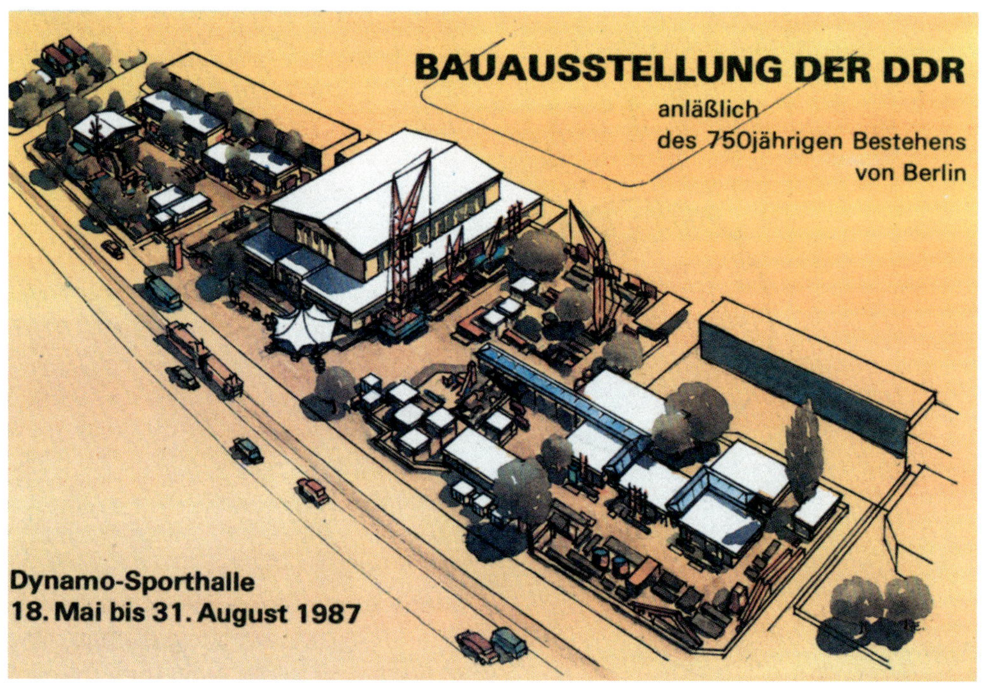

Fig. 3 Postcard for the *Bauausstellung der DDR* (Building Exhibition of the GDR) showing the exhibition grounds

Fig. 4 Prefabricated concrete-slab module with clinker and stucco on the outdoor grounds of the *Bauausstellung der DDR* (Building Exhibition of the GDR)

Fig. 5 Citizens' protest on Kurfürstendamm in front of the work *Randale* (Rampage) by Olaf Metzel, which had been created for the boulevard of sculptures, April 28, 1987

present and its derivation from the past (→ p.184). The area at the heart of historical Berlin, which the eastern part of the city had over the western part, served as an urban projection screen for the past, present, and future, which it had already been for centuries and continues to be today.

After all, the slogan of the celebration of West Berlin as the "Stadt der Gegenwart" (City of the Present) was true of both halves of Berlin. Here and there, one can observe a fragmentation of the past,[11] in a effort to make the history of the city the foundation of the present, in order to be able to build out of stories and images. The desired image of the present and the past that both cities were outlining in this way was, however, transparently an image campaign and hence quickly reached the limits of credibility and viability for the future.

PROTEST AT THE PARTY

The 750th-anniversary celebration in both parts of Berlin did not achieve without limitations its declared goals of making residents more satisfied with their living situation in a divided city and of reinforcing the formation of a city identity for outsiders. In the Federal Republic of Germany, the "upgrading of both halves of the city" was regarded "increasingly with mockery."[12] The press mercilessly shared the view that West Berlin "no longer had a proper function and tried to hide that with pure self-promotion."[13] In the city itself, there were protests, by everyone ranging from various citizens' action groups to "autonomous" groups (i.e., radical leftists and anarchists), against the high costs and enormous scope of the celebrations, which by the end of the summer of 1987 were even regarded by the Senate for Culture as having "grown too large" (fig. 5).[14] Clearly, many West-Berliners no longer recognized themselves or the actual situation of the city in the official program for the celebrations.

On the other side of the wall, the celebration did not improve the connection of GDR citizens to their capital. It even led to extraordinary protests on the part of the population and of regional governments, because extensive funding and large quantities of construction material were flowing to the capital. Cars in the outskirts of Berlin damaged and spray-painted with the slogan "Ärsche 750" (Asses 750), stickers with "821 Jahre Leipzig" (821 Years of Leipzig) and "781 Jahre Dresden," and trucks delivering construction materials marked "1026 Jahre Halle" all revealed the anger of other regions of the GDR. Money and materials were scarce there, and the historical building fabric was decaying,[15] while in Berlin there was an elaborate effort to construct a historical cityscape. The unmistakably artificial character of the latter met with skepticism in the capital as well: for example, it inspired the East Berlin artist Andreas Prüstel to create a daring collage of the Nikolaiviertel and Mickey Mouse (→ p.183).

The promise for the future that politicians associated with the anniversary was not fulfilled either. On the contrary. In celebrating two separate festivals, the city politics on both sides of the wall merely translated the familiar pair of "building and counter-building"[16] into the form "festivities and counter-festivities" and thus codified the status quo of the divided city, rather than offering a vision for the future. That is perhaps also the source of the bitter aftertaste for its citizens. Be that as it may, in 1989, two years later, Berliners from East and West celebrated together the end of the competition of systems.

ARCHITECTURE IN FILM AND ART

BERLIN CITYSCAPES IN FILMS FROM THE 1980s

Der Himmel über Berlin
Wim Wenders

Der *Himmel über Berlin* (released in English as *Wings of Desire*) is a partial historical document of Berlin cityscapes of the 1980s. Enormous vacant lots, empty expanses around the formerly central Potsdamer Platz, and the Berlin Wall create the backdrop of probably the most famous film about Berlin from the period just before the fall of the Berlin Wall.

Wim Wenders
Der Himmel über Berlin (Wings of Desire)
FRG/France, 1986–87
128'
Wim Wenders Stiftung – Argos Films

Stadtbild
Harun Farocki

Based on photographs of architecture and featuring conversations with photographers and architectural historians, Harun Farocki's *Stadtbild* (Cityscape) studies how the relationship to old and new architecture changed over the course of the postwar decades. The film's central reference point is the book *Die gemordete Stadt* (The Murdered City) by Elisabeth Niggemeyer and Wolf Jobst Siedler (1964). Like the book, Farocki's film also argues by means of images.

Harun Farocki
Stadtbild (Cityscape)
FRG, 1981
44'
Harun Farocki GbR

Insel der Schwäne
Herrmann Zschoche

Fourteen-year-old Stefan moves from a suburban idyll to the large housing development of Marzahn in northeast Berlin. Unfinished playgrounds and permanent construction pits characterize his new surroundings. Stefan gets into a conflict with an older student that escalates dangerously in the elevator shaft of a high-rise. The depicted hopelessness and dilapidation of the concrete-slab buildings were interpreted by GDR authorities as an open criticism of their housing construction policy.

Herrmann Zschoche
Insel der Schwäne (Island of Swans)
GDR, 1982–83
88'
DEFA-Stiftung

Die Architekten
Peter Kahane

East Berlin: a young architect and his collective are commissioned to design a culture center for a satellite city. Full of ambition, the group takes up its work, but their hopes soon turn to resignation. The film is a picture of failed architecture policy and a swansong to the GDR, which collapsed as it was still being shot. The model for *Die Architekten* (released in English as *The Architects*) was the Marzahner Promenade construction project that Michael Kny and Thomas Weber designed in the early 1980s in the collective of Wolf Rüdiger Eisentraut.

Peter Kahane
Die Architekten (The Architects)
GDR, 1989–90
102'
DEFA-Filmverleih/Deutsche Kinemathek

Cycling the Frame
Cynthia Beatt

In 1988, the filmmaker Cynthia Beatt followed the young Tilda Swinton on a bicycle tour of the island city of West Berlin, along the Berlin Wall. In the film, the actress rides her bicycle through green suburban idylls and gray concrete wastelands, always looking over to the eastern part of the city. *Cycling the Frame*: the title probably refers both to the film frame and to the "frame" of the city, the Berlin Wall, which seems like a strange foreign object to the British woman.

Cynthia Beatt
Cycling the Frame
FRG, 1988
27'
rbb Rundfunk Berlin-Brandenburg

TIMES ARE HARD BUT POSTMODERN

Artistic Installations by Isa Melsheimer

Isa Melsheimer, *Times Are Hard but Postmodern (Curtain),* 2013, fabric, yarn / *Tea and Coffee Piazza d'Italia in Post-Katrina Times,* 2013, fiber-reinforced concrete, ceramic

Isa Melsheimer, *Umlauftank* (Circulation Tank), 2012, reinforced concrete, houseplants, gouache on paper

Isa Melsheimer, *Stirling,* 2012, reinforced concrete

Isa Melsheimer, *Ungers,* 2012, reinforced concrete, houseplants

217 Isa Melsheimer, *Frei Otto / Westliches Haus,* 2012, reinforced concrete, lava vases

“AND WHAT’S IT LIKE LIVING HERE?”

On Living in Berlin Housing of the 1980s

Philine Schneider (Guerilla Architects)

At Guerilla Architects we work at the intersection of art and architecture, research and performance. We are a multidisciplinary collective and have set ourselves the task of researching and revealing the gray zones, resources, and hidden potential of (urban) spaces. The exhibition *Anything Goes? Berlin Architecture in the 1980s* offers us an opportunity to investigate the ideas of selected buildings of that period from the perspective of their residents. We are interested in their personal stories, in their perceptions of both the positive qualities and the weaknesses of the spaces; the changes they have experienced in their living surroundings, and what they imagine the future of their home to be.

Together with the photographer Phil Dera and armed with an audio recorder, we scattered out into the city, posted notices on doors, and spoke to people directly. We met them in playgrounds and on terraces, in parking lots and gardens, and we let them guide us around places that have a very special meaning to them.

Our expedition through the city took us to the following buildings: the LiMa residential court at Lindenstrasse 81–84 and Markgrafenstrasse 5–8 in Kreuzberg; the low-energy houses at Lützowufer 1–5 in the Tiergarten; the apartment buildings at Fraenkelufer 26/50 in Kreuzberg; the Spitteleck at Seydelstrasse 29–37 and Wallstrasse 1–8 in Mitte; and the Ernst-Thälmann-Park housing development on Greifswalder Strasse, Ella-Kay-Strasse 4/52, Lilli-Henoch-Strasse 1–20, and Danziger Strasse 105/109 in Prenzlauer Berg.

By processing the material that we collected on our visits, a contribution to the exhibition is being produced. The goal is to create a dynamic archive that will grow and evolve during the exhibition as visitors add material in regular workshops.

Spitteleck, view from Leipziger Strasse

Wohnhof LiMa (LiMa Residential Court), view of the courtyard façade

Wohnhof LiMa, view of the terrace

LIMA RESIDENTIAL COURT IN KREUZBERG

The client competition for the LiMa residential court at the time set the task that the future users participate in the interior design and management.[1] Fluid transitions between the private and public areas were meant to connect the urban space to the housing units. We discover an ensemble of large windows, terraces, stairs, and towers around a semicircular, communal, green courtyard; a manageable whole that is nevertheless also protected from prying eyes. During one meeting, the resident Gabriella Sarges talks about the initial phase of the building: “Back then, it was the first building by the Selbstbaugenossenschaft (Self-Construction Cooperative). Because they were building themselves, they also formed a community—that really played a role. They had different competencies and would exchange views. And they worked together, and some of them even fell in love.... Many people only ever moved away because they had separated.” We were informed about changes in ownership, planned renovations,[2] and changes related to the rights of neighbors to have a say about the use and self-management of common spaces. “We were allowed to decide who moves in here. That was stipulated in the rental agreements.... Also about [the use of] the 400-square-meter common room.... That’s no longer the case today.” She also told us about her favorite places: “This place is especially comfy.” She points to the sofa in front of the corner windows. “People come in here, and they relax—you can see it. This corner, this vestibule—you go through this passageway, and then you are home.” One special quality of the LiMa residential court is the many communal terraces, which can also be accessed freely from outside via open and permeable stairwells. This brings the outdoors right up to the

1 Eva Koch, "Wohnhof LiMa," http://f-iba.de/wohnhof-lima (all URLs accessed July 17, 2020).

2 Christoph Gunsser, "… in die Jahre gekommen: Wohnhof LiMa," https://www.db-bauzeitung.de/db-themen/db-archiv/wohnhof-lima.

3 Landesdenkmalamt Berlin, Siedlung Ernst-Thälmann-Park, www.stadtentwicklung.berlin.de/denkmal/liste_karte_datenbank/de/denkmaldatenbank/daobj.php?obj_dok_nr=09030002.

4 On this, see the essay by Andreas Butter, Julia Wigger, and Kathrin Meissner in this volume.

5 "Ernst-Thälmann-Park: Stadtumbau Massnahme 'Ausstattung mit Spiel- und Bewegungsangeboten,'" https://mein.berlin.de/projects/ernst-thalmann-park-stadtumbau-massnahme-ausstattu.

6 Anne Funk and Dirk Kaden, "Energiesparhäuser am Landwehrkanal," http://f-iba.de/energiesparhaeuser-am-landwehrkanal.

Ernst-Thälmann-Park housing development, view from the window

apartment doors. "People are always moving within this sphere of half-private, half-public. You can see everything in the court. There is social control, but at the same time the people are very relaxed." In order to protect the legacy of the building complex for the long term, Gabriella Sarges founded, together with several other residents, a neighborhood initiative which filed an application for monument protection this year. "We are a special house, and everyone should know that."

ERNST-THÄLMANN-PARK HOUSING DEVELOPMENT IN PRENZLAUER BERG

We meet Gabi Lehr and Andrea Sturm at the Ernst-Thälmann-Park housing development, which was listed on the historical register in 2014.[3] The ensemble for 4,000 residents is embedded in a park landscape that houses social and cultural institutions. At the same time, it is not far from Alexanderplatz, the former center of East Berlin, the capital of the GDR. The two women tell us: "The bookstore, the greengrocer—all the stores were here…. A butcher, and behind it was a store for dairy products. Then there was a grocery store. Later there was a Schlecker [drugstore]. Then there was a restaurant…. The workshops, the theater, the gallery. Basically, you had your whole cosmos here." The former gasometer on the grounds had to give way to the new buildings.[4] "That was symbolic, of course, demolishing the old and dirty and placing something here with a landscape and infrastructure for workers." In the GDR, the apartments were assigned to the residents. Gabi Lehr, one of the original residents, recalls: "We were very, very proud and very, very pleased that we got this apartment. It was like the grand prize in the lottery…. In GDR days, it was a privilege to live here." Gabi Lehr can also tell of the social composition of the residents: "It was really a very good mix living together here: the saleswoman, the former policeman, professors alongside workers. Because there were one-, two-, three-, and four-room apartments on every floor, you could check in on grandma in her one-room apartment."

The planning of the redesign of the grounds has been underway since 2017, with opportunities from the city for participation, such as neighborhood walks, park tours for children and teenagers, an online forum, and public workshops.[5] The two women feel comfortable here in the complex. Andrea Sturm, who has been living here for twenty-two years, tells us an anecdote from the neighborhood: "Erich Honecker was standing at our front door once and called out to someone from the building: 'And what's it like living here?'—'Yeah, thanks, Mr. Honecker, everything's great!'"

LOW-ENERGY HOUSES IN THE TIERGARTEN

On the grounds of the low-energy houses on Lützowufer, as children play, we talk to Vanessa Schulz, Nicholas Wenzel, and Winfried Walter about living in the buildings that served planners as a research field for low-energy buildings.[6] The concepts from back then hardly play a role any longer for the residents today. "There is a pleasant climate in terms of the space …, but in the winter it gets quite cool. I have a wall heater that I can adjust, and that wall is always warm," says Vanessa Schulz. Nicholas Wenzel states: "Often you forget that you are already heating." The buildings are spatially connected largely via the design of the shared outdoor space. "In the garden, children in particular gather. People know each other, but you have to walk around the building to get in here," Vanessa Schulz explains. Nicholas Wenzel says: "It's a little tricky to get back here…. It's not that intuitive."

He talks about the qualities of the apartments facing north and south: "There is a front and a back area, which you can separate very well. And this winter garden feels like two rooms…. It gives me the feeling that there are quite a number of different rooms, even though there aren't." Because of its immediate proximity to a planned building project, which included an intervention in the planted outdoor grounds, the residents formed a neighborhood group two years ago to prevent construction that is too dense. They all see the distance from other buildings and the outdoor greenery as contributing to the quality of the ensemble. "It is incredibly bright with the windows extending down to the floors, even back here, this calm, the birds," says Vanessa Schulz. And Nicholas Wenzel adds: "I especially appreciate the human-animal relationship here, for example these squirrels—we have an emotional connection to them. There is a beautiful tree standing in front of the winter garden, and two squirrels keep climbing it—like lovers. At some point, they were joined by a third one, and we were pleased. That is in part because there is so much vegetation here." Winfried Walter sums it up: "I love this apartment. We sit at the table and look toward the Landwehrkanal, and we have this south-facing winter garden. It's a beautiful building."

The meetings with the residents have left us full of impressions. All of them have developed intense connections to their living environments that go beyond the planning aspects of the buildings. The users have made the architectural features their own. These valuable personal experiences can contribute to the debate about possible architectures for the future.

Low-energy houses at the Landwehrkanal

Low-energy houses, view of the balcony and front yard

Locations of the Buildings Depicted in the Catalogue

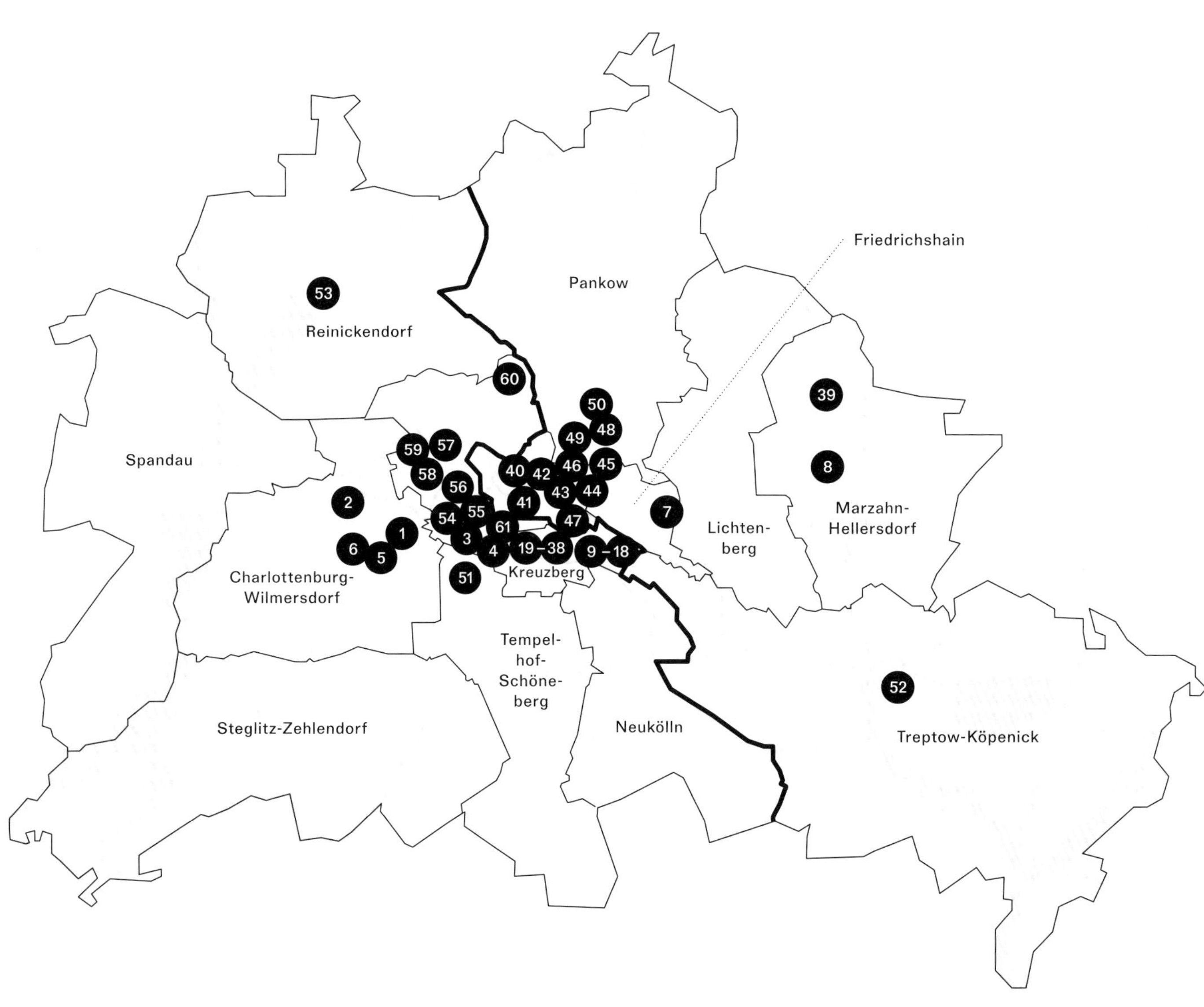

Among the digital programs on the homepage of the Berlinische Galerie, you will find audio tours which guide you to selected buildings in Berlin from the 1980s.

1 von Werder/Pompinon/Bayersdorff, residential building, Herderstrasse 16 →p.22

2 Hämer, redevelopment, Nehringstrasse 30 →p.25

3 Ungers, residential building, Lützowplatz (demolished) →p.39

4 Gregotti, gate house, Lützowstrasse 43–51 →p.116

5 Jahn, Victoria City Areal (unbuilt), Kurfürstendamm →p.124

6 Hadid, office building (unbuilt), Kurfürstendamm →p.140

7 Ettel/Enzmann, Bersarinplatz (unbuilt) →p.138

8 Grund/Neuer/Schweizer, stepped building, Lion-Feuchtwanger-Strasse →p.84

9 Smithson, redevelopment, Adalbertstrasse (unbuilt) →p.26

10 Regenbogenfabrik, Lausitzer Strasse 22 →pp.47, 58

11 Siza/Brinkert, residential building, Schlesisches Tor →p.48

12 Nylund/Stürzebecher/Puttfarken, Wohnregal (Residential Shelving), Admiralstrasse 16 →pp.54, 62

13 Kollhoff, residential building, Luisenplatz →p.120

14 Baller, residential building, Fraenkelufer 44 →pp.153, 154, 155, 172

15 Planschok(o), Schokoladenfabrik (chocolate factory) →pp.160, 161

16 Küenzlen, daycare center, Dresdner Strasse 128 →pp.162, 163

17 Küenzlen, redevelopment, Paul-Lincke-Ufer 44 →pp.164, 165

18 Siza, residential building (unbuilt), Fraenkelufer →p.169

19 Kollhoff/Ovaska, residential park at the Berlin Museum, Alte Jakobstrasse 129–133 →p.8

20 Frowein/Spangenberg, residential park at the Berlin Museum, Alte Jakobstrasse 129–133 →p.8

21 Abraham/Büttner/Neumann, residential/office building, Friedrichstrasse 32–33 →p.15

22 Riemann, southern Friedrichstadt (unbuilt) →p.28

23 Krier, southern Friedrichstadt (unbuilt) →p.27

24 Krier, residential building, Ritterstrasse →p.36

25 Krier, gate building, Ritterstrasse →p.36

26 Eisenman, Robertson, residential/office building (unbuilt), Kochstrasse 62–63 →p.52
and park (unbuilt), Checkpoint Charlie →p.53

27 von Beulwitz, self-built terraces, Wilhelmstrasse 120–121 →p.55

28 Rossi/Braghieri, residential/office building, Wilhelmstrasse 36–38 →p.115

29 Kreis/Schaad/Schaad, residential park at Berlin Museum, Lindenstrasse 15–17 →p.116

30 Hejduk, residential building (Berlin Masque), Charlottenstrasse 96–98 →pp.144, 146, 149

31 Hejduk, Victims (unbuilt), Prinz-Albrecht-Gelände →p.144

32 Office for Metropolitan Architecture (OMA)/Zenghelis, Zenghelis/residential building at Checkpoint Charlie →pp.4, 118, 140

33 Meyer / Bartnig, residential/office building, Friedrichstrasse 56 →p.85

34 Warhaftig, residential building, Dessauer Strasse 38–40 →pp.158, 159

35 Ettel/Enzmann, Diktatur (unbuilt), Prinz-Albrecht-Gelände →pp.187, 192

36 Libeskind, Jüdisches Museum, Lindenstrasse 9–14 →pp.188, 189, 196

37 Gisel, Ephraim-Palais (unbuilt), Lindenstrasse 9–14 →p.194

38 Hertzberger, residential building, Lindenstrasse 81–84, →p.220

39 Eisentraut/Kny/Weber/Senz/Bondzin, CBD Marzahn, Marzahner Promenade →pp.87, 88, 89, 96, 98, 138

40 Prasser/Schwarz/Bankert, Friedrichstadtpalast, Friedrichstrasse 107 →pp.82, 135, 185

41 Gisske/Prasser/Schwarz/Bankert/Swora/Meyer et al., redevelopment of Friedrichstrasse (partially built), Friedrichstrasse →pp.49, 50, 51, 106, 107

42 Prasser/Weiss, Passagen Friedrichstadt (partially built, demolished) →pp.83, 104

43 Gisske/Prasser/Bankert, residential/office building, Gendarmenmarkt →pp.80, 81, 92, 95

44 Rösler, Akademie der Künste, Gendarmenmarkt (unbuilt) →pp.78–79

45 Jentsch/Brabetz/Bendler, office building, Dircksenstrasse 38 →p.119

46 Stahn, redevelopment, Nikolaiviertel →pp.181, 182, 183, 194

47 Schmidt, Spitteleck, Seydelstrasse 29–37 →p.219

48 Krause/Kristen/Megow/Zache/Mücke/Schulz et al., redevelopments in Prenzlauer Berg →pp.24, 46, 68–75

49 Inhabitants, redevelopment, Hirschhof, Oderberger Strasse →p.70

50 Stingl, residential area, Ernst-Thälmann-Park, Greifswalder Strasse →p.221

51 Otto, Ökohäuser, Askanischer Platz →pp.156, 157, 175, 177, 179

52 Meyer, Narva factory (unbuilt), Schöneweide →p.119

53 Moore/Ruble/Yudell, residential area, Tegeler Hafen →p.123

54 Krier, urban villas, Rauchstrasse →pp.113, 114

55 Stirling/Wilford, WZB, Reichpietschufer 50 →pp.121, 130

56 Hollein, Kulturforum (unbuilt), Potsdamer Strasse →p.122

57 Reidemeister/Glässel, residential building (unbuilt), Moabiter Werder →p.125

58 Halfmann, Spreeufer (unbuilt) →p.125

59 Rossi, Deutsches Historisches Museum (unbuilt), Spreebogen →pp.186, 192

60 Kleihues/Schonlau, residential building, Vinetaplatz →p.23

61 Libeskind, Berlin City Edge (unbuilt), Gleisdreieck →p.127

LIST OF WORKS

Impulses and Confirmation

Hélène Binet, residential block, Vinetaplatz by Josef Paul Kleihues, Manfred Schonlau, ca. 1986, gelatin-silver print, Studio Hélène Binet, → p. 23 top

Otto Borutta, aerial view, view from the south on the historical area of the Luisenstadt, ca. 1965, black-and-white negative, 6 × 7 cm, repro 2020, Berlinische Galerie BG-AS 42/2016,695, → p. 6

Siegfried Büker, townhouse at Herderstrasse 16 by Hasso von Werder, Uwe Pompinon, Klaus Beyersdorff, ca. 1971, color print, 40 × 30 cm, Berlinische Galerie BG-AS 469.4.1/470.4.1/2047.2.1, → p. 22

Jürgen Holtfreter, poster for the exhibition *Diagnose: Zum Bauen in West-Berlin* (Diagnosis: On Building in West Berlin), 1968, offset print, 84 × 58.5 cm, Akademie der Künste AdK KS poster 10685, → p. 20

Edmund Kasperski, residential complex on Lützowplatz by Oswald Mathias Ungers, 1986, black-and-white negative, 6 × 6 cm, repro 2020, Landesarchiv Berlin F Rep 290 0276155, → p. 39 fig. 5

Josef Paul Kleihues, Manfred Schonlau, residential block of new buildings on Vinetaplatz, isometric drawing, 1971–77, slide, 3.6 × 2.4 cm, repro 2020, Baukunstarchiv NRW Baukunstarchiv NRW F-000-280, → p. 23 bottom

Rob Krier, idealized plan for southern Friedrichstadt, 1977, ink on tracing paper, 80 × 110 cm, Archive Rob Krier, → p. 27

Rob Krier, Ritterstrasse residential complex, building types, 1977, felt-tip pen, chalk on cardboard, 65 × 100 cm, Deutsches Architekturmuseum, Frankfurt am Main, 142-008-002, → p. 36 fig. 2

Rob Krier, Ritterstrasse residential complex, gate building, model, 1977, colored styrofoam on chipboard, 77 × 280 × 180 cm, Deutsches Architekturmuseum, Frankfurt am Main, 142-008-032 (9), → p. 36 fig. 3

Siegfried Nitsch, renovation Arnimplatz, 1974, gelatin-silver print, 23.8 × 30 cm, Berlinische Galerie BG-AS 17/2013,703, → p. 24

Peter Anatoljewitsch Ratschkov, modernism and postmodernism compared, excerpts from Peter Anatolyevich Rachkov's dissertation, "On Theoretical Concepts of Postmodernism," Moscow School of Architecture, ca. 1981, translated by Christian Schädlich, felt-tip pen on paper, 115 × 81.3 cm, Berlinische Galerie BG-AS 102/2019,4, → p. 12

Peter Riemann, urban islands, 1977, ink and colored pencil on yellow-tracing paper, 17 × 17 cm, Archive Peter Riemann, → p. 28 right
Peter Riemann, concept for southern Friedrichstadt, Cornell Summer Academy in Berlin, 1977, india ink and colored pencil on yellow tracing paper, 16.5 × 16.5 cm, Archive Peter Riemann, → p. 28 right

Aldo Rossi, Fabio Reinhart, Bruno Reichlin, Eraldo Consolascio, *La Città analoga* (The Analogue City), 1976, paper collage, felt, ink, gouache, and plastic film on paper, 230 × 240 cm, Paris, Centre Pompidou – Musée national d'art moderne AM 2012-2-371, → p. 34 fig. 1

Christian Schädlich, "Italienische Rationalisten" (Italian Rationalists) and "Rationalismus: The New York Five" (Rationalism: The New York Five), two sheets from a series of drawings on postmodernism, ca. 1982, ink on tracing paper, 29.7 × 21 cm, Berlinische Galerie BG-AS 102/2019,9–10, → p. 29

Gottfried Schenk/Mieterinitiative Sanierungsgebiet Klausenerplatz, residential and commercial building at Nehringstrasse 30, 1975, inkjet-print on Photo Rag Baryta, 31 × 45 cm, Archive Gottfried Schenk, → p. 25

Alison Smithson, study as part of the "Entwerfen in der historischen Strasse" (Designing on the Historical Street), 1975, felt-tip pen on back-and-white photocopy on paper, 21.5 × 57 cm, Berlinische Galerie BG-AS 1/2020,165, → p. 26

Tseng Kwong Chi, Keith Haring mural at the Berlin Wall, photograph, 1986, Muna Tseng Dance Projects, Inc., → p. 15 top

Unknown author, Brandenburg Gate with Berlin Wall, postcard, 1960s, Alfred Ziethen Verlag Sinthern, Archive Lutz Vetter, → p. 19

Unknown author, children playing by the Berlin Wall in West Berlin, postcard, ca. 1970, Archive Office for Metropolitan Architecture (OMA) Rotterdam, repro 2020, → p. 19

Oswald Mathias Ungers with Karl-Lothar Dietzsch, Georg Hagemann, Burkhard Meyer, Barbara Taha, Bernd Wippler, residential complex on Lützowplatz, isometric drawing, preliminary design, ca. 1980, diazotype, paper, colored pencil, 63.5 × 63.5 cm, Landesarchiv Berlin B Rep 168 (maps) no. 240, → p. 39 fig. 4

Oswald Mathias Ungers, Peter Riemann, *Die Stadt in der Stadt: Ein grünes Archipel* (The City in the City: A Green Archipelago), 1977, pencil, ink and colored pencil on tracing paper, 66 × 62.5 cm, repro Archive Riemann 2006, → p. 28 left

Gerd Wessel, "damit man es nicht so sieht" (so that it's not so visible), ca. 1975, ink and pencil on paper, 17.2 × 29.5 cm, Berlinische Galerie BG-AS 574.41, → p. 21

Beautiful Old City

Building Academy of the GDR, Peter Gerlach, basic research to plan the transformation of Prenzlauer Berg, 1976, diazotype, 53 × 50 cm, IRS Erkner/ scientific collection C_09_01-05, → p. 70 fig. 2

Building Academy of the GDR, urban development planning of Prenzlauer Berg, 1977, diazotype, 71 × 71 cm, IRS Erkner/scientific collection A_10_02-06, → p. 68 fig. 1

Dietrich von Beulwitz, self-built terraces, model, 1981–87, wood, cardboard, paper, plastic, metal, 38.5 × 41.5 × 22.5 cm, Berlinische Galerie BG-AS 4/2018,40, → p. 55 right

Dietrich von Beulwitz, self-built terraces, perspective of the surroundings, 1981–87, tracing paper, 60.4 × 61 cm, Berlinische Galerie BG-AS 4/2018,34, → p. 55 left

Robert Conrad, Gaudystrasse, 1987, gelatin-silver print, 48 × 32 cm, repro 2020, Archive Robert Conrad, → p. 45

Robert Conrad, in the courtyard of the building at Fehrbelliner Strasse 6, 1980s, gelatin-silver print, 48 × 32 cm, repro 2020, Archive Robert Conrad, → p. 43

Gerd Danigel, Gasometers, 1984, black-and-white negative, repro 2020, Archive Gerd Danigel, → p. 44

Gerd Danigel, Oderberger Strasse, June 9, 1989, black-and-white negative, repro 2020, Archive Gerd Danigel, → p. 72 fig. 4

Brigitte Deiters, façade design on Husemannstrasse, typological detailed studies, pre-1987, ink on paper, 39.08 × 41.38 cm, IRS Erkner/ Archive Brigitte Deiters, → p. 71

Eisenman/Robertson Architects with Thomas Leeser, public parks at Checkpoint Charlie, perspective, 1985, photo reproduction, paper, film, 92 × 61 cm, Landesarchiv B Rep 168 (maps) no. 1189 Bl. 3, → p. 53 bottom

Eisenman/Robertson Architects with Thomas Leeser, public parks at Checkpoint Charlie, site plan, 1985, colored pencil on cardboard, 29 × 21 cm, Landesarchiv Berlin B Rep 168 (maps) no. 48 Bl. 8, → p. 53 top

Edmund Kasperski, Wohnregal (Residential Shelving), Admiralstrasse 16, ca. 1986, color negative, 6 × 6 cm, Landesarchiv Berlin F Rep. 290 (01) no. 0016909_C, → p. 62 fig. 5

Manfred Kraft, celebration of the third anniversary of the Regenbogenfabrik (Rainbow Factory), March 24, 1984, gelatin-silver print, 1984, repro 2020, Umbruch Bildarchiv, → p. 58 fig. 1

Model workshop Ingenieurhochbau Berlin, operation project planning, multipart representation model around Friedrichstrasse, ca. 1987, scale 1:200, wood, plastic, metal, organic material, color, Berlinische Galerie BG-AS 34/2019, Quartier 108: → p. 49, Quartier 205: pp. 50, 51, Deutscher Dom, Konzerthaus/ Schauspielhaus, Franz. Dom: p. 92 fig. 2, Quartiere 205, 206: p. 104 fig. 2, Quartier 115: p. 107 fig. 5, Quartiere 107–109, 112–115, 202–205, 208, 210, 302, 402: p. 106; Passagen Friedrichstadt, p. 83 top

Jochen Moll, the façade of a squat in Kreuzberg, 1980, gelatin-silver print, Bildarchiv Preussischer Kulturbesitz, Mo 1476-78, → p. 60 fig. 3

Kjell Nylund, Peter Stürzebecher, Christof Puttfarken, Wohnregal (Residential Shelving), view, 1985–87, diazotype, watercolored, 94.9 × 127.7 cm, Architekturmuseum der TU München, → p. 54 left

Kjell Nylund, Peter Stürzebecher, Christof Puttfarken, Wohnregal (Residential Shelving), perspektive (isometry), 1985–87, tracing paper, quill, 46 × 88 cm, Architekturmuseum der TU München, → p. 54 right

Günter Schneider, residential and commercial building at Checkpoint Charlie by Eisenman/Robertson Architects with Thomas Leeser, ca. 1986, black-and-white negative, 4.5 × 6 cm, Landesarchiv F Rep 290, 0284765, → p. 52

Hans Seiler, view to the Kaiser-Wilhelm-Gedächtnis-Kirche (Kaiser Wilhelm Memorial Church) from Hardenbergstrasse, 1965, black-and-white negative, 6 × 6 cm, Landesarchiv Berlin F Rep. 290 (01) no. 0107661, → p. 60 fig. 2

SPIEGEL, magazine cover, 4/1981, SPIEGEL-Verlag Rudolf Augstein GmbH & Co. KG, → p. 61 fig. 4

Gabriele Stolze, everyday life in the Hirschhof, 1987–88, slide, 2.4 × 3.6 cm, IRS Erkner/ scientific collection C_98-D009, → p. 73 fig. 5

Südost Express (Southeast Express), cover, 1982, FHXB Friedrichshain-Kreuzberg Museum, → p. 65 fig. 6

Unknown Author, model drawing of Rykestrasse, 1988, photograph of drawing, 18 × 24 cm, IRS Erkner/ scientific collection D1_1_7_3-002, → p. 74 fig. 6

Unknown photographer, block between Swinemünder Strasse and

Zionskirchstrasse, 1983, Senatsverwaltung für Bau- und Wohnungswesen (Senate Department for Building and Housing), ed., *Stadterneuerung Berlin: Erfahrungen, Beispiele, Perspektiven* (Urban Renewal Berlin: Experiences, Examples, Perspectives) (Berlin, 1990), → p. 184, repro 2020, → p. 46

Unknown photographer, apartment building at Schlesisches Tor by Álvaro Siza Vieira with Peter Brinkert, 1984–85, Berlinische Galerie BG-AS 2/2016,7a-b, → p. 48

Werkfabrik (Work Factory) / Margarete Winkes, renovated house façade of the Regenbogenfabrik (Rainbow Factory), 1987, slide, 3.6 × 2.4 cm, repro 2020, Berlinische Galerie BG-AS 66/2019,28a, → p. 47 top

Werkfabrik (Work Factory) / Margarete Winkes, sketches for the redevelopment and conversion of an old factory site into a Regenbogenfabrik (Rainbow Factory) with a bicycle workshop, ca. 1983, collage (felt-tip pen, offset print on color print), 15 × 21.2 cm, Berlinische Galerie BG-AS 65/2019,65, → p. 47 bottom

The City as a Whole

Frank Dölle, casino, twenty-four-hour department shop in Quartier 205 Friedrichstrasse/Taubenstrasse – view from the north, 1988, watercolor, pencil, opaque white on paper, 45.3 × 58.5 cm, Berlinische Galerie BG-AS 80/2019,6, → p. 83 bottom

Dorothea Dutschmann, Kaulsdorf Nord residential complex, Rostock type by Iris Grund, ca. 1984, gelatin-silver print, 18 × 18.2 cm, Berlinische Galerie BG-AS 17/2013,629, → p. 84

Wolf Eisentraut, Michael Kny, Thomas Weber, study of Marzahn, 1983, offset print on paper, 29.5 × 42 cm, Berlinische Galerie BG-AS 93/2019,11a, → p. 96 fig. 6

Edmund Kasperski, Passagen Friedrichstadt (Friedrichstadt Arcades), 1991, black-and-white negative, 6 × 6 cm, Landesarchiv Berlin F Rep. 290 (01) no. 0328225, → p. 104 fig. 1

Christian Kloss, L'espaces d'Abraxas residential complex, 2010, digital photograph, Archive Christian Kloss, → p. 95 fig. 4

Michael Kny, Thomas Weber, center of Marzahn, 1987, slide, 2 × 3.5 cm, Berlinische Galerie BG-AS 93/2019,253, → p. 98, fig. 9

Michael Kny, Thomas Weber, department shop Marzahn, 1987, color slide, 2 × 3.5 cm, Berlinische Galerie BG-AS 93/2019,239, → p. 98, fig. 8

Michael Kny, Thomas Weber, Gallery M, 1991, slide, 2 × 3.5 cm, Berlinische Galerie BG-AS 93/2019,239, → p. 98, fig. 10

Kirsten Kofahl, *Arcades*, 2006, digital photograph, Archive Kirsten Kofahl, → p. 95 fig. 5

Dankwart Kühn, façade design Markgrafenstrasse, 1975, watercolor and ink on cardboard, 57.5 × 100 cm, Berlinische Galerie BG-AS 21/2017,2, → p. 94 fig. 3

Klaus Lehnartz, aerial view Gendarmenmarkt, 1968, slide, 6 × 6 cm, Photonet.de / Klaus Lehnartz, → p. 92, fig. 1

Harald Metzkes, *Aufbau von Marzahn* (Construction of Marzahn), 1984, oil on canvas, 180 × 130 cm, artist's property, → p. 86

Manfred Prasser, Peter Weiss, Passagen Friedrichstadt (Friedrichstadt Arcades), ca. 1986, Bundesarchiv Berlin DH1-36355, → p. 104 fig. 3

Werner Rösler, design for the Akademie der Künste (Academy of the Arts), Platz der Akademie (now Gendarmenmarkt), 1980, wax crayon on tracing paper, 242 × 75 cm, IRS Erkner, scientific collection, Legacy Werner Rösler IRS C 17 04-01-001 002, p→ p. 78–79

Unknown photographer, art on the building by Horst Bartnig, Friedrichstrasse, 1987–89, color print, 20.2 × 20.2 cm, Berlinische Galerie BG-AS 61/2019,3, → p. 85

Unknown photographer, Friedrichstadtpalast, ca. 1984, gelatin-silver print, 12.9 × 12.6 cm, Berlinische Galerie BG-AS 95/2012,35, → p. 82

Unknown photographer, Geissenweide restaurant complex, Biesdorf, 1978, gelatin-silver print, 23.1 × 29.5 cm, Berlinische Galerie BG-AS 17/2013,390, → p. 96 fig. 7

Unknown photographer, Marzahner Promenade, ca. 1988, color print, 20.4 × 19.8 cm, Berlinische Galerie BG-AS 108/2012,6, → p. 87

Unknown photographer, new residential and commercial building by Peter Meyer, Friedrichstrasse Quartier 202, 1989–90, color print, 19 × 24.2 cm, Berlinische Galerie BG-AS 61/2019,3, → p. 85

Gerd Zimmermann, main post office of Marzahn, 1991, color slide, 6 × 6 cm, repro 2020, Archive Gerd Zimmermann, → p. 88 top

Gerhard Zwickert, center of the third residential section of Marzahn with Marzahn S-Bahn (commuter rail station, 2003, black-and-white negative, 6 × 12 cm, repro 2020, Archive Gerhard Zwickert, → p. 89

Gerhard Zwickert, department store Marzahn, 2003, black-and-white negative, 6 × 12 cm, repro 2020, Archive Gerhard Zwickert, → p. 89

Gerhard Zwickert, main post office of Marzahn 2003, black-and-white negative, 6 × 12 cm, repro 2020, Archive Gerhard Zwickert, → p. 88 bottom

Gerhard Zwickert, patio in the Haus der Dienste (House of Services) Marzahn, 2003, black-and-white negative, 6 × 12 cm, repro 2020, Archive Gerhard Zwickert, → p. 89

Gerhard Zwickert, residential and commercial buildings on Gendarmenmarkt, 2003, color negative, 6 × 9 cm, repro 2020, Archive Gerhard Zwickert, p→ p. 80–81

Urban Diversity

Raimund Abraham, residential and commercial building by Raimund Abraham with Heike Büttner, Claus Neumann, Friedrichstrasse 32–33, 1980–87, gelatin-silver print, Archive Una Abraham, → p. 15

Hélène Binet, John Hejduk, residential complex with studio tower, 1988, gelatin-silver print, Studio Hélène Binet, → p. 117 right

Thomas Bomm, *Krier_Rauchstrasse*, 2018, color print behind acrylic glass, 59.4 × 84.1 cm, Archive Thomas Bomm, → p. 114 top

Siegfried Büker, residential complex on Alte Jakobstrasse 129–133 by Dieter Frowein, Gerhard Spangenberg, 1986, color print, 21 × 29 cm, private property, → p. 8 bottom

Robert Göllner, new construction of the Wissenschaftszentrum Berlin, ca. 1988, color negative, 10.2 × 17.2 cm, private property / Robert Göllner Photography-Archive, → p. 121

Zaha Hadid, office building Kurfürstendamm 70, 1986, acrylic on cartridge paper, 126 × 80 cm, Zaha Hadid Foundation / Zaha Hadid Architects, → p. 140 fig. 10

Jasper Halfmann, Spreeufer competition, axonometric projection, 1988–90, diazotype with corrective solution on paper, 71 × 91 cm, Berlinische Galerie BG-AS 134.15.5, → p. 125 right

John Hejduk, *Berlin Masque*, elevations and plans for guest towers and shopping booths, 1981, graphite and colored pencil on tracing paper, 117.1 × 92.5 cm, Canadian Centre for Architecture, John Hejduk fonds DR1998:0098:044, → p. 146 fig. 3

John Hejduk, *Berlin Masque*, plan for *masque*, 1981, graphite and colored pencil on tracing paper, 144.5 × 69.3 cm, Canadian Centre for Architecture, John Hejduk fonds DR1998:0098:045, → p. 146 fig. 4

John Hejduk, *Berlin Masque*, model, 1981, wood, color, 9.8 × 92.6 × 92.7 cm, Canadian Centre for Architecture, John Hejduk fonds DR1998:0098:109, → p. 144 fig. 1

John Hejduk, *Victims*, partial site plan, 1984, India ink and ink on paper, 98.5 × 137 cm, Canadian Centre for Architecture, John Hejduk fonds DR1998:0109:003:017, → p. 144 fig. 2

John Hejduk, *Victims*, sketch, 1984, quill and ink on yellow lined paper, 28 × 21 cm, Canadian Centre for Architecture, John Hejduk fonds DR1998:0109:002:001, → p. 117 left

Hans Hollein, model of the Kulturforum, 1983, wood, plastic, 51 × 140 × 140 cm, Berlinische Galerie BG-AS 2/2015, → p. 122

Helmut Jahn, competition for the Victoria City Areal, Kurfürstendamm/Joachimsthaler Strasse, model, 1988, plastic, wood, plexiglass, 37.5 × 41.5 × 30.8 cm, Berlinische Galerie BG-AS 103.1.1, → p. 124

Jochen Jentsch, Bernhard Brabetz, Klaus Bendler, administration building of the Wohnungsbaugesellschaft Mitte, Dircksenstrasse 38, 1984–87, ink, pencil, colored pencil, felt-tip pen on tracing paper, 40.5 × 56.5 cm, Archive Jochen Jentsch, → p. 119 bottom

Hans Kollhoff, residential development at Luisenplatz, urban design, 1982, Archive Prof. Kollhoff, → p. 120 bottom

Hans Kollhoff, Arthur A. Ovaska, Wohnpark am Berlin Museum (Residential Park at the Berlin Museum), axonometric drawing, 1986, Archive Prof. Hans Kollhoff, → p. 8 fig. 2

Rob Krier urban villa, Rauchstrasse 6, plan of ground floor, ca. 1980, 42 × 30 cm, ink on tracing paper, Landesarchiv Berlin B Rep. 168 (maps) no. 146, → p. 114 bottom

Rob Krier, competition entry Rauchstrasse Block 189 IBA, perspective, garden courtyard facing west with group of people in the foreground, 1980, ink on tracing paper, 47.5 × 45.5 cm, Landesarchiv Berlin B Rep. 168 (maps) no. 902, → p. 113

Dieter Leistner, gatehouses Lützowstrasse 43–51 by Vittorio Gregotti, 2020, repro of slide (10.5 × 12.7 cm), Archive Dieter Leistner, → p. 116 bottom

Dieter Leistner, residential building Lindenstrasse 15–17 by Werner Kreis, Ulrich Schaad, Peter Schaad, 2020, repro slide (10.5 × 12.7 cm), Archive Dieter Leistner, → p. 116 top

Daniel Libeskind, Berlin City Edge, model, 1987, cardboard, paper print, metal, wood on wooden base, 58.5 × 271 × 145.3 cm, Collection Frac Centre-Val de Loire, 9910618, photo: Olivier Martin-Gambier, → p. 127

Daniel Libeskind, Berlin City Edge, projection of Berlin psychocyber netics, urban concept and detail of the structure, 1988, laser reproduction on photo paper, 100.5×101 cm, Collection Frac Centre-Val de Loire, 994 01 10, → p. 126

Peter Meyer, industrial complex for the NARVA lightbulb factory Berlin, 1985, Xerox copy, colored pencil, 30×42 cm, Berlinische Galerie BG-AS 61/2019,19, → p. 119 top

Charles Moore, John Ruble, Buzz Yudell, residential complex at Tegeler Hafen, model, 1980–88, plastic, cardboard, paper, metal on wooden plate, 33×125×125 cm, Deutsches Architekturmuseum, Frankfurt am Main, 172-032-001, → p. 123

Ivan Nemec, residential development at Luisenplatz by Hans Kollhoff, Archive Prof. Kollhoff, → p. 120 top

Office for Metropolitan Architecture (OMA), Elia Zenghelis, residential building at Checkpoint Charlie, Friedrichstrasse 207–208, preliminary design, EG-Lichtdecke (EG-ceiling), 1981, Office for Metropolitan Architecture (OMA) Rotterdam, → p. 140 fig. 11

Office for Metropolitan Architecture (OMA), Elia Zenghelis, residential building at Checkpoint Charlie, site plan, 1980, watercolor on Xerox paper, ca. 82×166 cm, repro, Office for Metropolitan Architecture (OMA) Rotterdam, → p. 4

Office for Metropolitan Architecture (OMA), Elia Zenghelis, Zoe Zenghelis, residential building at Checkpoint Charlie, 1980, perspective, 1987, mixed technique, oil on cardboard, 88×148.5 cm, Deutsches Architekturmuseum, Frankfurt am Main, 186-001-002, → p. 118

Uwe Rau, residential and commercial building at the corner of Kochstrasse 1–4 and Wilhelmstrasse 36–38 by Aldo Rossi, Gianni Braghieri, 2020, repro slide, Berlinische Galerie, → p. 115

Andreas Reidemeister, Joachim Glässel, Atrium High-Rise at the Moabiter Werder, model photograph, 1989, slide, 9×12 cm, repro 2020, Archive Andreas Reidemeister → p. 125 left

James Stirling, Michael Wilford, and Associates, Wissenschaftszentrum Berlin, sketch of a site plan, perspective, 1979–87, ink and graphite on paper, 21×29.9 cm, James Stirling/Michael Wilford fonds Canadian Centre for Architecture AP140. S2. SS1. D57. P6. 17, → p. 121 bottom

James Stirling, Michael Wilford, and Associates, Wissenschaftszentrum Berlin, typological study, 1979–88, ink and colored pencil on paper, 77.3×83.5 cm, James Stirling/Michael Wilford fonds Canadian Centre for Architecture AP140. S2.SS1.D57.P15.5, → p. 130 fig. 2

Unknown author, Friedrichstadtpalast, postcard, ca. 1985, Archive Lutz Vetter, → p. 135 fig. 7

Robert Venturi, Denise Scott Brown, Steven Izenour, *Learning from Las Vegas* (Cambridge, MA, 1972), → p. 129 fig. 1

Gerd Zimmermann, main post office of Marzahn, interior view, color slide, 6×6 cm, repro 2020, Archive Gerd Zimmermann, → p. 138 fig. 8

Architecture for the People

Hinrich Baller, Torhaus (Gate House) on Fraenkelufer, ca. 1981, slide, 2.3×3.6 cm, repro 2020, Archive Hinrich and Inken Baller, → p. 154

Hinrich and Inken Baller, apartment building on Fraenkelufer/Admiralstrasse, ca. 1984, slide 2.3×3.6 cm, repro 2020, Archive Hinrich and Inken Baller, → p. 153

Hinrich and Inken Baller, building development at Fraenkelufer, interior view, ca. 1984, slide 2.3×3.6 cm, repro 2020, Archive Hinrich and Inken Baller, → p. 172 fig. 3

Reinhard Friedrich, building development at Fraenkelufer, courtyard view, 1984, slide 2.3×3.6 cm, repro 2020, Archive Hinrich and Inken Baller, → p. 172 fig. 4

Reinhard Friedrich, aerial photograph Fraenkelufer, ca. 1979, gelatin-silver print, 17.8×24 cm, Archive Hinrich and Inken Baller, → p. 169 fig. 1

Reinhard Friedrich, Torhaus (Gate House) on Fraenkelufer, detail, 1984, slide, 2.3×3.6 cm, repro 2020, Archive Hinrich and Inken Baller, → p. 155

Heiner Hoffmann, hammam and café in the Frauen-Stadtteilzentrum (Neighborhood Center for Women), 1979–88, slide, 35 mm film, Berlinische Galerie BG-AS 35/2020,2, → p. 161

Heiner Hoffmann, ecological planning for the conversion of a former chocolate factory into the Frauen-Stadtteilzentrum (Neighborhood Center for Women) in Kreuzberg, ca. 1984, slide, 35 mm film, repro 2018, BG-AS 35/2020,1, → p. 160 top

Declan Kennedy, rooftop greenhouse in the Frauen-Stadtteilzentrum (Neighborhood Center for Women), 1988, slide, 35 mm film, Berlinische Galerie BG-AS 35/2020,3, → p. 160 bottom

Martin Küenzlen / Oekotop GmbH Berlin, rooftop greenery, Block 108, 1986, color print, Berlinische Galerie BG-AS 62/2019,29, → p. 165

Martin Küenzlen / Oekotop GmbH Berlin, Kita Dresdner Strasse, 1983, colored pencil on cyanotype, 64×90.5 cm, Berlinische Galerie BG-AS 62/2019,52, → p. 162 top

Martin Küenzlen / Oekotop GmbH Berlin, Kita Dresdner Strasse, 1990, greenery inside, slide, Berlinische Galerie BG-AS 62/2019,68, → p. 163

Martin Küenzlen / Oekotop GmbH Berlin, winter garden windows, 1982–83, color print, 13.5×8.8 cm, Berlinische Galerie BG-AS 62/2019,15a-d, → p. 164

Martin Küenzlen / Oekotop GmbH Berlin, winter garden windows, interior view, 1982–83, color print, 13.5×8.8 cm, Berlinische Galerie BG-AS 62/2019,16, → p. 164

Frei Otto, Hermann Kendel, Ökohaus (Eco House), ca. 1991, color print on PE paper, 21.2×29.6 cm, Berlinische Galerie BG AS BG-AS 5/2014,13, → p. 156 bottom

Frei Otto, model of the Ökohäuser (Eco Houses) as open platforms, built-ins not yet installed, 1983, color print, 42×59 cm, Frei Otto Werkarchiv, saai/Karlsruhe FO_KB-P_1983-05_02-35, → p. 179 fig. 5

Frei Otto, model of the Ökohäuser (Eco Houses) with finished and planted platforms, design for Askanischer Platz, 1981, wood, hard foam, paper, plexiglass, metal, dried plants, 66×64×29 cm, Frei Otto Werkarchiv, saai/Karlsruhe M_057 Depot Münze 8A2, → p. 177 fig. 3

Frei Otto, model of the Ökohäuser (Eco Houses), design for Askanischer Platz, 1981, wood, wire, wool, 114×77.5×31 cm, Frei Otto Werkarchiv, saai/Karlsruhe, M_077 Depot Münze SES SFAS, → p. 157

Frei Otto, Ökologischer Bauplatz auf der Etage … umgebaut … im Selbstbau (Ecological Construction Site on the Floor … DIY Conversion), design for Askanischer Platz, April 1, 1981, scale 1:50, pencil on tracing paper, 42×59.4 cm, Frei Otto Werkarchiv, saai/Karlsruhe FO_PL-A2_1988-01-34, → p. 177 fig. 4

Frei Otto, sketch of an idea for a treehouse, 1980, watercolor on paper, 14.8×21 cm, Frei Otto Werkarchiv, saai/Karlsruhe FO_HS_80, → p. 156 top

Frei Otto, title page of "Anpassungsfähiges Bauen / Adaptable Building," June 1959, offset print, 42×59.4 cm, Frei Otto Werkarchiv, saai/Karlsruhe FO_PL-A2_1959.07-001, → p. 177 fig. 2

Frei Otto, Das übereinandergesetzte Eigenheim (The Stacked Single-Family Home), 1951, ink on cardboard, 42×59.4 cm, Frei Otto Werkarchiv, saai/Karlsruhe FO_PL-A2_1951.01-021, → p. 175 fig. 1

Álvaro Siza Vieira, design sketch of Fraenkelufer, sketchbook 45, Berlin, 1979, ink on paper, 20×30 cm, Canadian Centre of Architecture, Gift of Álvaro Siza, → p. 169 fig. 2

Unknown author, "Ich werf' die Autos raus … und werd' ein Kinderhaus" (I am throwing the cars out and becoming a house for children), invitation card, September 10, 1983, offset print, 15×21 cm, Berlinische Galerie BG-AS 62/2019,57a-b, → p. 162 bottom

Unknown photographer, hammam in the Frauen-Stadtteilzentrum (Neighborhood Center for Women), 2007, 35 mm film, Archive Schokofabrik, → p. 161

Myra Warhaftig, view of the eat-in kitchen, Dessauer Strasse 38–40, ca. 1987, slide, 24×26 cm, Karlsruhe Institute of Technology (KIT), Institute of Art and Building History, Department of Art History DP_220_00218, → p. 159 bottom

Myra Warhaftig, apartment building at Dessauer Strasse 38–40, view from the west, ca. 1993, slide, 24×26 cm, Karlsruhe Institute of Technology (KIT), Institute of Art and Building History, Department of Art History DP_220_00054, → p. 158

Myra Warhaftig, child-oriented housing, Dessauer Strasse 38–40, isometry and floor plan, 1987, ink on cardboard, 61×82 cm, Karlsruhe Institute of Technology (KIT), Institute of Art and Building History, Department of Art History PL_220_0027, → p. 159 top

A Future from the Past

Bauakademie der DDR (Academy of Architecture of the GDR), *Bauausstellung der DDR* (Building Exhibition of the GDR), postcard, 1987, 10.5×15.5 cm, Berlinische Galerie BG-AS 8/2020,2, → p. 202 fig. 3

Sibylle Bergemann, from the series *Das Denkmal* (The Monument), 1986, documentation of the building of the Marx-Engels Forum on Usedom and in Berlin, 1975–86, Legacy Sibylle Bergemann, OSTKREUZ; Courtesy Loock Gallery, Berlin, → p. 181

Hélène Binet, Jüdisches Museum (Jewish Museum) Berlin, 1996, two photographs, gelatin-silver print, Studio Hélène Binet, → pp. 188–89

Druckkombinat (Print Combine) Berlin, "Historical market 4/5 July 1987 around Alexanderplatz," 1987, poster, digitalization template: slide, Bundesarchiv Berlin, Poster Collection of the SED, Plak 102-072-019, → p. 184

Christian Enzmann, Bernd Ettel, *Diktatur* (Dictatorship), leporello, 1983, gelatin-silver print, 25×25×2 cm, Berlinische Galerie BG-AS 96/2019,2, → pp. 187, 192 fig. 2

Ernst Gisel, design for the reconstruction of and extension to the Ephraim-Palais, 1979, black-white-copy, 84.8×29.7 cm, Landesarchiv Berlin, E Rep. 300-70 no. 69, → p. 194 fig. 3

Daniel Libeskind, competition for the realization of the Jüdisches Museum (Jewish Museum Berlin), 1988, ink on tracing paper, 89.5×120.5 cm, Berlinische Galerie BG-AS 31/2020, → p. 196 fig. 5

Ingeborg Lommatzsch, protest poster at the boulevard of sculptures, April 28, 1987, black-and-white negative, 24×36, Landesarchiv Berlin, F Rep. 290 (02) no. 0284396, → p. 202 fig. 5

Klaus Oberst, historical parade, 4.7.1987, gelatin-silver print, 13×18 cm, Bundesarchiv, picture 183-1987-0704-058, → p. 199 fig. 1

Andreas Prüstel, *Disney-Spezial* (Disney Special), 1988, collage on cardboard, 44.5×39 cm (beam dimension), Berlinische Galerie BG-AS 24/2020, → p. 183

Aldo Rossi, Deutsches Historisches Museum (German Historical Museum) Berlin, model, ca. 1987, wood, glass, copper, plastic, textile fiber, metal, 41×135×136 cm, Deutsches Historisches Museum, L 94/106, → p. 186

Aldo Rossi, Deutsches Historisches Museum (German Historical Museum), Berlin, perspective view, 1988, pause on paper, 69.5×88.2 cm, Berlinische Galerie BG-AS 132.2.1, → p. 192 fig. 1

Christian Schädlich, building exhibition of the GDR, 1987, slide, 2.4×3.6 cm, Berlinische Galerie BG-AS 102/2019,1, → p. 202 fig. 4

Günter Stahn, Roland Korn, Heinz Mehlan, Rolf Ricken, design for the reconstruction of the Ephraim-Palais, 1978, ink on tracing paper, 65×84 cm, Berlinische Galerie BG-AS 5.93.1.7, → p. 194 fig. 4

Unknown photographer, postcard of Friedrichstadtpalast, Archive Lutz Vetter, → p. 185

Unknown photographer, view of the historical Nikolaiviertel, ca. 1980, gelatin-silver print paper, 20.9×30.5 cm, Berlinische Galerie BG-AS 17/2013,74, → p. 182 top

Unknown photographer, rebuilt Nikolaiviertel, 1987, gelatin-silver print, 17.4×23.7 cm, Berlinische Galerie BG-AS 17/2013,522, → p. 182 bottom

Architecture in Film and Art

BERLIN CITYSCAPES IN FILMS FROM THE 1980s

Cynthia Beatt, *Cycling the Frame*, FRG, 1988, 27', rbb Rundfunk Berlin-Brandenburg, → p. 211

Jürgen Böttcher, *Konzert im Freien*, GER, 2001, 88', Deutsche Kinemathek, n.p.

Die Tödliche Doris, *Naturkatastrophenballett*, FRG, 1983, 1'52'', contribution to the WDR-Rockpalast/ Käthe Kruse, n.p.

Harun Farocki, *Stadtbild* (View of the City), BRD, 1981, 44', Harun Farocki GbR, → p. 208

Peter Kahane, *Die Architekten* (The Architects), GDR, 1989–90, 102', DEFA-Filmverleih / Deutsche Kinemathek, → p. 210

Riki Kalbe, *Bodenproben*, FRG, 1987, 31', Arsenal – Institute for Film and Video Art e.V., n.p.

Kain Karawahn, *The Berliner Summer Night Dream*, FRG, 1984, 1'33'', Kain Karawahn and Video Forum Collection of the Neuer Berliner Kunstverein, n.p.

Ulrike Ottinger, *USINIMAGE*, FRG, 1987, 10', Ulrike Ottinger Filmproduktion, n.p.

Wim Wenders, *Der Himmel über Berlin* (Wings of Desire), FRG/FR, 1986–87, 128', Wim Wenders Foundation – Argos Films, → p. 207

Herrmann Zschoche, *Insel der Schwäne* (Island of Swans), GDR, 1982–83, 88', DEFA-Stiftung, → p. 209

TIMES ARE HARD BUT POSTMODERN

Isa Melsheimer, *Frei Otto / Westliches Haus (West House)*, 2012, reinforced concrete, lava vases, → p. 217

Isa Melsheimer, *Stirling*, 2012, reinforced concrete, → p. 215

Isa Melsheimer, *Tea and Coffee Piazza d'Italia in Post-Katrina Times*, 2013, fiber-reinforced concrete, ceramic, → p. 213

Isa Melsheimer, *Times Are Hard but Postmodern (Curtain)*, 2013, fabric, embroidery thread, → p. 213

Isa Melsheimer, *Umlauftank (Circulation Tank)*, 2012, reinforced concrete, houseplants, gouache on paper, → p. 214

Isa Melsheimer, *Ungers*, 2012, reinforced concrete, houseplants, → p. 216

PHOTO CREDITS

ADN: p. 185
Esra Akcan: pp. 149, 150
Hinrich and Inken Baller: pp. 153–55, 172 figs. 3, 5
Estate of Sibylle Bergemann, OSTKREUZ; Courtesy Loock Galerie, Berlin: p. 181
Dietrich von Beulwitz / Berlinische Galerie: p. 55
Hélène Binet: pp. 23 top, 117 right, 188–89
Thomas Bomm: p. 114 top
Siegfried Büker: p. 8 bottom, 22
Robert Conrad: pp. 43, 45
Gerd Danigel: pp. 44, 72 fig. 4
DEFA-Stiftung / Christa Köfer, p. 210
DEFA-Stiftung / Waltraut Pathenheimer, p. 209
Brigitte Deiters / IRS Erkner: pp. 71 figs. 3, 73 fig. 5
DER SPIEGEL 31 (1981): p. 61 fig. 4
Phil Dera: pp. 219–23
Frank Dölle / Berlinische Galerie: p. 83 bottom
Wolf-Rüdiger Eisentraut, Michael Kny and Kollektiv: p. 96 fig. 6
Christian Enzmann, Bernd Ettel: pp. 138 figs. 9a–9b, 187, 192 fig. 2
Ernst Gisel / gta Archiv ETH Zurich: p. 194 fig. 3
Hildegard Göllner: p. 121 top
Zaha Hadid Architects: p. 140 fig. 10
Jasper Halfmann / Berlinische Galerie: p. 125 right
John Hejduk / John Hejduk fonds, Canadian Centre for Architecture: pp. 117 left, 144, 146
Harun Farocki GbR: p. 208
Heiner Hoffmann: pp. 160 top, 161 top
Max and Lilli Hollein: p. 122
Jürgen Holtfreter / Akademie der Künste, Berlin, Kunstsammlung: p. 20
Helmut Jahn / Berlinische Galerie: p. 124 left
Jochen Jentsch: p. 119 bottom
Declan Kennedy / Anja Kennedy: p. 160 bottom
Christian Kloss: p. 95 fig. 4
Michael Kny, Thomas Weber: p. 98 fig. 8–10
Kirsten Kofahl: p. 95 fig. 5
Hans Kollhoff / Arthur A. Ovaska: p. 8 fig. 2
Hans Kollhoff: p. 120 bottom
Wilmar König: p. 15 fig. 2
Manfred Kraft / Umbruch Bildarchiv: p. 58 fig. 1
Rob Krier: p. 27
Rob Krier / Deutsches Architektur Museum: p. 36
Rob Krier / Landesarchiv Berlin: pp. 113, 114 bottom
Martin Küenzlen / Oekotop GmbH Berlin / Berlinische Galerie: pp. 162 top, 163–65
Dankwart Kühn / Berlinische Galerie: p. 94 fig. 3
Dieter Leistner: p. 116
Daniel Libeskind / Berlinische Galerie: p. 196 fig. 5
Daniel Libeskind / Collection Frac Centre-Val de Loire: pp. 126–27
Ingeborg Lommatzsch / Landesarchiv Berlin: p. 202 fig. 5
Adolf Loos / Albertina, Vienna: p. 134 fig. 6
Harald Metzkes, VG Bild-Kunst, Bonn, 2020: p. 86
Peter Meyer / Berlinische Galerie: pp. 85, 119 top
Jochen Moll / Bildarchiv Preussischer Kulturbesitz: p. 60 fig. 3
Ivan Nemec: p. 120 top
Siegfried Nitsch / Berlinische Galerie: p. 24
Klaus Oberst / Bundesarchiv: p. 199 fig. 1
Frei Otto Werkarchiv, saai, Karlsruhe: pp. 156 top, 157, 175 fig. 1, 177 figs. 2–4, 179 fig. 5
Office for Metropolitan Architecture (OMA) / Elia Zenghelis / Zoe Zenghelis: p. 118
Office for Metropolitan Architecture (OMA) / Elia Zenghelis / Matthias Sauerbruch: pp. 4, 140 fig. 11
photonet.de / Klaus Lehnartz: p. 92 fig. 1
Manfred Prasser, Peter Weiss / Bundesarchiv DH1-36355: p. 104 fig. 3
rbb Rundfunk Berlin-Brandenburg: p. 211
Legal successors of Bauakademie der DDR, Institut für Städtebau and Architektur / IRS Erkner: pp. 68 fig. 1, 70 fig. 2
Legal successors of Druckkombinat Berlin / Bandesarchiv Berlin, Plakatsammlung der SED: p. 184
Legal successors of Ernst Gränert: p. 133 fig. 4b
Legal successors of Carl Krause / IRS Erkner: p. 133 fig. 4a
Legal successors of Edmand Kasperski / Landesarchiv Berlin: pp. 39 fig. 5, 62 fig. 5, 104 fig. 1
Legal successors of Eisenman / Robertson Architects with Thomas Leeser / Landesarchiv Berlin: p. 53
Legal successors of Reinhard Friedrich: pp. 169 fig. 1, 172 fig. 4
Legal successors of Andreas Prüstel: p. 183
Legal successors of Uwe Rau: p. 115
Legal successors of Werner Rösler / IRS Erkner: pp. 78–79
Legal successors of Hans Seiler / Landesarchiv Berlin: p. 60 fig. 2
Legal successors of Alison Smithson: p. 26
Legal successors of "Südost Express" / FHXB-Museum / Archiv Südost Express, Berlin: p. 65 fig. 6
Legal successors of Oswald Mathias Ungers / Landesarchiv Berlin: p. 39 fig. 4
Legal successors of Werkfabrik / Berlinische Galerie: p. 47
Legal successors of Alfred Ziethen Verlag: p. 19
Peter Riemann: p. 28 right
Peter Riemann / Legal successors of Oswald Mathias Ungers: p. 28 left
Andrea Rossetti: pp. 214–16
Aldo Rossi / Centre Pompidou MNAM-CCI / Eredi Aldo Rossi: p. 34 fig. 1
Aldo Rossi / Deutsches Historisches Museum / Eredi Aldo Rossi: p. 186
Aldo Rossi / Berlinische Galerie / Eredi Aldo Rossi: p. 192 fig. 1
Tomari Ruccius and Orly Fatal-Warhaftig: pp. 158, 159
Christian Schädlich / Berlinische Galerie: pp. 12, 29, 202 fig. 4
Gottfried Schenk: p. 25
Karl Friedrich Schinkel / Kupferstichkabinett, Staatliche Museen zu Berlin h_00108228: p. 130 fig. 3
Alvaro Siza / Canadian Centre of Architecture, ARCH281716, Alvaro Siza fonds, Gift of Alvaro Siza: p. 169 fig. 2
Günter Schneider / Landesarchiv Berlin: p. 52
Günter Stahn, Roland Korn, Heinz Mehlan, Rolf Ricken / Berlinische Galerie: p. 194 fig. 4
James Stirling / Michael Wilford fonds Canadian Centre for Architecture: pp. 121 bottom, 130 fig. 2
Gabriele Stolze: p. 73 fig. 5
Jonas Stürzebecher / Architekturmuseum TU München: p. 54
Tseng Kwong Chi: Muna Tseng Dance Projects, Inc. / The Keith Haring Foundation: p. 15 fig. 1
Unknown author / Berlinische Galerie: p. 162 bottom
Unknown photographer / Archiv Andreas Reidemeister: p. 125 left
Unknown photographer / Baukunstarchiv NRW, Bestand Josef Paul Kleihues: p. 23 bottom
Unknown photographer / Berlinische Galerie: pp. 48, 82, 84, 87, 96 fig. 7, 135 fig. 7, 182
Unknown photographer / Legal successors of Bauakademie der DDR / Bauinformation: p. 74 fig. 6
Unknown photographer / Schokofabrik: p. 161 bottom
Florian Urban: p. 106 fig. 4
Gerd Wessel: p. 21
Wim Wenders Stiftung – Argos Films: p. 207
Gerd Zimmermann: pp. 88 top, 138 fig. 8
Ute Zscharnt: p. 133 fig. 5
Gerhard Zwickert: pp. 80–81, 88 bottom, 89

From Secondary Literature

Senatsverwaltung für Bau- und Wohnungswesen, ed. *Stadterneuerung Berlin: Erfahrungen, Beispiele, Perspektiven*. Berlin: Senatsverwaltung, 1990, pp. 184, 46.
Venturi, Robert, Denise Scott Brown, and Steven Izenour, *Learning from Las Vegas: The Forgotten Symbolism of Architectural Form*. Cambridge, MA, and London, 1972, p. 129.

Markus Hawlik: p. 122
Gunnar Klack: p. 124
Olivier Martin-Gambier: pp. 126–27
Georges Meguerditchian / Centre Pompidou MNAM-CCI: p. 34
Ludger Paffrath: pp. 49–51, 83 top, 92 fig. 2, 104 fig. 2, 106 figs. 1–5, 7–10, 13, 15–19, 107 fig. 5
Anja Pienkny: p. 73 fig. 5
A. Psille / Deutsches Historisches Museum: p. 186
Bernd Seeland: p. 159 top
Manuel Weidt: p. 86
Anja-Elisabeth Witte: pp. 8 bottom, 12, 19 top, 24, 26, 28 left, 29, 47, 48, 55 left, 73, 80–82, 84, 85, 87–89, 94, 96, 98, 106 figs. 6, 11, 12, 14, S. 115, 121 top, 129, 135, 138 fig. 8, 153, 154, 156 bottom, 162–65, 169 fig. 1, 172, 183, 185, 192 fig. 2, 194 fig. 4, 196, 201, 202 figs. 3, 4

ACKNOWLEDGMENTS

The exhibition has received backing from the following artists and photographers:

Horst Bartnig
Sibylle Bergemann
Hélène Binet
Thomas Bomm
Siegfried Büker
Robert Conrad
Gerd Danigel
Robert Göllner
Klaus Lehnartz
Dieter Leistner
Isa Melsheimer
Harald Metzkes
Ulrike Ottinger
Gottfried Schenk
Gerhard Zwickert

Many important objects have been donated to the museum in the context of preparations for this exhibition. We would like to express our immense gratitude to the following institutions, families, and individuals for the confidence they have shown in the Berlinische Galerie:

Dietrich von Beulwitz
Susanne Brinkert
François und Linde Burkhardt
Waltraud von Demandowsky-Parow
Frank Dölle
Wulf Eichstädt
Christian Enzmann
Bernd Ettel
Renate Feder
Achim Felz
Margot Gerke
Hendrikje Herzberg
Klaus Just
Hermann Kendel
Antja Kennedy
Declan Kennedy
Wolfgang Kil
Michael Kny
Dorothea Krause
Martin Küenzlen
Jürgen Ledderboge
Günther Ludewig
Peter Meyer
Jörg Müller
Moritz Müller
Leo Pompinon
Christian Schädlich
Solweig Steller-Wendland
Jonas Stürzebecher
Thomas Weber
Peter Weiss
Manfred Zache

It is thanks to the substantial support of the following institutions that the former special building projects of the GDR for the center of Berlin around Friedrichstrasse could be shown in the form of thirty-nine representative models:

Stiftung Deutsche Klassenlotterie Berlin (DKLB-Stiftung)
Kulturstiftung der Länder
Der Regierende Bürgermeister von Berlin, Senatskanzlei – Kulturelle Angelegenheiten

The following institutions and individuals have assisted us with our research or kindly provided individual loans:

Conny Apel
Hinrich Baller
Inken Baller
Dieter Bankert
Hanne Bolz
Gianni Braghieri
Christian Enzmann
Bernd Ettel
Dieter Frowein
Hildegard Göllner
Brigitte Groihofer
Edgar Haas
Sigrid Heger
Jochen Jentsch
Eva-Maria Jockeit-Spitzner
Hans Kollhoff
Rob Krier
Kjell Nylund
Peter Riemann
Ulrich Schaad
Michael Wiedemann
Antje Zimdars-Weigelt

Akademie der Künste, Baukunstarchiv, Berlin: Tanja Morgenstern
Architekturzentrum Wien: Monika Platzer
Baukunstarchiv NRW, Dortmund: Regina Wittmann
Canadian Centre for Architecture, Montreal: Giovanna Borasi, Catherine LaRivière, Caroline Dagbert
Deutsches Architekturmuseum (DAM), Frankfurt am Main: Peter Cachola Schmal, Wolfgang Welker, Katja Leiskau
Deutsches Historisches Museum, Berlin: Sabine Witt, Karen Klein, Jörg Rudolph, Nicole Schmidt
Frac Centre – Val de Loire: Paul Laurent
Friedrichstadt-Palast Berlin: Annegret Blume-Swenson, Nora Hawich, Gero Konietzko
Karlsruher Institut für Technologie (KIT), Institut für Kunst- und Baugeschichte: Martin Papenbrock, Anna Krüger
Karlsruher Institut für Technologie (KIT), saai Archiv für Architektur und Ingenieurbau: Georg Vrachliotis, Joachim Kleinmanns, Martin Kunz
Landesarchiv Berlin: Andreas Matschenz, Thilo Mrosek, Aileen Tomzek
Landesdenkmalamt Berlin: Christoph Rauhut, Sabine Schulte, Thorsten Dame
Leibniz-Institut für Raumbezogene Sozialforschung, Erkner: Andreas Butter, Kai Drewes, Anja Pienkny
Musée national d'art moderne Centre Pompidou, Paris: Bernard Blistène
OMA, Rotterdam: Nuria Ribas Costas, Talitha van Dijk
Stiftung Topographie des Terrors: Ulrich Tempel
Ungers Archiv für Architekturwissenschaft (UAA), Cologne: Anja Sieber-Albers
Universität der Künste Berlin, Universitätsarchiv: Dietmar Schenk
Wissenschaftszentrum Berlin für Sozialforschung: Harald Wilkoszewski, Dirk Reimann, Lisa Heck
Zaha Hadid Architects: Henry Virgin

The authors of the texts and the exhibition curator would like to thank the following individuals, whose cordial support, research, inspiration, and criticism have proved essential for the development of insights into Berlin's epoch of building during the 1980s:

Inken Baller
Dieter Bankert
Christian Enzmann
Bernd Ettel
Helmut Geisert
Stefanie Heckmann
Joachim Kleinmanns
Martin Kunz
Maurice Lahde
Haila Ochs
Manfred Schonlau
Jürgen Schöne
Jürgen Tomisch
Lutz Vetter
Wolfgang Voigt

COLOPHON

This catalogue is published in conjunction with the exhibition: *Anything Goes? Berlin Architecture in the 1980s*, January 29 – April 26, 2021

Berlinische Galerie
Berlin's Museum of Modern Art, Photography and Architecture
Alte Jakobstrasse 124–128
10969 Berlin

Tel +49 (0) 30-78 902-600
Fax +49 (0) 30-78 902-700
bg@berlinischegalerie.de
www.berlinischegalerie.de

Exhibition

Curator:
Ursula Müller
Academic Advisory Council:
Dr. Andreas Butter, Leibniz-Institut für Raumbezogene Sozialforschung
Prof. Marco De Michelis, IUAV Università Iuav di Venezia
Prof. Dr. Stanislaus von Moos, Universität Zürich
Prof. Dr. Kerstin Wittmann-Englert, Technische Universität Berlin
Prof. Dr. Gerd Zimmermann, Bauhaus-Universität Weimar
Academic assistance:
Nuno de Brito Rocha, Anna-Maria Nitschke, Antonia Wolff
Support:
Dr. Verena Pfeiffer-Kloss
Registrar:
Frank Schütz
Conservation:
Andreas Piel, Maria Bortfeldt
Mounting:
Sabina Fernández-Weiss
Head of installation:
Wolfgang Heigl
Film program:
Ursula Müller, Antonia Wolff
Film compilations of documentary footage:
Dirk Schaefer
Tactile stations:
Annette Müller, Robert Niemann and Students of Technical University Berlin, Department Modell+Design.
Specialist advising:
Christine Rieger, Dirk Sorge, art guides, Reiner Delgado, social affairs officer of the Deutscher Blinden- und Sehbehindertenverband (DBSV)
Exhibition architecture:
David Saik, Berlin
Exhibition setup:
RT Ausstellungstechnik, Berlin
Public relations:
Bureau N

Cooperation and media partners:

Funded by:

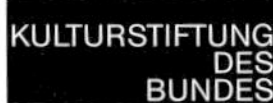

Catalogue

Editors:
Dr. Thomas Köhler, Ursula Müller
Concept:
Ursula Müller
Editorial staff:
Dr. Verena Pfeiffer-Kloss, Ursula Müller, Antonia Wolff, Anna-Maria Nitschke
Copyediting:
Dawn Michelle d'Atri
Translations:
Steven Lindberg (D), Claudia Marra (I)
Graphic design:
Lars Egert, Zurich
Typeface:
Parma (Dinamo)
Image editing:
HIGHLIGHT BERLIN
Production, Kerber Verlag:
Jens Bartneck
Project management, Kerber Verlag:
Martina Kupiak

Cover illustrations:
Front: Hélène Binet, residential complex with studio tower by John Hejduk (detail), 1988, gelatin-silver print, Studio Hélène Binet
Back: Gisela Stappenbeck, Entrance to the new Friedrichstadtpalast, 1984, bpk/Gisela Stappenbeck

Printed and published by:
Kerber Verlag
Windelsbleicher Strasse 166–170
D – 33659 Bielefeld
Tel. +49 5 21/9 50 08-10
Fax +49 5 21/9 50 08-88
info@kerberverlag.com

Kerber publications are distributed worldwide by:
ACC Art Books, Sandy Lane, Old Martlesham, Woodbridge, IP12 4SD, UK
accartbooks.com
uksales@accartbooks.com

Artbook | D.A.P.
75 Broad Street, Suite 630, New York, NY 10004, USA
artbook.com / orders@dapinc.com

The German National Library lists this publication in the German National Bibliography: dnb.de

ISBN 978-3-940208-67-5 (Museum edition)

ISBN 978-3-7356-0700-3 (Bookstore edition)

Web App

Concept and text:
Dr. Verena Pfeiffer-Kloss
Organization:
Linus Lütcke
Design and technical implementation:
3pc GmbH Neue Kommunikation

Berlinische Galerie

Administration